THE PRACTITIONER INQUIRY SERIES

Marilyn Cochran-Smith and Susan L. Lytle, *Series Editors*

Coming Out of School   L.S. Lowry, 1927

UNPLAYED TAPES

TAPES

a personaL history of
coLLaborative
teacher research

STEPHEN M. FISHMAN & LUCILLE MCCARTHY

 National Council of
Teachers of English
Urbana, Illinois

 Teachers College
Columbia University
New York & London

Cover and frontispiece art used by permission of Tate Gallery, London/Art Resources, New York, and Mrs. Carol A. Danes

NCTE Stock Number: 55731-3050

Published simultaneously by the National Council of Teachers of English, 1111 W. Kenyon Road, Urbana, IL 61801-1096 and Teachers College Press, 1234 Amsterdam Avenue, New York, NY 10027.

Teachers College Press ISBN: 0-8077-3967-7

Library of Congress Catalog-in-Publication Data

Fishman, Stephen M.
    Unplayed tapes : a personal history of collaborative teacher research /
Stephen M. Fishman, Lucille McCarthy.
        p. cm. — (The practitioner inquiry series)
    Includes bibliographical references and index.
    ISBN 0-8141-5573-1 (acid-free paper)
        1. Action research in education–United States–Case studies.
    I. McCarthy, Lucille Parkinson, 1944–.   II. Title.   III. Series.

LB1028.24 .F52 2000
370'.7'2—dc21   99-056501

This book was typeset in Palatino and Trajan by The Visual Pair, LLC.
The typefaces used on the cover are Trajan and Disturbance.
The book was printed by Automated Graphic Systems, Inc.

FOR BARBARA WALVOORD AND SAM WATSON

Mentors, Colleagues, Friends

THE THINGS IN CIVILIZATION WE MOST PRIZE are not of ourselves. They exist by grace of the doings and sufferings of the continuous human community in which we are a link. Ours is the responsibility of conserving, transmitting, rectifying and expanding the heritage of values we have received that those who come after us may receive it more solid and secure, more widely accessible and more generously shared than we have received it.

— JOHN DEWEY, *A Common Faith* 1934/1962a, p. 87

CONTENTS

ACKNOWLEDGMENTS

I n the quotation we have chosen for our epigraph, John Dewey says our task is to reshape our traditions so we pass them on to future generations in more usable form. Our own efforts to do this have relied from the very start on the conversation and counsel of many people. Over the past decade, at various times and in various ways, we have benefited from the generosity of the following colleagues: Charles Bazerman, Carol Berkenkotter, Linda Brodkey, Marilyn Cooper, Peter Elbow, Michael Eldridge, Janet Emig, Joseph Harris, Donald Jones, Kenneth Kantor, Barry Kroll, Susan Lytle, John Mayher, Susan McLeod, Marian Mohr, Thomas Newkirk, Patrick Shannon, Louise Smith, Francis Sullivan, Barbara Walvoord, and Sam Watson.

We are also indebted to our editors at NCTE and Teachers College Press: Michael Greer, Zarina Hock, Jane Curran, and Carol Collins. All are thoroughly professional, and all leaven their expertise with large doses of patience, flexibility, and good humor.

Finally, a huge thank-you to our families for their ever-present love and support.

INTRODUCTION

Steve Fishman and Lucille McCarthy

The past quarter century has seen a resurgence of interest in teacher research, not only in the United States, but also in Britain, Continental Europe, Canada, and Australia. The appeal of teacher research is its power to enhance instructor practice—specifically, to improve teacher judgment, sensitivity, and theoretical understanding. Given the importance of teachers in any plan for educational reform, it is not surprising that significant efforts are underway to incorporate practitioner inquiry into both preservice and inservice training for primary and secondary school teachers (Cochran-Smith, Garfield, & Greenberger, 1992; Hursh, 1995; Zeichner & Gore, 1995). And at the college level, Writing Across the Curriculum (WAC) programs, which continue to expand, urge university teachers to examine their own classroom practices (Walvoord, Hunt, Dowling, & McMahon, 1997).

WHY THIS BOOK?

An Integrative Approach to Teacher Research

Although teacher research is arguably our most promising opportunity for educational reconstruction, there is little agreement about how to do it. In fact, theorists are currently engaged in vigorous clashes about its nature, purposes, and methods. Without denying that debates among spokespeople for different paradigms of teacher research can be valuable and productive, our book argues for an integrative rather than an either/or approach. Our conciliatory orientation seeks to preserve the best that various research paradigms offer rather than to expose—as is often the aim among opposing theorists—the worst aspects of competing models. That is, in combining a variety of methods and research report genres, we seek to maintain a productive dialogue among these opposed alternatives rather than stage an agonistic debate to declare one the victor.

By supporting an integrated methodology we do not mean to suggest that our orientation is best or universally ideal. We can certainly envision research settings in which less blended techniques and genres are more appropriate. However, a multiple methods approach has been fruitful for us, and we forward it as an attractive teacher-research model. In effect, we urge experimentation with different amalgamations, ones in which practitioner inquirers combine methods and research report genres to meet the special challenges presented by their own research situations.

An Integrative Approach to the Study of Teacher Research

Our book also uses an integrated approach to tell the story of recent teacher research. That is, in *Unplayed Tapes*, we take responsibility for all aspects of practitioner inquiry, joining discussion of the history of the field, its theory, and its various research techniques with presentation of our own classroom studies. Whereas many teacher-research books focus primarily on only one of these concerns—for example, theory (see Ray, 1993; Schon, 1983), or practical advice (see Brause & Mayher, 1991; Brookfield, 1995; Hubbard & Power, 1993), or actual classroom studies (see Newman, 1990, 1998; Patterson, Santa, Short, & Smith, 1993)—we believe it is empowering for teacher-researchers to speak to all of these issues. In fact, we are wary of the many collections of practitioner studies which, although well intended, are framed and theorized by a university researcher whose name appears on the cover. This implies a weakness in teacher-generated knowledge, suggesting that an outsider, a university-based theorist, is required to secure space for teacher voices. Admittedly, given the devaluing of teacher perspective within the educational hierarchy, this approach has been necessary and, certainly, has served an important function.

However, despite the significant role such collections of practitioner studies have played, we encourage teacher-researchers to speak more fully for themselves. Our efforts to integrate in this volume all facets of practitioner inquiry—its history and theory, its techniques, and our own actual studies—will, we hope, strike a blow for increased practitioner voice. Ultimately, our aim is to offer our version of the new instructor-based knowledge for which Cochran-Smith and Lytle (1993) and others appeal: knowledge generated by fully empowered teacher inquirers.

Speaking Personally about Teacher-Research History, Methods, and Collaboration

We choose to tell the recent history of teacher research in terms of our own 10-year collaboration for three reasons. First, in significant ways, our work together, including our disagreements about the purposes and methods of teacher research, reflects larger discussions which have shaped the movement. Second, because we bring contrasting skills and attitudes to our work, we have been forced to face head-on the internal clashes which have plagued the teacher-research field—charges that it is either too narrowly personal or too narrowly academic. Finally, our type of collaboration, an inside classroom teacher and an outside university-based researcher, is often maligned as potentially exploitive. However, in this book, we show the workings of a long-term, insider-outsider arrangement, illustrating its benefits as well as our struggles to avoid its pitfalls.

As we have said, in recounting the history of recent teacher research by opening the unplayed tapes—the private conversations—behind our published research reports, we do not mean to suggest that inside-outside collaborations are best or that our own studies of Fishman's college philosophy classroom provide a model of teacher research that is ideal for all occasions. Rather, we want to show how a collaborative, integrative approach has worked for us. In doing so, we also answer calls by teacher-researchers for more behind-the-scenes glimpses into how enduring partnerships survive as well as how experienced researchers actually carry out their work (see Hubbard & Power, 1993, p. xv).

Our Personal Account of the History of Teacher Research

The generally qualitative nature of teacher research suggests that at least one appropriate vantage point for its history is from the inside, from an intimate, close-up perspective rather than a more distant point of view. Our approach is, therefore, something like studying the French Revolution by focusing on the life of one family and relating it to larger Assembly debates, royal proclamations, and military engagements. In other words, we believe that presenting the recent history of teacher research in personal terms—our own particular experience of the broader issues and conflicts of the movement—may be a more accessible and effective approach than one which remains general and detached.

We limit our historical account of teacher research to the past quarter century, although its roots certainly go back further—at least as far as John Dewey's 1904 call for the reform of teacher education. Its sources also include the broad initiative known as action research (see Altrichter, Posch, & Somekh, 1993; Noffke & Stevenson, 1995). In fact, commentators who emphasize the social and political ramifications of teacher research find its origins in the 1930s in the action research of John Collier and Kurt Lewin (see Hopkins, 1985, pp. 43-61; Noffke, 1997). However, it is only since the late 1970s that numerous forces have coalesced to generate new ways of testing and shaping pedagogic theory through teacher inquiry.

Therefore, in Chapter 1 of this volume, Fishman starts our history of teacher research with the late 1970s work of British historian and educationist Lawrence Stenhouse and American compositionist Ann Berthoff. He focuses on this period because it marks the beginning of the recent resurgence of teacher research, and he spotlights these two scholars because their theoretical statements about teacher inquiry are cited throughout subsequent commentaries and research reports. By highlighting these two theorists, Fishman does not mean to slight other influential contemporaries like James Britton (Britton, Burgess, Martin, McLeod, & Rosen, 1975), Patricia Carini (1979), Dixie Goswami (Goswami & Stillman, 1987), Donald Graves (1983), Lee Odell (1987), or Donald Schon (1983). But, as he reconstructs events, the conceptions of practitioner inquiry offered by Stenhouse and Berthoff immerse us quickly in the history of oppositional currents shaping both the field and our own 10-year collaboration.

As Fishman explicates their positions in Chapter 1, Stenhouse becomes associated with analysis, academic voice, and systematic data collection, whereas Berthoff becomes the standard-bearer of narrative, personal voice, and teacher perspective. Although both Stenhouse and Berthoff share the view that qualitative teacher research is more helpful to classroom practitioners than experimental research, in their different emphases they spawn contrasting approaches in subsequent second-generation literature.

Our history of teacher research begins in the late 1970s, not only because this period initiates the resurgence of teacher research, but also because it marks the time that both of us enter the field. McCarthy enrolls in graduate school at the University of Pennsylvania in 1981 and publishes her initial classroom study in 1985 (McCarthy & Braffman). Fishman attends his first Writing Across the Curriculum (WAC) workshop in 1983 and publishes his first classroom account 2 years later (1985).

Ameliorating Methodological Clashes within Teacher Research

In addition to providing a historical account of recent teacher research, our primary reason for writing this book is to influence the future of practitioner inquiry based upon our experience. Specifically, we argue that future teacher research should consider reconciling various aspects of classroom study which, at the present time, are seen as mutually exclusive. That is, emphasis is either on narrative or analysis, classroom data or theory, personal or academic voice, and teacher or student perspective. That the field finds itself in this position is understandable. As Cochran-Smith and Lytle (1993) point out, teacher research was born in opposition to traditional experimental classroom study. The original struggle thus made room for qualitative, naturalistic accounts of classrooms alongside more quantitative, scientific-paradigm ones. But now that respectability for qualitative research has been achieved, the present conflict pits teacher-researchers who favor teacher story and retrospective against those who advocate systematic methods of data collection and analysis.

A sign that this clash is getting stronger rather than weaker is evidenced by the 1998 Annual Convention of the Conference on College Composition and Communication. The convention theme, "Historias y Cuentos [Stories and Tales]: Breaking with Precedent," and the large number of plenary sessions devoted to teacher stories seemed driven as much by opposition to systematic social science research as by affirmation of the value of narrative ways of knowing. And the 1998

American Educational Research Association (AERA) convention suggests that the teacher story versus social science conflict is, in addition, being fueled by postmodern theory. In a session titled "Emotions and Educational Inquiry," it was clear that numerous educational researchers who employ personal narrative and humanities-based writing in their studies build their work on such postmodern figures as Lyotard (1992) and Foucault (1978). This postmodern educational research, like narrative inquiry in composition studies, is presented as directly opposed to positivist social science techniques of classroom investigation (see Constas, 1998). The position we take in this volume is that both alternatives—analytic and narrative—can be enhanced by integrating their contrasting features.

Current Bifurcation of Teacher Research

As Fishman shows in Chapter 1, systematic, carefully triangulated data collection, presented in an academic voice, has been criticized by some teacher-researchers as too removed from the everyday concerns of practitioners. Their objection is that such work is inaccessible because of its technical language and because the personal histories and motives of the researchers are hidden (see Bissex & Bullock, 1987; Ray, 1993). By contrast, university-based researchers see teacher stories as insufficiently systematic, too local, and too little connected to broader academic and social issues (see Applebee, 1987).

The long and the short of it is that we agree with both these criticisms. Systematic classroom inquiry can adopt an academic voice that severely limits its audience, its analytic language and global point of view serving as a barrier for classroom teachers who might otherwise be interested readers. Conversely, teacher stories can be so meagerly theorized, thematized, or academically contextualized that their authors miss important chances to mine the material at hand and reveal their work's broader significance. Therefore, in our own classroom studies, as we show in subsequent chapters, we attempt to address these criticisms. We do this, first, by exploring multiple classroom perspectives (student, teacher, and outside researcher) and, second, by fully employing our different research and reporting strengths.

Integrating Narrative and Analysis, Personal and Academic Language, Data and Theory, Teacher and Student Perspective

Although our joint studies always attend closely to Fishman's teacher perspective, we are able to contrast it not only with McCarthy's outsider point of view but also with Fishman's students' perspectives, which McCarthy elicits from interviews and pupil texts. In other words, our collaboration gives us increased opportunities to triangulate among teacher, researcher, and student points of view. It also allows us to experiment in our reports with ways to accommodate insider narratives with outsider analysis, personal concerns with academic ones, and classroom data with explanatory theory.

This integrative work, however, did not come easily to us. When we began our first collaborative study, McCarthy had just completed two investigations of other teachers' classrooms, and Fishman had struggled to publish a couple of single-authored accounts of his own Introduction to Philosophy course. But our need and desire to publish was about the only goal we had in common, and it did not take long for us to realize our approaches to classroom studies were diametrically opposed. Whereas McCarthy's publications followed the American Psychological Association (APA) scientific report form and stressed academic language, Fishman wrote teacher narratives in a personal voice. Whereas her emphasis was on student perspectives and systematic data collection, he focused on the teacher's point of view and sought to highlight theory. In the course of defending our opposing tendencies, we had to teach each other about our different approaches and skills. As a result of this stepping into each other's shoes, we began to realize the value of each other's orientations, and our ideas of teacher research expanded. Thus, over time, we have integrated our opposing approaches in various ways, creating blends that seem to answer charges that teacher research is either overly academic or overly personal, too global or too local.

Exploring an Insider-Outsider Collaboration

The final reason for our personal history of teacher research is to provide a close-up study of a type of practitioner inquiry—an insider-outsider collaboration—about which the current teacher-research movement is ambivalent. On the one hand, theorists are extremely wary of conjoint projects between teacher insiders and university-based researcher outsiders. They fear that such arrangements may lead to practitioner exploitation, preventing teachers from generating their own questions about their classrooms and discouraging them from developing enough research skills to carry on independently once the outside-researcher leaves (Cochran-Smith & Lytle, 1993; Feldman & Atkin, 1995). On the other hand, many theorists recognize the value of cooperation among teacher-researchers who are *peers*, arguing that such equal-status collaboration encourages a critical perspective, a level of reflection often absent from single-authored studies (Feiman-Nemser & Melnick, 1992; Flores & Granger, 1995; Stevenson, Noffke, Flores, & Granger, 1995).

The position we adopt in this volume is that collaboration can be harmful or helpful depending upon the relationship that develops between co-investigators. Partnerships involving university-based researchers, in our view, are no more inherently dangerous than partnerships involving teachers on the same school corridor, at the same grade level, and with similar years of experience. Central to successful collaborative teacher research, as we see it, are opportunities to develop common goals, to view each partner's unique abilities as equally valuable, and to divide the research load so that both parties believe they are contributing and profiting in comparable ways. Put simply, when each of us recognized we could achieve our goals better by working together than apart, we were highly motivated to talk things through and make the adjustments necessary to keep our shares of the research fair and mutually rewarding. A final reason, then, for this personal history—the unplayed tapes of our decade of collaborative inquiry in Fishman's college philosophy classroom—is to point to potential benefits of this form of teacher research. We organize these benefits around two categories: developing community and coming to know what we know.

Developing Cooperative Community

The primary value of collaborative work, as we have experienced it, is the development of cooperative community. In the course of our five classroom studies, we have come to feel that the process and product of our research is totally shared, that interest and delight in each other's professional and personal growth is genuine. For us, this development is noteworthy because academic life is often competitive and atomizing. Even in the classroom, their many contact hours with students notwithstanding, teachers tend to experience isolation (see Lytle & Fecho, 1992, p. 296).

Despite the fact that classroom practice is often a lonely activity, many teachers acknowledge—in the midst of their own isolation—that learning itself, paradoxically, is a social or communal process. Given this view of knowledge as socially constructed, collaborative research offers teachers a chance to investigate the rhythms and challenges of cooperative community, the conditions which promote participants' dependence on and care for the performance and success of one another (see Bisplinghoff

& Allen, 1998; Pradl, 1992). Put differently, collaborative classroom research can provide an antidote to the isolating aspects of academic and school life. In doing so, it may help teachers better understand the ins and outs of the cooperative learning they often want for their students.

Seeing One's Teaching and Research Anew

A second potential advantage of collaborative research is the chance to become an outsider to one's own practice. This provides a rich source of dissonance, often generating clashing perspectives which stimulate investigation and fresh insight. Our own conflicts, as we later show, help us better articulate our different views of teaching and research. And our continuing discussion of these differences forces us to examine the theories or assumptions underlying our opposing perspectives.

DEFINING TEACHER RESEARCH

As the field's clashes about the nature of practitioner inquiry suggest, any account of teacher research quickly confronts the problem of definition. This is because, as we have said, it is a movement or form of inquiry which is highly amorphous: its audiences, settings, methods, and purposes vary markedly. Reflecting these differences, Lytle (1997) presents 16 different names by which teacher-researchers have identified their work, including practitioner inquiry, action research, critical action research, and collaborative action research (p. 20).

Who Does Teacher Research?

Although Lytle (1997) emphasizes the great variety of answers to the what, when, why, and how of teacher inquiry, she suggests there is agreement about the "who" of it. That is, she believes teacher research means, at the least, teachers studying their own classrooms. But even this point appears open to debate. It does not seem far-fetched that some theorists would argue that our own studies of Fishman's college philosophy classroom—ones he conducted with McCarthy, a university-based composition specialist—should be excluded from any list of genuine examples of teacher research. Their argument would be based upon an idealization of the teacher-researcher as a primary or secondary school practitioner, laboring alone or in connection with a small, peer support group (see Feldman & Atkin, 1995, p. 128). Such a paradigm would exclude someone like Fishman, a university professor collaborating with an outside-researcher, and for this reason, we find it too limiting. Nevertheless, we sympathize with its dignifying of the K-12 classroom practitioner, a vision underscoring a reforming purpose which, in our view, can unite teacher-researchers, no matter their place on the educational ladder.

This reforming element seeks increased respect for teachers and improved instruction for students (see Banford et al., 1996; Bissex & Bullock, 1987; Beyer, 1996; Cochran-Smith & Lytle, 1993; Hall, Campbell, & Miech, 1997; Patterson et al., 1993; Short et al., 1996). And despite our many differences, we suggest that teacher-researchers at all levels generally share these goals. Although Fishman teaches at a university, his concern, like that of instructors at primary and secondary schools, is to study the art of teaching and, as a consequence, perfect his own practice. Like these instructors, he, too, wants greater voice in the educational process—in the development of pedagogy, educational theory, and curriculum. Admittedly, our collaborative classroom studies take place in a setting and for an immediate purpose that is quite different from grade school teachers' contexts and purposes. That is, Fishman meets young adults 3 hours per week for 14 weeks, and, given his university's demands, his immediate goal is to contribute to published conversations in academic journals. By contrast, K-12 practitioners have many more contact hours with students and, generally, exert their influence for change not in journals but at teacher collaboratives, school board meetings, and PTA functions. However, to define teacher research as inquiry conducted only by K-12 instructors who have no connection to university-based outsiders may serve, in the long run, to maintain long-standing class distinctions and to lose opportunities for our mutual benefit. Rather than bicker about how to rank-order our disparate stations and approaches to teacher research, historical evidence from other reform movements suggests each of us can become better at what we do if we take an inclusive view, one which opens all participants to new avenues of conversation with one another (see Dewey, 1920/1962b; Walvoord, 1996).

Our claim that teacher-researchers generally share the goals of enhanced practitioner respect and improved student instruction is a broad one. Yet, not surprisingly, even this position has its opponents. Its critics would argue that our view of teacher research as a quest for increased practitioner power ignores wider political and social objectives. Indeed, theorists who insist that teacher research should aim not just at improved practice but also at increased justice in school and society would criticize our focus on Fishman's teaching as too individualistic (see Zeichner & Gore, 1995, p. 16). Although we agree that a more ideologically focused approach is frequently called for, we fear that making political and social liberation—however that might be interpreted —a necessary goal of teacher research may discourage or devalue practitioners whose first concern is classroom management (see Chandler, 1998; Schuyler & Sitterly, 1995). Such a liberatory position would frown on studies which, for example, explore questions about how to encourage high school pupils to read *The Scarlet Letter* (Hirtle, 1993) or, for that matter, to read anything at all (Cone, 1994).

Our stance regarding these conflicting agendas is, once again, an integrative one. We see each of these currents or orientations as having merit and as capable of being perfected, modified, or cobbled together depending upon the circumstances in which teacher-researchers find themselves.

ORGANIZATION OF THE PRESENT STUDY

We start our book, as we have indicated, with an account of developments in teacher research in the late 1970s and 1980s. In Chapter 1, Fishman surveys the literature, identifying what he calls the opposing "charter conceptions" of practitioner inquiry espoused by Lawrence Stenhouse and Ann Berthoff. He then traces the influence of these theorists in subsequent second-generation literature in the current teacher-research resurgence.

In Chapter 2, we speak more personally, each of us placing ourselves within the historical context Fishman provides in Chapter 1. In his half of Chapter 2, Fishman characterizes himself as a "Berthoffian zealot," whereas McCarthy, in her half, defines herself as a "Stenhousian social scientist." After describing the researchers we were when we met in 1989, we outline our reasons for agreeing to collaborate.

In the body of the book that follows (Chapters 3 through 10), we present four paired chapters. In the first member of each pair (Chapters 3, 5, 7, and 9), we open the unplayed tapes behind four of our published studies, describing our debates as collaborators, our disagreements about how to conduct our classroom studies and write our research reports.

Throughout, we highlight ways we attempt to ameliorate the either/or dualisms which we see as plaguing the teacher-research field. In the second member of each pair (Chapters 4, 6, 8, and 10), we reprint these four studies, the public outcomes of our behind-the-scenes negotiations.

In our concluding chapter, we offer teacher-researchers specific tips about how to integrate theory and data, insider and outsider perspectives, and contrasting methodologies. We also look back over our decade of collaborative teacher research and identify what we think are its salient ingredients. Finally, we consider the effects of teacher research on both of us and reflect on our motives, on the engines that drive us forward year after year into classroom inquiry.

CHAPTER ONE

CHARTER CONCEPTIONS OF TEACHER RESEARCH

Steve Fishman

✳

S econd-generation studies in the field of practitioner inquiry—for example, *Seeing for Ourselves* (Bissex & Bullock, 1987), *Inside/Outside* (Cochran-Smith & Lytle, 1993), and *The Practice of Theory* (Ray 1993)—anchor themselves in two charter conceptions of teacher research. The first is Lawrence Stenhouse's (1975, 1981/1985h) view that teacher research is both systematic and self-critical. Stenhouse sees teacher research as reflective inquiry which involves established methods of data collection and analysis, peer review, and publication.

The second, quite different, conception of teacher research is from Ann Berthoff (1979/1987a). Berthoff claims that practitioner inquiry is *re-searching* experiences teachers already have, a form of "inventing" in which we speak or write to "know what [we]...mean" (p. 30). That is, according to Berthoff, teachers already have in their memories all the information they require for fruitful inquiry into their classrooms. I call both of these definitions of teacher research "charter conceptions" because Stenhouse's and Berthoff's efforts to develop a new category of classroom studies have helped chart the course of this emerging field.

Alongside these charter definitions, and equally pervasive in the second-generation literature, are two widely shared justifications or goals for teacher research. The first is that practitioner inquiry leads to increased power and greater justice for teachers, and the second is that it leads to more effective classroom instruction. Much published teacher research suggests that practitioner inquiry does indeed empower instructors by giving them new voice and increasing their confidence and motivation. Whether or not it actually improves teaching is more difficult to ascertain. Some observers claim practitioner inquiry and better teaching go hand in hand (Bissex, 1987, p. 4; Patterson & Shannon, 1993, p. 8), whereas others worry that research can take energy and attention from classroom work (Campbell, 1998; Elbow, 1993, pp. 57-58). This debate aside, however, these two goals for practitioner inquiry—teacher empowerment and improved instruction—are mentioned by nearly all commentators.

STENHOUSE AND BERTHOFF: GENERATING EITHER/OR DUALISMS

In a number of ways, the charter definitions of Stenhouse and Berthoff are similar. Both are rooted in unhappiness with traditional educational research. Stenhouse (1978/1985f) argues that psychostatistical studies override teacher judgment rather than strengthen it because these studies ask teachers to slavishly apply rather than test and evaluate research results (p. 27). By contrast, according to Stenhouse, naturalistic or ethnographic studies—what he calls "the illuminative approach" (p. 26)—are preferable because they ask teacher readers to imaginatively step into the targeted classroom and appraise the credibility and usefulness of research conclusions in light of their own experience (1981/1985h, p. 12). Unlike statistical research, case studies do not assume that what works in one classroom will necessarily work in others. Instead, the assumption is that case studies, rather than providing prescriptions for teachers to follow, offer hypotheses for them to test (1978/1985f, p. 29). It is this case study approach which Stenhouse recommends for teacher research.

In parallel ways, Berthoff (1979/1987a) also criticizes traditional educational research. She maintains that standard quantitative research provides no "direction" for teachers because it focuses, not on reforming practice, but on advancing science by means of fresh data collection (p. 29). Like Stenhouse, Berthoff wants educational research to be based on teachers' questions. Otherwise, she says, it is pointless (p. 30). Stenhouse's way of putting this is that teachers should make researchers accountable to them rather than vice versa (1981/1985h, p. 19).

But despite Stenhouse's and Berthoff's similar doubts about the fruitfulness of traditional research for classroom practice, these theorists differ in their orientations toward practitioner inquiry. First, they disagree about the relation of outside and inside classroom reseachers. Whereas Stenhouse (1980/1985c) believes university-based outsiders and practitioner insiders have mutual need for one another (p. 109), Berthoff (1979/1987a) sees them in opposition. Teachers, she says, will only become researchers if they keep university people out of the schools (p. 30). Second, Stenhouse emphasizes that practitioner inquiry is systematic, empirical, and self-critical, with roots in naturalistic case study. This means, for Stenhouse, that data collection is not a hindrance but an expectation of teacher research. In sharp contrast, Berthoff says that teachers already have in memory all the information they need for successful classroom inquiry.

A final difference between the charter conceptions of Stenhouse and Berthoff is that Stenhouse underlines, in ways Berthoff does not, that teacher research is an ongoing social practice in which we add to, and perfect, the work of others. Whereas Berthoff (1979/1987a) simply calls for dialogue among teacher-researchers (p. 29), Stenhouse (1981/1985h) goes further, calling for publication and peer review. He declares, "Private research for our purpose does not count as research" (pp. 16-17). This is because, for Stenhouse, making research public is a way to share, profit from criticism, and join "a community of critical discourse" (p. 17).

STENHOUSE'S VIEW OF PRACTITIONER INQUIRY: ANALYTIC, ACADEMIC, AND DATA-ORIENTED

Stenhouse's training as a historian lies behind much of what he says about teacher research. He tells us the case-study approach is appropriate for practitioner inquiry because, like historical research, it casts its readers in an active, evaluating role (1981/1985h, p. 12). As Stenhouse views history, it does not simply supply descriptive generalizations. Instead, it uses careful documentation to get *inside* events—accessing the thinking of their key players—in order to build a rich, detailed account. When historians are successful, their readers, drawing upon their own knowledge, use their own judgment to evaluate the historian's interpretations (1979/1985e, p. 31).

Systematic Inquiry

Stenhouse's background helps make understandable his insistence that teacher research be "systematic inquiry," that it supply "the recognizable characteristics and context" of the data collected (1981/1985h, p. 12). He believes that only in this way can it achieve its essential, "illuminative" function (1978/1985f, p. 26). To quote Stenhouse: "I conclude that research can only markedly improve the act of teaching if it offers descriptions of cases or retrospective generalizations about cases sufficiently rich in detail to provide a comparative context in which to judge better one's own case" (1979/1985d, p. 50). Systematic inquiry, for Stenhouse, then, involves structured data collection which results, ideally, in case studies illuminating particular classroom practices and developing teacher readers' professional judgment.

Self-Critical Inquiry

As for what Stenhouse (1981/1985h) means by teacher research being "self-critical" (p. 8), I am less clear. He seems to require a combination of three related activities. First, as I have already said, Stenhouse believes teacher research should be published in order to profit from peer review (p. 17). This way, as he puts it, such research can be "coordinated with the work of others" (1979/1985g, p. 120). Second, he talks about the importance for practitioner inquiry of "critique" or "critical theory" (1982/1985b, p. 54). I take him to mean teacher-researchers need to examine the ideological assumptions behind particular classroom practices—their often unstated reasons for valuing certain student habits and behaviors.

Finally, Stenhouse (1979/1985g) believes teacher-researchers should generate criticism by becoming outsiders to their own research, finding continuities and discontinuities as they retrospectively analyze their own development and work (p. 120). Teacher colleagues and university researchers, he says, may help in this critical process, and to this end he encourages teacher-researchers to elicit alternative perspectives on their own classrooms. He writes, "An elementary school teacher who wishes to improve his or her teaching of science will record teaching or invite a colleague in as observer, and will, if possible, bring in an outsider to monitor the children's perceptions as a basis for 'triangulation'" (1980/1985c, p. 107).

Stenhouse's insistence that teacher knowledge and self-criticism are the result of careful documentation, multiple data sources, and varied perspectives can be traced to classical Greek thought. Plato, for example, distinguishes *doxa*, or mere belief, from *episteme*, or knowledge. Knowledge, unlike belief, is tested and warranted. To say we know something—as opposed to saying we believe something—suggests we can present evidence or grounds for our claim. It implies we have subjected our ideas to scrutiny, related them to the ideas of others, and explored their consequences by acting on them as if they were true.

Although Stenhouse is frequently cited in second-generation commentaries on teacher research, his stress on the self-critical aspect of systematic inquiry does not always receive high priority. This may be because, compared to Berthoff's approach to teacher research, Stenhouse seems more demanding and, therefore, less immediately empowering of teachers. To better compare Berthoff's charter definition with Stenhouse's, I now offer more details about her view that practitioner inquiry is re-searching what we already know.

BERTHOFF'S VIEW OF PRACTITIONER INQUIRY: NARRATIVE, PERSONAL, AND TEACHER-CENTERED

By contrast with historian Stenhouse, Berthoff's expertise is in composition and rhetoric. As a result, her conception of teacher research draws heavily upon her understanding of language, her view that, in both written and spoken forms, language is a means of discovery. She uses this feature of discourse to argue that teacher research is less about systematic data collection and more about reflecting on what, in some sense, we already know.

Re-searching What We Already Know

One way to interpret Berthoff's view of practitioner inquiry as re-searching our experience is that teacher inquiry is a process of making explicit what was formerly only tacit. And this notion that knowledge is within us, waiting to be awakened by the appropriate questioning, also has classic origins. Plato—puzzled by how we could learn new truths or recognize truth in claims which are allegedly unfamiliar—argues that all knowledge is at some level already known to us. We have to train ourselves to re-cognize the forms (or truths) of everyday things, but if we discipline our minds, we can do it.

I point to the historical roots of the Stenhouse-Berthoff conflict—the tension between science and story—to show how fundamental it has been in Western thought. In fact, John Dewey (1920/1962b) claims that the clash between science and story, reason and imagination, analysis and tradition, cost Socrates—who sided with rational analysis—his life. Whereas Greek story and mythology, Dewey tells us, vibrated with collective wisdom and emotion, the developing matter-of-fact knowledge or science of the Greek working class was, by comparison, dry and abstract. The loyalties these competing epistemologies attracted were so powerful, according to Dewey, that for arguing that story is an insufficient justification for morality, for insisting upon warrants more consistent and rational than priestly tales, Socrates was tried and, ultimately, put to death.

Similar conflicts have continued throughout the intervening period into modern times. Descartes, for example, takes up the knowledge-is-re-cognition position when he argues that to know something is to have a clear and distinct idea of it. Like Plato, Descartes trusts that we have a rational faculty or power which recognizes true ideas, or at least can do so when not unduly influenced by sensation and emotion. What is especially enlightened about Descartes, and why each of us is in his debt, is that Descartes extends rationality to all people, whereas Plato reserves it for an aristocratic or expert few. We are also in Descartes' debt because, by making reason universal, he paves the way for the view that everyone is entitled to respect and self-determination.

Although it may seem a bit of a reach to connect Descartes and Ann Berthoff, when Berthoff calls teacher research a form of re-searching or re-collecting our experience, she empowers all of us as teachers, works toward granting all of us respect and self-determination in our professional stations. I connect Berthoff and Descartes, despite the fact that the basis for Berthoff's re-searching theory of knowledge is very different from Descartes'. Whereas Descartes empowers us by appeal to a rational faculty with which we are born—a faculty which can reveal innate or a priori truths—Berthoff empowers teachers by appeal to our storehouses of experience, a rich memory accumulated over years of practice. Teacher research, as Berthoff (1978/1981) sees it, is a matter of tapping into these experiences, organizing and articulating them.

Collections of teacher research indicate that Berthoff is correct about the empowering potential of practitioner inquiry. Asking teachers to reflect on their years of practice, assuring them that such reflection is valuable to themselves and others, yields dramatic results. Published anthologies show that practitioners who journal, brainstorm, or freewrite about their experiences in a supportive, encouraging situation feel fresh energy and self-respect (see Bissex & Bullock, 1987; Cochran-Smith & Lytle, 1993; Hall et al., 1997; Patterson et al., 1993). Why does this happen, and how does it work?

Inventive Re-searching

A closer look at Berthoff's position suggests teacher research is more than simply recovering what we already know. It actually creates it. She tells us: "Inventing as a way of understanding is a truth known to poets as well as cognitive psychologists. A version of that dialectic is the one we all know concerning the composing process: you can't really know what you mean until you hear what you say" (1979/1987a, p. 30). As I understand her, Berthoff claims that journaling, brainstorming, and freewriting may seem like simple acts of self-expression, putting into words what we already know, but, to the contrary, these activities involve an important element of creativity. When an impulse toward expression brings us to speak or write, the act of articulation often presents us with more than thoughts or feelings previously formed. The point of utterance frequently disciplines and shapes our ideas in ways which surprise even ourselves. At these times we do not so much recover our beliefs as give birth to them. We speak or write not to communicate our views but to create them.

If then, for Berthoff, teacher research is properly understood as discovery rather than recovery, why does she speak as if teacher inquiry is simply coming to know what we meant all along? Why does she say, quoting Coleridge in another context, that language and writing allow us "to know our knowledge" (1978/1981, p. 57)? One reason may be that when we describe our self-discoveries, we sometimes engage in an odd sort of discourse. In these situations, when we are surprised by our self-discoveries, it seems strange to say we have come to know what we already know. Since we do not fully recognize our new ideas, we feel uncomfortable calling them our own. Yet we can hardly assign them to someone else. Faced with this puzzle, we can attribute our ideas to the divine muse or to forces for which we are only a vehicle. However, most of us are uneasy with such attributions, and so it seems less mysterious to say that at some implicit level we knew our "new" discoveries all along.

A second reason Berthoff may describe teacher research as re-searching or re-covering our knowledge is to support the empowerment goal of practitioner inquiry. She says to teachers, in effect, "You know more than you take credit for," and this is exhilarating. As teachers, we are energized when we begin brainstorming or journaling, unsure we have anything to say, only to find—20 minutes later—that we need more time and paper. Thus, Berthoff's view of practitioner inquiry as knowing our own knowledge moves teachers out of subordination to university-based or outside researchers. It announces that teachers already possess valuable information and occupy a privileged position regarding classroom studies.

Valuing Teacher Wisdom and Voice

Regarding the two frequently stated goals of practitioner inquiry, it is obvious that, although Berthoff certainly implies that instructors who engage in practitioner inquiry will improve their teaching, the central thrust behind her charter conception is the desire for greater justice for teachers. I believe Berthoff's foundational role in second-generation literature is the result of her efforts to stretch the idea of educational research to include previously silenced or ignored school voices. That is to say, Berthoff's definition echoes a chord which in the 1980s and 1990s has sounded for greater inclusiveness in the educational picture.

With regard to primary and secondary school teachers, for example, the National Writing Project (established at the University of California Berkeley in the early 1970s) has sponsored summer institutes the past quarter century predicated on the view that practitioners bring important wisdom to these institutes. NWP leaders see themselves as facilitators—rather than authorities—whose primary function is helping teachers articulate and refine what they already know about pedagogy and curriculum.

In similar ways, and across a similar span of time, composition theorists like Peter Elbow (1973) and Donald Murray (1968) have promoted the idea that good writing comes with frequent practice, and frequent practice comes when students have bona fide reasons for writing. This means valuing their personal experience, the knowledge and skills with which students enter our classrooms. It also means less focus on correct or outside models of writing and more focus on internal standards. Put another way, it suggests that if we provide assignments which let students "own" their compositions and write on topics they know and care about, they will be motivated to perfect their work. They will become equal and active partners—rather than subordinate and passive recipients—in constructing their own essays.

Likewise, advocates of the whole language approach to literacy give young children credit for their ability to recognize and use written words, although these children are unable to articulate any grammatical rules or conventions. Sounding much like Berthoff speaking about teachers' implicit knowledge of their classrooms, whole language proponents claim young students have already begun to develop written literacy before they enter school because, living in a print culture, they have personal and social needs to do so. Just as Berthoff says practitioner inquiry must start with teachers' questions, so Kenneth Goodman (1989/1996), a key whole language theorist, says reading should begin with what students already know. Since reading, like all language, is "social-personal invention," teachers need to be aware of students' existing abilities and provide situations for students to use and build upon them (p. 83).

On reflection, it is no accident that these reforming teacher and student movements occur simultaneously. Freeing teachers from the yoke of university-based, outside research parallels freeing students from the passive role of consumers of externally generated truths about literacy. In both movements, the guiding idea is that people whose personal experiences and concerns are valued—and who are allowed to actively express and reflect on those experiences and concerns—will develop the self-esteem and motivation necessary to perfect their nascent skills.

Alongside the practitioner inquiry and students-as-active-learners movements, I find similar reforming efforts for yet another, often-ignored segment of the educational community: parents. In recent classroom studies, teacher-researchers have begun exploring the relation of classroom and home literacies, granting unusual authority to parents, asking them to be co-researchers (Headman, 1993), co-designers of curriculum (Paley, 1995), and co-respondents to their children's reading and writing (Jumpp, 1996; Larsen, 1998; Shockley, Michalove, & Allen, 1995). Instead of adopting an authoritative stance toward students' parents, these teacher-researchers offer parents equal partnerships, enlisting their active input into their children's literacy development.

As I explain in Chapter 3, Lucille McCarthy and I, in our collaborative classroom inquiries, have enjoyed many of the empowering, as well as utilitarian, benefits of Berthoff's (1979/1987a) call "to think about the information we have" (p. 30). Reflections on my teaching experiences fueled my midcareer renewal of interest in my students' writing and my own teaching strategies. Given the low value normally placed on teachers' practical wisdom at all levels of instruction, I cannot praise highly

enough the confidence-building which Berthoff's views have stimulated.
But as I explain later, there are difficulties in presenting teacher research,
as well as student learning, as simply knowing our knowledge. As important as personal knowledge is for active learners, there are problems in
assuming that knowing is primarily an internal affair of personal discovery
or that teacher research is appropriately done only by and for oneself.

STENHOUSE, BERTHOFF, AND SECOND-GENERATION TEXTS

As I have explained, Stenhouse's definition of teacher research pays special
attention to the systematic, critical aspects of practitioner inquiry, whereas Berthoff stresses its experiential and inventive aspects. Of course,
these are bold-letter characterizations intended to distinguish these two
theorists. To be fair, we also need to keep in mind ways in which their
ideas overlap, as I noted above. Stenhouse's (1981/1985h) view of
criticism is, actually, a broad one which includes discussion among peers
(p. 18), and he makes clear that the function of teacher research is to raise
questions about applied pedagogy. By the same token, Berthoff
(1979/1987a)—despite her emphasis upon re-searching or coming to
know our knowledge—says, like Stenhouse, that practitioner inquiry
means teachers dialoguing together (p. 29). And, also like him, she maintains that theory and practice need each other, going so far as to say
teachers should not be allowed to swap "recipes" for classroom exercises
unless they also swap theories (p. 32).

However, in the second-generation literature, the gap between
Stenhouse and Berthoff becomes large. Although there is some blurring,
the majority of second-generation authors lean toward Stenhouse,
stressing connections between practitioner inquiry and other, more traditional forms of research. These theorists underline the importance for
practitioner inquiry of written findings, documentation, peer criticism,
and literature reviews (see Altrichter et al., 1993; Cochran-Smith & Lytle,
1993; Hubbard & Power, 1993; Mohr & MacLean, 1999). By contrast, the
minority more disposed toward Berthoff place a questioning attitude at
the heart of teacher research (see Bissex & Bullock, 1987; Ray, 1993). In
this latter group some even claim—in the ultimate effort to empower
teachers—that all good teachers, whether they know it or not, are
teacher-researchers (Patterson & Shannon, 1993, p. 8). This Berthoff-based
approach emphasizes practitioner inquiry as personal questioning and

downplays it as cumulative, perfectable, and social. For example, Ruth Ray (1993) writes: "teacher research is best seen as a process rather than a product. Therefore, no matter what the findings, the research is 'successful' if it has led teachers to question, challenge, and learn from their experiences in the classroom" (p. 113).

The Stenhouse and Berthoff orientations I have outlined leave theorists of teacher research with difficult choices. If they lean toward Stenhouse, they risk making practitioner inquiry seem time-consuming and difficult. But if they incline toward Berthoff, they risk stretching the concept of practitioner inquiry so that it seems unrealistically easy. In the long run, this latter alternative may restrict the development of teacher research as well as the advancement of classroom instruction. To illustrate the potential difficulties of an overly facile approach to teacher research, I relate my own early efforts at classroom study.

Fresh from my first Writing Across the Curriculum workshop in 1983, I wanted to explore the difference my changed pedagogy was making for my students. After considerable discussion with my workshop leaders, they assured me teacher research required no more than a writing pad and the determination to note anything in my classes which provoked my curiosity. I tried this for a year and got nowhere. I also watched helplessly as a graduate student attempted to build a master's thesis around a study of one of my introductory philosophy courses. The master's candidate likewise failed, ultimately throwing up his hands in frustration at his mountain of notes and audiotapes. And then when, the following semester, I was finally able to write about my classes, I discovered, like other teacher-researchers, that it is not easy to find readership (see Shannon, 1993, p. 2). My initial work focused on my excitement about helping students develop their own voices and become active learners. Although this was new and exciting for me, my theme and my narrative treatment proved to be old hat for most audiences, and my first efforts at publication were failures.

These early experiences as a teacher-researcher are one reason I say the tensions between the Stenhouse and Berthoff orientations are not easily resolved. Stenhouse's approach may be discouraging initially, but in the long run it may contribute more to the development of teacher inquiry. On the other hand, although Berthoff's point of view may lead teacher-researchers to be a little naive about the task ahead, it may contribute more to practitioner confidence and self-esteem. I turn now to specific ways second-generation documents take up and enrich the Stenhouse and Berthoff definitions of teacher research.

Second-Generation Followers of Stenhouse

In their influential volume, *Inside/Outside: Teacher Research and Knowledge* (1993), Marilyn Cochran-Smith and Susan Lytle rely heavily on Stenhouse's charter conception of practitioner inquiry. They define teacher research as teachers' systematic and intentional study of their own classes and schools (pp. 7, 23-24). In clarifying what they mean by *systematic*, they also echo Stenhousian themes, calling for ordered ways of gathering information, documentation of experiences, and maintenance of written records (p. 24). Cochran-Smith and Lytle's overall justification for teacher research is a realignment of teachers' relationship to educational knowledge and the university-based "brokers of [that] knowledge" (p. 43). They tell us practitioner inquirers are uniquely positioned as insiders to explore the ways students and teachers construct knowledge, curriculum, and class procedures (see also Cochran-Smith & Lytle, 1998, 1999).

Seeking additional support for teachers' unique position, Cochran-Smith and Lytle move beyond Stenhouse to draw upon Clifford Geertz's theory of interpretative anthropology. Using his notion of local knowledge, they conclude that practitioner inquiry is a way for teachers to "know their own knowledge," that is, their "local knowledge" (1993, p. 45). This conclusion sounds like a repeat of Berthoff's view that teacher research is re-searching our experiences. However, despite the fact that Cochran-Smith/Lytle and Berthoff all work toward empowering teachers, the similarity suggested by their emphases on self-knowledge is misleading.

Berthoff, as already noted, believes teacher-researchers require no new information and can rely on the heuristic qualities of self-expression as their research tool. By contrast, Cochran-Smith and Lytle use Geertz (1983) to argue not that teachers need no new information but that, relative to outside-researchers, they are in a privileged position to obtain the local information they need. Cochran-Smith and Lytle write:

> [Geertz] suggests that ultimately anthropologists can't really represent "local knowledge"—what native inhabitants see—but can only represent what they [the anthropologists] see through—that is, their interpretive perspectives on their own experiences. Borrowing Geertz's term, we use local knowledge to signal both what teachers come to know about their own knowledge through teacher research and what communities of teacher researchers come to know when they build knowledge collaboratively. (1993, p. 45)

By casting teachers in the role of "native" anthropologists, Cochran-Smith and Lytle support the idea that practitioner inquiry is more than simply researching information we already have. In their appeal to Geertz, they put teachers in the position of privileged natives who are immersed in the data yet who can, at the same time, stand back and employ self-critical techniques. Using these strategies, teachers make explicit for themselves the assumptions and expectations underlying their classes. They gain insight, for example, into what counts as learning in their schoolrooms, who has access to it, and how it is presented, sustained, and evaluated (1993, p. 45).

Mapping Insider-Outsider Collaborations

Although Cochran-Smith and Lytle follow Stenhouse (1980/1985c, p. 107) when they use Geertz to privilege teachers as researchers, they part company with him when they use Geertz to bar university outsiders. Granting that Cochran-Smith and Lytle interpret Geertz fairly—that outside-researchers, no matter the duration or quality of their interactions with natives, can never understand local knowledge—then outside-researchers can never be much help to teachers. (For a parallel critique of outside-researchers, see Feldman & Atkin, 1995, p. 135.)

By restricting the role of university experts, Cochran-Smith and Lytle are obviously working to further teacher liberation. If outsiders are conceptually barred from the habits, language, and meaning of classroom culture—always limited to their own experiences and interpretative lenses—then it is practitioners who hold the keys to classroom worlds. And in many instances, keeping outsiders away is probably a good thing. As I follow exchanges along Internet teacher research lines (e.g., Xstar at listserve@lester.appstate.edu), I read accounts of university researchers exploiting practitioners, imperialistically mining teacher data and stories to secure degrees, publications, and promotions. These sorts of researcher-practitioner arrangements are exploitive and, often, counterproductive for classroom reform. However, I believe, as I expect Stenhouse would, that Cochran-Smith and Lytle's interpretation of Geertz as barring all university outsiders from access to native culture goes too far.

If we take seriously the idea that anthropologists—no matter their efforts to achieve participant-observer status—can never transcend their own experiences and points of view, then it is difficult to envision how anyone understands anyone else at all. Such a stance would lead us down a skeptical path, toward a view of knowledge which would also make it difficult for teacher-researchers to gain access to their own students' worlds. Although teachers and students co-construct classroom culture, they hardly inhabit similar places in that culture. Likewise, difficulties in understanding others' worlds would arise for teachers visiting one another's classes. If outsiders can never understand the groups to which they are not native, how can any outside teacher comment perceptively on a colleague's practices? Yet, contrary to this exclusionary view of local knowledge, we do seem able to perceptively enter other worlds, learning, for example, about our students' "underlife" (Brooke, 1987) or insightfully discussing a colleague's classes.

Cochran-Smith and Lytle, then, use their understanding of local knowledge to exclude outside-researchers and privilege inside ones. In addition, there is another assumption which seems to undergird their negative attitude toward university experts. This second assumption is that collaboration among peers, rather than among teachers on disparate rungs of the educational ladder, is likely to be more equitable and less exploitive. However, I see no reason why this is necessarily the case. A researcher does not have to go down the ladder to generate an unfair research situation. As McCarthy explains in the following chapter, as a graduate student studying college classrooms, she was in a position to unfairly criticize and exploit professors who held much higher rank. In other words, I do not believe that restricting collaboration in the classroom to teachers of equal rank solves the exploitation problem Cochran-Smith and Lytle seek to remedy. In fact, although I applaud their goal of empowering teachers as researchers, I fear their harsh view of university outsiders may, potentially, restrict rather than forward practitioner inquiry. As an alternative remedy to this exploitation problem, I suggest another approach to the outsider-insider distinction.

Insiders and Outsiders Alternate Roles

The frequent unfairness of classroom collaboration, as I see it, has less to do with university outsiders being strangers or holding higher educational rank and more to do with the sort of relationship outsiders and insiders develop. When Cochran-Smith and Lytle downplay the value of outsider-insider collaborations, they undoubtedly have exploitive outsider-insider arrangements in mind—ones in which researchers see practitioners and students as objects rather than co-agents of research. But outsider-insider collaborations do not have to be exploitive. As

McCarthy and I show in later chapters, outsider-insider arrangements can take on a variety of configurations. For example, in certain arrangements, although classroom practitioners are the only ones in the investigative spotlight, researchers consult with classroom teachers about project design, data collection, and reporting style (see Walvoord & McCarthy, 1990). In even more equitable forms—ones we call, in later chapters, democratic collaborations—the university outsider's research and teaching may come in for as much scrutiny as the activities of the insider practitioner. (For more on outsider-insider relationships, see Anderson & Herr, 1999; Banks, 1998; Bisplinghoff & Allen, 1998; Brodkey, 1996; Cole & Knowles, 1993; Durst & Stanforth, 1996; Elliott, 1991; Jordan & Jacob, 1993; Schulz, 1997; Ulichney & Schoener, 1996; Wagner, 1997; Wasser & Bresler, 1996.)

Despite Cochran-Smith and Lytle's distrust of outside, university researchers, the end result of their approach to teacher research, as I see it, is to ask teachers themselves to become outsiders to their own locales. That is, when they invite teachers to systematically study their own classes—to describe and analyze their local knowledge—they are, in effect, asking teachers to disengage from their normal activities, change their usual professional gaze, and view their classrooms in a highly reflexive way. Generally, teachers have their hands full just doing the insider work of keeping class going, getting students to respond directly to one another, deciding how and when to intercede with information or advice. Most times, teachers have, at best, only a felt sense of the organizing principles of their classrooms, for instance, of when, how, and who gets to question another class member's remarks. As I interpret it, the upshot of Cochran-Smith and Lytle's conception of teacher research is actually to help practitioners become outsiders, see their classes in new light, and uncover the tacit rules and expectations driving their school cultures.

Interestingly, John Dewey—whom Cochran-Smith and Lytle view as one of the earliest proponents of teacher research—argues that all learning, all genuine communication, requires that we become outsiders to our own beliefs and experiences. Being stuck in our own views means our modes of communication have become routine, and in this situation we cannot grow. Dewey (1916/1967) writes:

> Try the experience of communicating, with fullness and accuracy, some experience to another...and you will find your own attitude toward your experience changing.... The experience has to be formulated in order to be

[handwritten margin note: Support for writing ↓ knowing?]

communicated. To formulate requires getting *outside* of it, seeing it as another
would see it, considering what points of contact it has with the life of another
so that it may be got into such a form that... [the listener] can appreciate its
meaning. (pp. 5-6, emphasis added)

Teacher research for Cochran-Smith and Lytle is, then, as I see it, an example
of what Dewey calls learning. That is to say, teacher research, for them,
enables practitioners to view their experiences from another's perspective, to move back and forth between outsider and insider stances.

In sum, if I am correct in my interpretation of Cochran-Smith and
Lytle, their goals for teacher research are best met by ensuring that
"outsider" status in the classroom is allowed for teachers as well as
university researchers. The real point is not that university outsiders as
outsiders are dangerous but that they are dangerous when they forbid
teachers to share their status. For university researchers to limit instructors'
opportunities to be outsiders to their own local knowledge is a little like
16th-century Spanish colonials barring Native Americans from mounting
horses. Colonials did this to prevent natives from experiencing the new
perspectives and strategic advantages of horseback riding. My claim with
regard to teacher inquiry is that, in our zeal to overcome the hegemony
of outside-researchers, we should be cautious about concluding there is
something wrong with getting on horses altogether. Quite the opposite,
the point of inviting peers into our classrooms is to make it easier to
notice or question the too-familiar. And just as university researchers
need to help teachers become outsiders to their classrooms, teachers,
in turn, need to help university researchers see their own research methods
in fresh ways. In other words, if a collaborative inquiry is to be fully
equitable and reciprocal, there needs to be a mutually informing alternation of outsider and insider positions.

In Chapter 3, Lucille McCarthy and I discuss ways that we, as teacher-
researchers, struggle to alternate our outsider and insider positions in
order to challenge one another's assumptions about teaching, ways of
learning, and disciplinary knowledge and research. We describe how
McCarthy—the outside-researcher—occasionally encourages me—the
practitioner inquirer—to mount the researcher's horse to see my own and
her classes from new angles. We also detail how I urge her at times to
dismount to get different views of her focus students and her research
practices as well as her own teaching. In the arrangement which emerges
in our collaboration, it is not so much the researcher having to answer to

the teacher (as Stenhouse would have wished) or the teacher answering to the researcher (as is usually the case) but, rather, the two of us attempting to work together while, at the same time, encouraging one another's growth.

At this juncture, I leave Cochran-Smith and Lytle, theorists who incline toward Stenhouse's orientation, to discuss the work of two other second-generation theorists, Glenda Bissex and Ruth Ray, who incline toward Berthoff. Whereas Cochran-Smith and Lytle stress the need for systematic data collection and analysis, Bissex and Ray, following Berthoff's lead, stress the importance of personal knowledge for teacher research.

Second-Generation Followers of Berthoff

In her introduction to *Seeing for Ourselves: Case-Study Research by Teachers of Writing*, Glenda Bissex (Bissex & Bullock, 1987) builds on Berthoff's notion that practitioner inquiry is a form of rethinking or reobserving which requires no new information (p. 4). Bissex tells us such inquiry demands nothing fancy—no control groups, statistical analyses, or disciplinary language. In fact, much the opposite, it begins with personal questions and concerns (a teacher's "wonderings"), it employs straight talk, and its audience is, properly, the teacher herself, her students, or her school community (pp. 3-4). In addition, Bissex works to promote teacher research by pointing out both the shortcomings of academically structured classroom investigations and the advantages of personally framed practitioner narratives (p. 8).

Personal Questions and Voice versus Academic Questions and Voice

To establish her point about the personal quality of successful practitioner inquiry, Bissex analyzes the openings of two pieces of educational research: the first, an article from *Research in the Teaching of English (RTE)* by Donald Rubin and Gene Piche (1979), and the second, an article by Nancie Atwell from *Language Arts* (1984). The Rubin and Piche study is written in impersonal prose, employs heavy doses of parenthetical citations, and strives to make a place for itself in an ongoing published conversation. In direct opposition, Atwell adopts a neighborly tone, provides the context of her school situation, and retraces steps she has taken in her search for a research topic. Bissex (1987) concludes that the authoritarian, distanced voice of Rubin and Piche, as contrasted with the narrative, intimate style of Atwell, shows "their research has been conducted in different worlds for different audiences" (p. 9).

Bissex's contrast is vivid and telling. She adds weight to the view that much academic prose is so specialized and impersonal it can only keep an expert's attention. And it is true that parenthetical citations can serve as warning signs—I call them "Beware, Big Dog" signs—announcing that only those who are familiar with the cited materials can proceed safely with their reading. In 1987, when Bissex writes, the debate over the legitimacy of teacher stories was in its early stages, and her comparison argues well for them. However, just as too sharp a line between outsider and insider may prove counterproductive, so also may too thorough a distinction between academic research and practitioner retrospective.

As Stenhouse (1981/1985h) points out, all research involves criticism, and an important way to achieve this is by making it a community affair, encouraging peer sharing, discussion, and review (pp. 16-18). Although Rubin and Piche's *RTE* style may be clumsy and their citations too numerous, what they intend in their opening is to enter into conversation with their peers, to make themselves vulnerable to critical review. They assume, as Stenhouse makes explicit, that research, like all practices, cannot be successfully engaged in by oneself. It takes community work, no matter how physically alone one may be at various periods of the process. (I note that Berthoff [1979/1987a] adopts a similar position insofar as she says teacher-researchers must be in dialogue with one another [p. 29], but she emphasizes this less vigorously than Stenhouse.)

Contrary to Bissex's implication that Rubin and Piche are detached from their work, I believe they are not necessarily, in using academic language, ignoring or setting aside their own questions. Bissex, understandably—as she fights for practitioner narrative's legitimacy—makes it seem an either/or affair: either you start with other studies and use academic language (like Rubin and Piche) or you start with your own questions and employ a personal voice (like Atwell). But, however understandable from a justice-for-teachers standpoint, Bissex's either/or strategy is too limiting.

McCarthy's and my experience with classroom studies—our own efforts to integrate academic and personal concerns—suggests that Stenhouse and Bissex are *both* correct. Good research is not just disciplinary, nor is it just personal: it is both. Stenhouse is correct when he says that research is a critical practice requiring peer review, but Bissex, following Berthoff, is also correct when she maintains that personal questions are a crucial starting point for research. Rubin and Piche may present a citation-filled opening, yet their Stenhousian purpose—to locate the place where their own concerns and those of their fellow researchers coincide—is important to their community membership. Without it, they may end up talking to themselves in unproductive ways. Alternatively, if they lose sight of Berthoff's emphasis on real-life, personally-rooted questions, their work will lack energy and drama, be no more than idle academic chatter with little chance to influence action.

Personal Knowledge and Expression versus Academic Knowledge and Exposition

A related, second-generation book, which also focuses on clashes between personal experience and academic knowledge in classroom research, is Ruth Ray's *The Practice of Theory: Teacher Research in Composition* (1993). As the title suggests, Ray, writing 6 years after Bissex, works to shape a balanced approach, calling for integration of practice and theory, invention and criticism, personal and academic knowledge. Interestingly, Ray, like Bissex, also takes issue with a study from *Research in the Teaching of English:* "Conventions, Conversations, and the Writer: Case Study of a Student in a Rhetoric Ph.D. Program" by Berkenkotter, Huckin, and Ackerman (1988). Ray criticizes this study, however, not for the authors' impersonal style, but for their approval of graduate rhetoric programs which require *students* to adopt an impersonal style.

In their article, Berkenkotter et al. focus on one graduate student's efforts to write successfully as a Ph.D. candidate at Carnegie Mellon University. The authors (one of whom is "Nate," the student at the center of the inquiry) rely on careful examination of Nate's written texts to show his gradual adoption of "the language of his [newly chosen] discipline" (Berkenkotter et al., 1988, p. 15). However, in doing so, he must give up what the authors see as the personal, "expressive" prose of his under-graduate work in order to take on the formal, knowledge-of-the-academy prose required by Carnegie Mellon's graduate faculty (p. 19). Ray argues that the *RTE* authors "see expressive writing as inferior to expository writing" when they characterize Nate's expressive writing at Carnegie Mellon as a regression, a sign he is still "wrestling" with new ideas rather than truly understanding them (p. 144). Just as significantly, Ray sees Berkenkotter et al.'s view that academic discourse is superior to personal prose as discounting personal experience in favor of academic knowledge.

As I have already said, Ray, unlike Bissex, looks for ways to integrate personal experience and disciplinary knowledge. However, the details of her integration and its effect on teacher research are not fully clear. At times, it sounds as if Ray believes personal or expressive writing should be a stepping-stone, something to rely on until more mature, academic prose is mastered (p. 153). At other times, she argues that personal writing should be seen as an alternative way of knowing in academia, a way of resisting and challenging the status quo (p. 154). Yet, despite her talk of integrating these two voices, she concludes by echoing Berthoff. The value of writing about one's own classroom is, Ray says, "to come to a personal understanding of the field through reflection on and analysis of one's own experiences as a teacher and researcher" (p. 156). So despite her efforts to avoid language hierarchies and dichotomies—specifically, the split between academic and personal knowledge—Ray seems, in the end, to limit practitioner inquiry, keeping it within the bounds of the personal. I believe this harms teacher research because Ray loses sight of the possibility that greater interaction among different ways of knowing would allow what she calls "personal knowledge" to challenge and, in turn, be informed by disciplinary understanding (p. 82).

In subsequent chapters Lucille McCarthy and I discuss our own efforts to integrate narrative and analysis, personal knowledge and disciplinary understanding: to ameliorate, in short, the Berthoff-Stenhouse tensions, the either/or dualisms I have just outlined. To do this, we open the unplayed tapes—the private conversations—behind our own collaborative inquiries. These tapes illustrate ways in which McCarthy as a social scientist and I as a product of Writing Across the Curriculum workshops reflect major forces which collide and challenge one another in the teacher-research movement. As later chapters reveal, our collaboration is never entirely smooth, and our skirmishes, despite their idiosyncracies, reflect larger battles still being waged by practitioner-researchers. These chapters also show changes in our collaboration, a movement away from insider-outsider asymmetrical roles to a more balanced arrangement in which McCarthy and I are equally agents and objects of research.

However, before turning to details about McCarthy's and my conflicts over the nature of classroom research—and our efforts to reconcile our differences—each of us offers, in Chapter 2, a brief account of our backgrounds and the developments which led us in 1989 to undertake our initial joint study.

CHAPTER TWO

On the Path toward Collaborative Classroom Inquiry

Steve Fishman and Lucille McCarthy

I n this chapter each of us presents our history in ways which reveal current clashes in the teacher-research movement. Whereas Fishman was trained in a Berthoffian environment, one focused on the inventive power of writing and personal voice, McCarthy was trained in a very different corner of the teacher-research field. As a student in an English education doctoral program, she focused on systematic data collection, analysis, and development of an academic, social science voice.

THE INSIDER-TEACHER'S STORY
Steve Fishman

The Making of a Berthoffian Zealot

It all began innocently enough. In spring of 1983 I was shamed by faculty friends into attending a Writing Across the Curriculum (WAC) workshop sponsored by my university's English Department. It was a 3-day affair in the North Carolina mountains about 2 hours from campus. Since I enjoy neither travel nor adventure, I attended only to please Sam Watson and Leon Gatlin, longtime colleagues who were organizing the workshop and were having difficulty garnering faculty recruits. Watson and Gatlin were co-directors of the National Writing Project site at the university, and, as a result, the retreat highlighted classroom techniques and approaches featured at their summer institutes. These included honoring teachers' own practical wisdom, attending to the writing *process* as much as to the finished *product*, urging teachers to compose in their classes along with their students, and, in general, fostering a spirit of equality in the schoolroom. Despite my distaste for adventure, I would prove highly susceptible to these aspects of the workshop.

Indeed, in retrospect, I was, my reservations notwithstanding, a prime candidate for a WAC program. I had been teaching philosophy at the same institution—University of North Carolina Charlotte—for 15 years and had become uncomfortable with the sorts of residues students were taking from my courses. During these years, I taught in a way which was guided more by unthinking imitation than serious reflection. That is, I taught classic philosophic texts, used a mix of informal lecture and Socratic questioning, and, in general, mimicked the instruction I myself had received as an undergraduate and graduate student. Although it took me a long time to stop and ask myself about goals for my courses, the seeds of dissatisfaction with my own unthinking and imitative approach had been planted long before my first workshop.

As an undergraduate, I had been bothered by the gap between my personal concerns and the foci of my college courses, a dissatisfaction which continued through graduate school. Trying to suppress my sense that something was wrong with the teaching I was receiving, I attributed my difficulties to my own lack of ability and motivation. However, despite completing my Ph.D. at Columbia University in 1967 and achieving tenure in a philosophy department in a relatively short period, I continued to feel estranged from the academic community. It was these seeds of unhappiness which the workshop unexpectedly legitimized while appearing to offer alternatives to the teaching strategies I had myself long employed. What in particular about the workshop appealed to me?

Berthoffian Consequences of Attending a Writing Across the Curriculum Workshop

Using Personal Writing to Teach Philosophy
The first thing I noticed was the emphasis on the heuristic power of writing, its potential to bring forward personal knowledge. Ann Berthoff's idea—very much alive at the retreat—that all discovery begins with personal writing seemed to offer a way to demystify the abstract

and difficult philosophic reading I felt obliged to assign. I thought these apparently distant texts might seem less remote to students if they were understood as rooted in personal writing. I thought that if pupils could see work by Hume and Kant and Mill as products of many diary entries, letters, and drafts, they might feel less intimidated. They might see, perhaps, that their own work, although pale in comparison to the celebrated corpus, paralleled the tentative first steps behind the published philosophic texts they were reading.

Using Freewriting to Make Teaching More Student-Centered

A second feature of the workshop was its suggestion that teachers see the function of instruction as not so much to convey information as to help pupils find techniques for making their own way into course material. In particular, I was impressed with freewriting. My first evening at the workshop all participants were asked to freewrite about an article which Dixie Goswami, the workshop leader, had given everyone to read. This experiment was especially significant for me because it revealed that writing could be used not just to report but also to discover. Without knowing it, I was experiencing what Berthoff, quoting Coleridge—as I noted in Chapter 1—calls language's ability to help us "know our knowledge" (1978/1981, p. 57).

Although I fear sounding melodramatic, it was truly a watershed experience for me. It stimulated what appeared to be voices and rhythms that were mine yet unfamiliar, and I was astonished by them. Shortly after the retreat—in my first published attempt at teacher research (1985)—I described the significance of the writing I did at this initial workshop:

> On the first day I was asked to freewrite for ten minutes about an assigned article. The article was dull. But the writing, the ten minutes—that's all, no-more-time-to-be-spent—was the promised reward which made the reading bearable. It was the right instruction at the right time. Looking back, I see that moment as my watershed. I suddenly looked at writing differently, more confidently, for what could be expected of me in ten minutes of writing? Chances were good that, limited to one-sixth of an hour, I'd not embarrass myself. Once unburdened of the requirement that I have something memorable or correct to say, words poured out. I was free of worry about failing— failing to please those who might read my work, failing to prepare enough, failing to edit enough.

The second day's assignment was writing to be shared with a group, but I took it to be personal writing, primarily for myself rather than other workshop participants or journal editors or dissertation committees in philosophy. What happened? Voices, rhythms, emotions, and breath. I had always wondered where *I* had been in my previous writing. *I* hadn't been there at all; it was writing without passion, humor, or life. And now I knew why. I had put imitation above honesty. In trying to be part of a tradition, in trying to be as profound and authoritative as acknowledged luminaries in my field, my writing had lost its connection to the intimacies of my own life.

On the second day I realized there was something of my own inside that wanted to come out, and I began remystifying my life, putting awe and value in a new place, in myself. That day I found the joy of writing about what really mattered to me. It was therapeutic. It soothed my hunger for creative activity. It gave me a reason to be. (pp. 331-32)

Given my enthusiasm about what happened to me at that 1983 WAC workshop, it is no wonder that my first concern was making similar experiences available to my students. So when I returned to campus for summer session that year, I radically altered my teaching in hopes my students could also know the heuristic power of writing. Instead of focusing exclusively on canonic works, I downplayed these in favor of students' own texts about issues at the center of class discussion. Instead of speaking from the front of the classroom, I directed my students to form a circle, changing my own position within that circle from session to session in an effort to reduce the traditional privilege attending the instructor's voice. And, finally, I jettisoned exams which tested students' mastery of assigned readings and replaced them with two lengthy papers, each requiring multiple drafts.

Abandoning My Own Academic Writing for Narrative
My new focus on writing in the classroom resulted in some professional changes for me as well. In spring 1984, I enrolled in Sam Watson's advanced composition course and spent much of the time working on expressive writing in the form of short stories. Unfortunately for my academic work, I succeeded in publishing the initial ones, and thus I diverted my attention from philosophy to begin a 7-year period of short story work. Although this was something of a professional detour, I ultimately found such writing valuable insofar as it gave me insight into the types of habits—the daily composing and journaling—which I believe all successful writers, no matter their field, must develop.

I also continued to attend WAC workshops. In fact, between spring 1983 and spring 1990 I attended 12. At the second one, in 1984, I met Barbara Walvoord, who was the workshop leader. Walvoord focused her presentation on doing research in one's own classroom, and I caught the bug. But despite my enthusiasm about beginning such research, I had little understanding of what to do. When I consulted with Sam Watson, it turned out he had no experience researching classrooms either. Like many English teachers in the WAC movement, he saw himself as a consultant about improved writing instruction, not classroom research.

Still determined to do the sort of research Walvoord had spoken about, I audited an English Department course on classroom research and even traveled to Clemson University to speak with Dixie Goswami about it. But, despite these efforts, I still could not get the hang of it. Everyone was telling me how simple teacher inquiry is. "All you need is a question and a notebook," they said, "and you're set. Just go to class and write down everything relevant to your question." Although I tried it repeatedly, it got me nowhere. I could find no patterns to my observations, no clear answers to my questions, or at least nothing I could organize well enough to share with others.

In retrospect, I see that Walvoord and Goswami—both long-standing Berthoffians—were themselves beginning to respond to Stenhousian influences. This was reflected in their suggestions that I enact some simple form of systematic inquiry—framing a question and collecting relevant data. But with my limited understanding of and patience for the tasks of participant observation, I became frustrated. Still, I refused to give up. Desperate to understand student learning in my class and, at the same time, eager to make my classroom research respectable in the eyes of my department, I turned to a genre with which I had had prior success: the short story. This approach helped me write two accounts of my newly implemented WAC strategies. One of these, from which I have already quoted, appeared in 1985, and the other was published in 1989, both in a journal called *Teaching Philosophy*.

My First Teacher-Research Narrative: Pure Berthoff

The first of my two articles is a five-page narrative, more reflective of Berthoff's suggestion that we analyze information we already have than of Stenhouse's charge to use systematic inquiry techniques. In this article, I employ a before-and-after plot in which my WAC workshop becomes, in effect, a conversion experience, with my new classroom techniques the vehicle for a happy journey into the promised land. To be fair to the piece, however, I do make some effort to contextualize the expressivist writing I had adopted. Claiming that freewriting, for example, is a tool of self-discovery, I connect my new pedagogy to Socrates' motto about knowing thyself and to Pascal's claim that discoveries about the world always pale in comparison to discoveries about oneself.

In employing the before-and-after approach I was, without realizing it, following a popular genre of teacher research. Absent any knowledge of other classroom studies, absent any understanding of alternative pedagogical theories, by comparing my new self to my old self I gave my piece some conflict, a way to explore the experiences upon which I based my claims for personal writing in the classroom. I quote from the "after" part of my 1985 article:

> In the year and a half since the workshop, I have come to see anthologies of classic philosophic works as too intimidating, too carefully drawn, too removed from their contexts. They give me and my classes too little idea of where philosophic pieces come from and how they evolve. Not only was I starting my beginning students with the polished, mature work of great minds, but before my students' memories dried, I was stressing orthodox criticisms of these works—the fallacy of Plato's third-man argument, Anselm's mistaken identification of an idea with the reality it represents, the import of A. J. Ayer's theory of verifiability for Descartes' *cogito* and so on. This was like taking a first-day student of pottery to see a Cellini exhibit in Florence and pointing out that Cellini was really second-rate at glazes. . . .
>
> I am also trying to do less *talking* about philosophy now and more *showing*. My most effective tool is my own writing, even completing and sharing some of the writing tasks I assign as class requirements. In sharing my rough drafts and journals and letters, I want to be the guide who says: "I'm writing philosophic pieces about human values and community. You're welcome to watch me, help me, ask questions of me. In turn I want the same chance, to be allowed to watch and help and ask questions as you move forward with your own work." (pp. 332-33)

Although I would not have put it in these terms at the time, I had become a zealous convert to Bertoffianism. I was unwittingly following her instruction to teacher-researchers to employ no special data-gathering methods but simply to reflect on their own teaching experiences.

My Second Teacher-Research Narrative: Berthoff
with Hints of Stenhouse

In my second *Teaching Philosophy* article, the one I wrote 4 years later (1989), I begin in the exact same before-and-after way, once again celebrating my WAC workshop discovery. However, by the third paragraph I seem to be hearing the faint Stenhouse message behind Goswami's and Walvoord's suggestions for teacher inquiry. Instead of contrasting my later pedagogy to my own earlier one, I very quickly, in the second article, consider the work of other teachers who have tried to instruct students about philosophic writing. In other words, I no longer simply talk about myself; I now compare myself with other practitioners.

In addition, in order to support my views about teaching philosophic writing, I introduce, for the first time, student texts as evidence for my claims alongside appeals to my own experience. Somehow I had heard enough to learn the importance of making copies of student work. Although this is a far cry from Stenhouse's systematic inquiry, it was at least a start at using student data. More specifically, when I argue for the superiority of freewriting over traditional outlining as a precomposition technique, I am able, in my second article, to offer a student's own account of successful freewriting.

Another hint in my second piece that I felt a need for additional evidence to support my claims was my use of a letter I received that semester from my student assistant, David Stegall. David was a senior philosophy major bound for graduate school and enrolled in a department practicum to obtain experience in the classroom. For his three credits, David discussed all aspects of my Intro to Philosophy classes with me, and on occasion, when I had to be out of town, he took full responsibility for my teaching. After one such day of substitution, he wrote a letter describing how he failed to stimulate satisfying discussion in my 11:00 class but then introduced freewriting at the opening of the 1:00 period to reverse things. What struck him was the power of this writing technique to prepare students for class conversation, to help them generate something to say about assigned readings.

In preparing my second *Teaching Philosophy* article, I sensed—although I could not have used this language—the value of triangulation. I realized I could use David's letter to provide another perspective on my classroom, one that supplemented my own, suggesting to my readers that I was not seeing my class through rose-colored glasses or simply finding what I hoped to find. This was another step away from the before-and-after genre, although a small one, I admit. Even my most casual readers might complain that one student success story in a classroom is hardly convincing evidence for a pedagogy. Further, they might point out that quoting from my student assistant's letter—especially a pupil I was grading at the end of the semester—is not a strong basis for trustworthy claims. But David's letter is not a straightforward testimony for personal writing in the classroom. It actually reveals an initial resistance to the writing strategies I was employing in Intro to Philosophy. I quote from David's letter as it appeared in my second teacher-research article (1989):

> The truth is that I thought the successes and failures of this semester were solely a product of your charisma. On days when you were animated, classes were a success; on days when you were empty or tired, classes limped along. I feared being asked to evaluate classroom techniques because I really felt that it was you and not the techniques which made the difference. But after last Friday's classes I've come to see things differently.
>
> I went into your 11:00 Intro class, mumbled for a while about trying to find themes within a journal, and broke the class up into three groups. It was terrible. The students had nothing to say to each other and left at least as confused and lost as they were beforehand. While eating lunch and waiting for your 1:00 Intro class, I reflected on the failure of the 11:00 class. One thing I'm beginning to learn is that it is useless to agonize over the past. So instead of feeling dejected, I tried to think of another way, another technique, to breathe life into the class. I walked into the 1:00 class and got myself and the other students to take five minutes or so to write down what they thought their final essay might be about if they were writing it today. It worked. Tom read what he had written, and his first sentence was, "Write about that which refuses to go away." It was like a bolt of lightning; the class, we, had forgotten that simple, yet profound, key you always stress.
>
> Then Richard spoke, saying he might write his essay on the "circle," the message that our moving the desks and getting into a circle sends each day. He went on to say that he had simply started writing a list of things that came to mind when he thought of what the semester had meant. We all paused to make our own lists, and as we began to share the lists, something magical happened. John asked me, "Our lists tell us what we have gotten from this course. What is it that you have received from the course?" And I was honest. I spoke of cynicism causing me to lose the courage to believe and

care. I spoke of how the openness and depth of the words of these students had given me something I could believe in. I said a lot of things... and the students sensed I was honest, and, as they smiled and nodded their heads in agreement, I felt loved. I felt alive.

So what are the techniques that work? The power of getting in a circle. The pausing in class to write. The earnest honesty of the teacher. These are all one needs to make the classes successful. (pp. 370-71)

As I examine this article from the distance of nearly a decade, David certainly seems to be a subordinate who wants to please me, one of his major professors. However, what makes his letter somewhat convincing is the conflict he himself expresses at the opening. In effect, he says, Steve, you have been telling me how great these new techniques are, but I do not believe you. I do not want to come right out and say it, but I really suspect it is your own energy and not the techniques that are important. So David is a reluctant supporter of my view that writing can be an effective way to stimulate student thinking and discussion. Small groups are not successful for him in the 11:00 class, but when freewriting works and gives him an excited and productive discussion in the 1:00 class, he changes his mind about this approach. The fact that his corroboration comes only after an initial skepticism adds weight to his testimony.

Although I now see development in my teacher-research approach between my first and second pieces, I cannot say the second piece left me with a clear idea about how to do future work. That is, my second piece explores differences between my own approach to student philosophic writing and the approaches of two published peers, and in it I introduce new sorts of classroom data. But after I finished, I had no idea what to do next. I certainly wanted to know more about my students' learning as well as ways to improve my teaching, but filling more notebooks with daily, several-page, after-class reflections did not seem a promising springboard to future work. In 1989, after my second piece appeared, I still felt there were teacher-research secrets I did not know. I went from workshop to workshop, hoping someone would finally say, "Here's how you do it," but no one did.

The Insider-Teacher Takes On an Outsider-Collaborator

Rowing in this sea of confusion, I once again encountered Sam Watson, one of the organizers of the first workshop I attended 6 years earlier. Sam, knowing by now I was hooked on exploring teaching and learning in my classroom, talked me into being a presenter at the 1989 Convention of the Conference on College Composition and Communication in Seattle. Along with Barbara Walvoord and Toby Fulwiler, Sam had organized an elaborate panel of WAC leaders as well as converts from a variety of disciplines. Among the presenters was Walvoord's colleague in composition studies, Lucille McCarthy, a newly appointed assistant professor at the University of Maryland Baltimore County. I was impressed with McCarthy's classroom research skills, and believing that I had gone as far as I could by myself, I invited her to join me in a study of my Introduction to Philosophy class. In doing so, I expected to learn enough about teacher research, ultimately, to do it on my own. (For a similar account of a teacher-researcher seeking help from a university outsider, see Isakson & Boody, 1993.) My collaboration with McCarthy did eventually teach me a great deal about classroom inquiry, but this did not turn out to be its primary significance for me, as I make clear in Chapter 3.

As for why McCarthy accepted my invitation, that requires some understanding of the evolution of teacher research in America in the decades of the 1980s and 1990s. As McCarthy describes her own graduate and postgraduate experiences with classroom inquiry, we learn not only why she decides to join with me in a collaborative classroom study but also more about the struggle between Berthoffian and Stenhousian views in the classroom research field.

THE OUTSIDE-RESEARCHER'S STORY
Lucille McCarthy

Why did I accept Steve Fishman's invitation in 1989 to join him as outside investigator in his classroom? Although the outsider role is comfortable for me—both by disposition as well as training—it was Steve himself who interested me. I recall thinking after our initial conversations that I had never met a teacher more driven to understand his own classroom. He seemed fearless in his willingness to turn the spotlight on himself, to reflect upon his mistakes and revise his pedagogy. By contrast, although I have spent as long in the classroom as Steve (some 30 years) and share many of his questions about teaching and learning, I am more comfortable looking outside myself for answers. I prefer putting others on stage, listening and questioning in an effort to understand their perspectives.

For this reason—and others I describe later—I was open to Fishman's request to observe his classroom, and eventually, he and I agreed to collaborate. Unfortunately, however, we failed to articulate clearly our assumptions about teacher research and the roles each of us expected to play. This would cause no small amount of conflict during our initial study, as Steve explains in the next chapter.

To understand the outsider role I assumed I would adopt with Fishman—that is, the researcher I actually was in 1989—I need to say more about two previous research experiences. The first is my doctoral training in the early 1980s at the University of Pennsylvania; the second is a collaborative project I carried out between 1985 and 1989 with my colleague Barbara Walvoord.

The Making of a Stenhousian Researcher

When I began my Ph.D. program in 1981, I had taught 14 years of high school English and had spent the previous year as an adjunct instructor of composition at Loyola College in Maryland. It was this latter experience that convinced me I needed the doctorate—both to bring my understanding of composition pedagogy up to date as well as to prevent a lifetime of part-timer exploitation. At Penn's Graduate School of Education, it was assumed that doctoral candidates would become social scientists, specifically, ethnographers of communication. Dell Hymes, the eminent sociolinguist, was dean at the time, and my courses featured research tools which would enable me to analyze the interaction of language and social life. In particular, I would be prepared to enter classroom "discourse communities," identify participants' ways of speaking and writing, and, thus, understand something about the challenges facing student newcomers in various academic situations (Hymes, 1972). Put differently, my graduate education promised to equip me to figure out, as anthropologist Clifford Geertz puts it, "how others, across the sea or down the corridor, organize their significative world" (1983, p. 151). I would be able to ascertain, "What is going on here? What do these people think they're up to?" (Geertz, 1976, p. 224).

Among the social science tools I learned to use at the University of Pennsylvania were observation and interview techniques drawn from anthropology, protocol analysis taken from cognitive psychology, and text analysis schemes based upon theories of conversational interaction. I gained facility with terms like "triangulation," "negative case," and "trustworthiness," and I counted events whenever I could. I understood intuitively in that era that numerical data—from composing-aloud transcripts, for example—had a special persuasive power in the field. In composition studies as in education, qualitative inquiry in the 1980s was only beginning to gain respect, and in order to be published in prestigious journals, naturalistic inquirers had to mimic the approaches and language of traditional, scientific paradigm work.

My Dissertation: A Data-Extraction Arrangement

In my dissertation (1985), therefore, I adopted an objective outsider stance, and, combining several of my newly learned methodologies, I observed the experiences of one college student, Dave Garrison, as he wrote in three disciplines during his freshman, sophomore, and junior years. I likened Dave to a stranger in foreign lands, a traveler who, in each new academic territory, struggled to learn an unfamiliar language. In my inquiry into Dave's writing in various disciplinary classrooms, his teachers were important elders—"native speakers" I dubbed them—in each different academic setting. I needed these teachers' insider perspectives, so I observed and interviewed them. But after eliciting information from them, I left the scene to construct their stories by myself.

This was entirely appropriate to the research model I was employing, one I now refer to, borrowing from Wagner, as a "data-extraction arrangement" (1997, p. 15). For Wagner, data-extraction studies focus directly on teaching practices, and they are designed by outside researchers who enter the classroom only long enough to extract information for distribution elsewhere, often to policymakers at higher administrative levels. In this model, researchers and teachers play distinct roles: the former are *agents* of inquiry, the latter their *objects*.

Although my dissertation study resembled Wagner's data-extraction inquiries, it did not fit his definition exactly. Coming from a composition program, I was interested in understanding one student's learning to write, not in generalizing about pedagogy. Like Janet Emig (1971), who had directed my master's thesis 20 years earlier at the University of Chicago, I focused on pupil composing rather than, in any direct way, on teacher techniques. And, of course, I never thought of my audience as policymakers.

Despite these differences, however, my relationship with my research objects was extractive. Neither Dave nor his teachers helped me plan or conduct the research, and I offered them no voice in the report. In fact,

Dave's teachers actually understood very little about my project, and as far as I know, none ever read my findings or benefited in any way from participation. And just as they were ignorant of my inquiry outcomes and methods, I understood their classrooms in very limited fashion. I extracted from them only what I needed to better understand Dave's struggles—enough, that is, to satisfy my dissertation committee.

Of course, data-extraction arrangements like mine risk exploiting or frustrating students and teachers, who are, generally, lower in the educational hierarchy than the researcher. But my own experience suggests that institutional status is only one factor determining how exploitive or cooperative a research arrangement is. Although I was a lowly graduate student/adjunct composition instructor interviewing long-tenured, full professors, I was in a position, if I evaluated their teaching negatively, to do them harm they would have no way to counter. Thus, more important to successful outsider-insider cooperation than relative rank is, I suspect, a belief shared by both that they are equally responsible for the project.

It is, of course, easy to be critical of one's dissertation in hindsight, to point to things one would do differently given one's subsequent research experiences. To be fair to myself and my dissertation advisers, however, I was pleased with the project when I completed it 15 years ago. It answered genuine questions I had, and it was well received by those who read it. Nevertheless, I now see my data-extraction approach with its detached outside-researcher stance as limiting for me as well as for my informants. We all could have learned more, I believe, had I granted them more voice. And not only was it an inefficient use of resources, I also now see it as unjust—especially when I criticized the teachers.

Overall, then, my social science training at Penn did little to prepare me to collaborate with students and teachers. This is understandable. In schools of education in the early 1980s, as I have noted, researcher objectivity was the name of the game. The practitioner inquiry movement—with its valuing of teacher knowledge and insistence upon researcher-practitioner cooperation—had not yet fully blossomed (see Noffke, 1997).

Reporting My Qualitative, Data-Extraction Study in a Traditionally Quantitative Journal

I eventually reported my dissertation in an article titled "A Stranger in Strange Lands: A College Student Writing Across the Curriculum" (1987). Although it appeared in *Research in the Teaching of English* (RTE) at about the same time as Steve Fishman's pieces appeared in *Teaching Philosophy,* our reports could hardly have been more different. By contrast to Steve's Berthoffian narratives of teaching experience, my article closely follows Stenhouse. I base my case study on evidence provided by systematic, social science inquiry rather than personal reflection, and I set my work, much more than Fishman does, within the existing literature of my field. In these ways, then, "A Stranger in Strange Lands" exemplifies the "illuminative method" Stenhouse praises (1979/1985g). However, what Stenhouse would not admire is the absence of teacher voice.

But my article silences not only Dave's instructors, it also suppresses me. Whereas Fishman's style is personal and self-revealing—a style Geertz calls "author-saturated"—mine is academic and "author-evacuated" (1988, p. 9). As researcher I tell little about myself, focusing instead on methodological issues required by *RTE*'s American Psychological Association (APA) format. I model my article on two qualitative studies published in *RTE* just ahead of mine (Dyson, 1984; Herrington, 1985) and present my case study in scientific dress. In what I now recognize as a "compatabilist" effort (Smith, 1997) to gain space for qualitative work in a traditionally quantitative journal, I organize Dave's story using the five-part scientific report form. In my methods section, I go so far as to equate naturalistic and scientific research, assuring my readers I have met, in my qualitative study, agreed-upon standards of "validity" and "reliability" (1987, p. 243). I explain:

> Validity of the findings and interpretations in this study were insured by employing the following techniques. (1) Different types of data were compared. (2) The perspectives of various informants were compared. (3) Engagement with the subject was carried on over a long period of time during which salient factors were identified for more detailed inquiry. (4) External checks on the inquiry process were made by three established researchers who knew neither Dave nor his professors. These researchers read the emerging study at numerous points and questioned researcher biases and the bases for interpretations. (5) Interpretations were checked throughout with the informants themselves. (See Lincoln & Guba, 1985, for a discussion of validity and reliability in naturalistic inquiry.)

In this passive-voiced account, I construct myself as a white-coated researcher, an inquirer whose biases have been eliminated, and whose conclusions can, therefore, be trusted. It is almost as if my methods, working by themselves, generate my research conclusions. Throughout my report, it appears as if it is not I who speak but my data:

The protocol data explain...
The text analysis data provide further insight into...
Evidence from interviews and observation shows... (1987, pp. 245, 249, 253)

In sum, my academic style—with its distanced outsider stance and Stenhousian documentation—contrasts sharply with Fishman's Berthoffian appeal to personal experience. These clashing approaches would, like our failure to articulate fully our expected insider-outsider roles, cause misunderstanding when we began to work together.

In addition, one of my conclusions in "A Stranger in Strange Lands" would produce yet more trouble. It is the advice I give teachers in the disciplines at the article's close. Despite my failure to actually collaborate with Dave's instructors, I speak as outside expert, telling all such teachers how best to help student "strangers" in their classrooms:

> For teachers in the disciplines, "native speakers" who may have used the language in their discipline for so long that it is partially invisible to them, the first challenge will be to appreciate just how foreign and difficult their language is for student newcomers. They must make explicit the interpretive and linguistic conventions in their community, stressing that theirs is one way of looking at reality and not reality itself.... [They] must then provide student newcomers with assignments and instructional supports which are appropriate first steps in using the language of their community. (1987, p. 262)

As Fishman explains in the next chapter, this is advice he could not easily accept.

My Dissertation Adviser

My dissertation was directed in part by a scholar now at the forefront of the teacher-research movement, Susan Lytle. Lytle and her colleague, Cochran-Smith (1993), have made important contributions to the second-generation literature—contributions which Fishman, in Chapter 1, places in the Stenhouse camp. It is no surprise, then, that in the early 1980s Lytle's emphasis with her graduate students was on systematic inquiry. Specifically, she taught me protocol analysis and helped me use this method to attend closely to my student informant's thinking and writing. Today, in the late 1990s, were I Lytle's student, she and I agree that she would direct me, in addition, to listen closely to instructors—and not only listen, but also include them in designing and carrying out the inquiry. In fact, she might even urge me to go further, to get help from teachers to become an outsider to my own research, focusing our gaze from time to time on my methods so I too might become the object of joint inquiry.

In 1985, however, when I left the University of Pennsylvania, doctorate in hand, I was a researcher who preferred to study the classrooms of others from a neutral outsider stance. What caused me to alter this approach?

Learning to Collaborate with Classroom Teachers: The Clinical Partnership

My decision, eventually, to join forces with Fishman was influenced by a second research experience, one shaped by Barbara Walvoord, my English Department colleague between 1981 and 1988 at Loyola College in Maryland. A National Writing Project (NWP) site director and Writing Across the Curriculum (WAC) authority, Walvoord placed great faith in teacher self-reflection, espousing, in fact, in the early 1980s, the same Berthoffian viewpoint I was later to hear from Fishman. Walvoord's role in my professional development began in 1985 when she asked me, at the close of my doctoral work, to join her in-progress study of student writing in four college classrooms. Walvoord was collaborating with the classroom teachers, and it was as I watched her and her partners over the next 4 years that I became convinced of the benefits of conjoint inquiry for both researcher and teacher.

Walvoord had initiated her project 3 years earlier, in 1982, and it involved her pairing with a teacher from each of four disciplines—business, biology, psychology, and history—to study that instructor's classroom. Each disciplinary teacher understood and helped modify Barbara's research design and joined her in carrying out the inquiry. Although Walvoord would, ultimately, be first author on three of their four joint chapters—her outsider voice dominant as framer and explainer—she consulted her teacher partners at every stage of the writing (see Walvoord & McCarthy, 1990).

Why, then, did Walvoord need me? The answer lies in my newly acquired Stenhousian inquiry techniques. Although Walvoord was working with teachers to investigate their classrooms, she had been trained in methods of literary analysis rather than social science, and she was coming to understood—as Fishman would several years later—that no matter how much she and her colleagues benefited from writing their teaching narratives, these stories are hard to publish. Barbara told me, "I can't just work with these teachers in any way I want and hope to get us a voice. I need your methodological and theoretic grounding." Realizing that Walvoord and I could learn a great deal from each other, I signed on. In this 7-year study, I played the role, as we explain in our book (1990), of the "writing specialist . . . [who] helped shape and guide data analysis, critiqued emerging chapter drafts co-authored by the [researcher-teacher] pairs, [and,] with Walvoord co-authored introductory and concluding chapters" (p. 1).

In Walvoord's and my work, then, I, for the first time, began to see teachers as co-researchers. In contrast to my own history of distanced outsider inquiry, Walvoord never considered not collaborating with teachers. They were her "starting place," she said, a very different relationship, obviously, from the ones I had with Dave's instructors. Walvoord's teacher collaborators were her friends before the study began, equal-status academics with whom she had worked in NWP and WAC projects and with whom she enjoyed mutual respect and trust. In fact, Walvoord says, she invited these four instructors to collaborate precisely because she knew they were "secure, student-oriented teachers who were open to change" (Walvoord & McCarthy, p. 47). So whereas I had assumed I did not need the participation of classroom teachers, Barbara believed she could not do without it. She saw herself (like Dave) as going into foreign academic territories, and she wanted insider experts to guide her. These teachers understood local language and customs, she told me, in ways she could never hope to do. As I watched Walvoord and her teacher colleagues work together, I saw she was right.

The distance between outside-researcher and teacher-insider in Walvoord's study was, then, much less than in my data-extraction dissertation. In what Wagner (1997) calls a "clinical partnership," Walvoord and her colleagues were co-agents of inquiry as they examined classroom events, and the teacher-insiders, as well as the outside-researcher, stood to profit from the study. Although Walvoord and her partners did occasionally focus on their own collaboration, it is the instructors and their students who are the primary objects of joint analysis. The pairs never actually turned their research gaze on outsider Walvoord herself; neither her inquiry methods nor her own classroom were of interest in this situation. Rather, because research outcomes spotlighted the teachers, it was they, not Walvoord, who learned about themselves. In sum, clinical partnerships, as opposed to data-extraction agreements, offer benefits to both insider and outsider, but the focus of both types of arrangement remains primarily on the teacher-insider.

Reporting Walvoord's Clinical Partnership Study

Unlike data-extraction reports, which are characterized by asymmetry of power and voice, in clinical partnerships outsider and insider are valued equally. Walvoord and her teacher partners managed their multiple perspectives by blending their voices in a point of view they call the "negotiated we" (Walvoord & McCarthy, 1990, pp. 44-45.) To achieve their co-authored chapters, Walvoord generally initiated the drafting process, attempting to capture her and her partner's conjoint analysis. The teacher partner then responded, confirming or resisting Walvoord's interpretations and making revision suggestions. Although the "negotiated we" voice is far from perfect in its ability to represent teacher perspectives—privileging, as it does, Walvoord's language and requiring that conflict be leveled rather than preserved—it is, nevertheless, a major advance over the distanced-outsider style I adopted in "Stranger."

Clinical Partnership and Teacher Change

Perhaps the greatest advantage of a clinical partnership, by comparison to a data-extraction agreement, is its potential for instructor growth. Because Walvoord's teacher partners were collecting and examining data along with her, they too became outsiders to their own classrooms. From this new vantage point, they could learn how their techniques were working, which were succeeding, which were going wrong, and why. This was a powerful impetus to change. Unlike my own "seduction and betrayal" of teacher informants (Newkirk, 1996), Walvoord offered her colleagues the opportunity to analyze and critique their classrooms, a chance to see their teaching anew. For example, when Ginny Anderson, the biology teacher, examined protocol and interview data revealing her students' confusion about her assignment, she could pinpoint the places they took wrong turns. In subsequent semesters, Anderson was able to adjust her pedagogy, intervening in student processes in ways that helped them produce higher quality work.

As Walvoord's six-member project drew to a close in 1989, I was convinced of the value of outsider-insider collaboration. I had witnessed the researcher's enriched comprehension of the classroom and the teachers' excitement and renewal. In fact, I was so sold on this sort of researcher-teacher partnership that I wanted one of my own. Just then Fishman came on the scene.

The Outside-Researcher Takes on an Insider-Teacher

Joining forces with Fishman seemed a reasonable thing to do, then, because I thought it would allow me to cooperate—as Walvoord had done—with a disciplinary teacher. And from the start, Fishman and I saw we needed each other. He was, as he has explained, repeatedly frustrated in his efforts to study his classroom by himself. To do such research, he had concluded, he needed an outsider's help. For my part, like Walvoord, I wanted an insider-teacher who would help me understand his world. What I did not know at that time was that eventually I would come to need not only Fishman's perspective as teacher insider but also his ability to read and write theory. Although my academic area, composition studies, places high value on systematic inquiry, it is actually driven by theory. Fishman, as a philosopher, it turned out, is far more skilled in theoretic analysis than I, and my eventual dependence upon his theoretic skills wrought unanticipated, and significant, changes in our collaborative agreement.

However, in 1989, when I agreed to work with Fishman, I believed I was contracting for the sort of clinical partnership I had observed in Walvoord's project. That is, I believed Fishman and I were positioned, as insider and outsider, to share responsibilities and reap rewards which, if somewhat different for each of us, would be valuable to us both. Although I was right about shared responsibilities and mutual benefits, as things unfolded, Fishman's and my collaboration took some unexpected turns.

CONCLUSION
Steve Fishman and Lucille McCarthy

To summarize, we began our research with considerably different views about teacher research. With regard to its purpose and perspective, we were starkly opposed. Fishman was teacher-centered, interested in reflecting on his own successes and failures in his classroom. By contrast, McCarthy was student-centered. Although she had learned from Walvoord that collaborative classroom research could lead to teacher change, this was not her primary objective. Instead, she wanted to understand the nature of Fishman's philosophic discourse and his students' experiences as they learned to read and write it.

With regard to the relationship of personal and disciplinary knowledge, narrative and academic analysis, Fishman, as a good Berthoffian, assumed that teacher stories were the best way to report classroom research. By contrast, McCarthy was committed to careful analysis presented in an academic voice. And while Fishman's skin crawled at the sight of parenthetical academic citations, McCarthy thought they were as important as commas and periods.

Finally, on the question of insider-outsider arrangements and their potential for exploitation, Fishman wanted total equality, and although McCarthy said she agreed, we had very different notions of what that equality meant. Fishman expected to have an equal say over the research questions, data analysis, and writing, whereas McCarthy assumed equal meant Fishman's understanding her research design and helping her carry it out. She expected him to be both a good informant and sensitive respondent to her emerging findings and drafts, but she had no notion their collaboration would develop into a more democratic arrangement, one which, on occasion, turned the research focus from Fishman onto her.

In the chapter that follows, we describe these events, the ways our negotiations over our differences reflect the history of core conflicts within teacher research. We also describe the development of what we call our integrative approach as we work to reconcile these core oppositions.

OUR INITIAL STUDY: THE BERTHOFF-STENHOUSE BATTLEGROUND

Steve Fishman and Lucille McCarthy

O ur initial study, "Boundary Conversations: Conflicting Ways of Knowing in Philosophy and Interdisciplinary Research," was published in *Research in the Teaching of English (RTE)* in December 1991. In this chapter, we present the unplayed tape, the private research discussions which lie behind our study. First, Fishman describes three memorable events which shaped our work during our first examination of his Introduction to Philosophy classroom, and then McCarthy follows with her perspective. Our research disagreements are instructive, we believe, because, although neither of us knew it at the time, they reflect misunderstandings, conflicts, and challenges in the teacher-research field in general. Specifically, our disagreements focused on ways to fashion an equitable collaborative research arrangement and meet criticisms that teacher research is either too narrowly personal or too academically abstract.

EVENT 1: SOCIAL SCIENCE QUESTIONS AND PERSONAL, NONACADEMIC ANSWERS
Steve Fishman

The first event I recount occurred early in our collaboration when McCarthy asked me, "What is philosophy, and how do you teach it to your Intro students?" Not suspecting my long-standing difficulties with this question, she expected a simple, straightforward answer. Instead, I responded, "I don't know. It's a complicated, 2500-year story, tied loosely to puzzles about reality." This did not satisfy McCarthy, and as the two of us pursued this question, we began to discover just how different our orientations were, not only concerning classroom research, but also about larger issues such as learning, truth, and the relationship of the academic disciplines.

McCarthy's interrogation touched a sensitive nerve. As an undergraduate I had struggled from the outset with the question, What is philosophy? I remember overhearing a conversation in the library between two graduate student instructors which symbolized my field's inability to clearly define itself. When one asked the other, "What do you say at the opening of the course about the nature of philosophy?" the other instructor replied, "It's best to avoid that question altogether. Just tell them they'll figure it out by the end of the semester."

Nevertheless, in trying to explain myself to McCarthy, I went on to describe philosophy as a field built more around classic texts than around a shared project or clear-cut methodology. However, when McCarthy pressed me about what exactly I wanted for my students, I offered an answer that was more reflective of my time with Writing Across the Curriculum and National Writing Project people than my years in graduate school. "What I really want for my students," I said, "is for each of them to fall in love with one of their own sentences."

McCarthy nodded politely at me, but she could not help wondering outloud, "How can you teach philosophy if you don't know what it is? You're not teaching biology or business. You're teaching philosophy, and I don't see your students learning to write philosophically if you don't tell them how."

Although McCarthy and I did not yet recognize it, we represented not just differences between Berthoff and Stenhouse about teacher research but also sharp differences in our concepts of knowledge and preferred ways of knowing. McCarthy, a psychology major in college, did her graduate training, as she outlined in the previous chapter, in a social science-oriented English education program. Her inclination was to view problems as solvable through field investigation, and she saw citations to other people's work as a way of building directly upon the findings of her predecessors. To her, knowledge is cumulative, and publications prior to 1970 seem like old news, road posts long since replaced by better maps and signals. She found it strange, then, that I was unable to clearly define philosophy's methods and could say I spent my whole mature life reading John Dewey and still did not fully understand him.

Thus, when McCarthy questioned me about the nature of philosophy, she acted very much in the spirit of a social science field worker. She reflected Stenhouse's view (1982/1985b) that good historical case studies are written from an insider's point of view. As he points out, histories of trade unions employ the language of trade unionists, horticultural histories employ the language of horticulturists, and so on (p. 53). Therefore, McCarthy's instinct as a social scientist-outsider—one now wanting to work cooperatively with a teacher-insider—was to ask me, the native, about my local culture. In effect, her initial response to my answers implied, "You cannot be much of a wise elder in your community if you cannot tell me about the special language you speak, what counts as proof and knowledge for your people, and the written genre with which your people are familiar."

For my part, I had no idea why McCarthy was so insistent with her questioning. Whereas *her* initiation in English education featured discrete tools for exploring and studying social problems, *mine* offered no explicit instruction about how to conduct philosophic research. As both an undergraduate and graduate student, I followed course reading lists and my professors' discussions of their assignments, but I received no direct advice about how to read philosophic texts or write philosophic papers. I just assumed if I read the assignments over and over, some new and personal angle, some fresh, original criticism would come to me which would be acceptable to my professors.

Further, whereas McCarthy, like Stenhouse, saw the world as a Balkanized map of discrete disciplinary kingdoms—each with its specially flavored discourse and ways of seeing the world—I assumed philosophy was the queen of the sciences. If I was not precisely sure what philosophy was, I at least knew that its focus was extremely general and abstract, and somewhere I had picked up the idea that the disciplines served up information which philosophy then wove into synoptic tapestries.

...ven my background, it is understandable why I found Berthoff's approach to writing valuable. Whereas I, as a student, only knew to sit on a chair hoping for private inspiration, I could at least now, thanks to Berthoff, give my students some prewriting strategies, a kind of head start toward fresh interpretations. This turning inward also went along with my tacit philosophic training that learning comes from reflection on one's own experience. McCarthy's view—had she fully articulated it for me—that I was living in a world quite foreign to the worlds of, say, biology or business or law would have shocked me. I simply saw the world in simpler, more naive terms.

Although as McCarthy and I began our collaboration, we were, obviously, deeply divided by our views of classroom research knowledge, and our disciplinary training, our immediate skirmishes were about the nature of student initiation. We could not get very far with our study of my Intro to Philosophy class until we clarified our ideas about the purpose of college courses and the roles of reading and writing within them. But these conflicts over student initiation, as I will show, quickly brought out our major differences, ones which mirrored opposing positions in the world of teacher research.

Conflict over Student Initiation: Knowledge as Social versus Knowledge as Personal

Despite my acknowledgment that McCarthy was correct to question the adequacy of my classroom instructions about philosophic writing and reading, I bridled at her idea that I was teaching classes of apprentice philosophers. Whereas she—reflecting her sociolinguistic view that knowledge is socially constructed—saw me as a tribal elder initiating novices into the ways of the philosophic discipline, I—reflecting my romantic view that knowledge is personal discovery—saw myself facilitating something more open-ended, something I might have described as each student's personal journey toward enlightenment. Although I avoided mentioning it to McCarthy, whenever she spoke of my students as apprentices, what came to my mind was the distasteful image of student plumbers being trained in a lock-step, overly routinized fashion. To me, her view of students as philosophic inititiates cast me in the uncomfortable role of a know-it-all prescribing exactly what pupils need to achieve professional success. Her notion that every college class was really a guided introduction to foreign lands just seemed to rob pupils of the chance to use their own intelligence to create their own ways.

However, the best I could do in defense of my position—my belief that students are not clay to be molded into predetermined professional forms—was to mumble about the importance of doubt and uncertainty for pupil growth. "If I try to tell my students exactly what they must do in their papers," I asked McCarthy, "how in the world will they ever experience the joy of figuring things out for themselves?"

As my discussions with McCarthy continued, each of us trying to convince the other of the value of our own particular view of student initiation, our conflict helped us become more self-conscious about what lay behind our differences. We began to see that our own fight represented a larger debate within composition studies about the nature of knowledge. We came to see that McCarthy's view was championed by the so-called social constructionists, theorists like Bartholomae (1985) and Bizzell (1982), who claim that under the banner of student self-discovery (which I was attempting to unfurl) pupils are denied instruction in the conventions and ways of thinking required for entry into professional and academic life. By contrast, we came to see that my view was defended by people like Harris (1989) and Pratt (1987) who charge social constructionists with being utopian, that is, with seeing discourse communities as far more discrete and neatly bounded than they, in fact, really are. According to Harris and Pratt, students speak a number of overlapping communal languages, and to learn the discourse of an academic discipline does not require that they abandon already familiar ways of speaking and knowing.

In sum, our collaborative classroom study led McCarthy and me to see our differing views of student initiation in a larger context. At the same time, our mutual respect led us to step into each other's shoes and attempt to modify our original positions, to blend what initially seemed to be irreconcilable points of view.

Debates over Student Writing: Academic versus Personal Voice

As I have just shown, in the early stages of Lucille McCarthy's and my first collaborative study we debated about student initiation, and this led us to questions about implicit versus explicit instruction and the nature of knowledge construction. Our discussions also swirled around ways to teach writing. As McCarthy has already outlined, when we first met, she had just completed her book-length study with Barbara Walvoord, the focus of which was student strategies for successful writing in disciplinary courses. It was quite natural, therefore, that McCarthy set out to examine something similar in my own classroom. As a result, not long after asking me, "What is philosophy?" she followed up with, "What counts as good writing in your class?"

But McCarthy found my answer to her second question no more satisfactory than my answer to her first. "I'm not sure what I want," I said. "I guess I want students to show they've been reflecting, that they've put something original, something of themselves, into their work." McCarthy was again troubled by my response. "Your students must be confused," she told me. "Unless you're giving them carte blanche and anything goes, many won't get it. You don't give them all A's, do you?" Under further questioning, I admitted I provided no formal models of writing for my students, and in an even more damaging confession, I revealed that most of my students did poorly on my essays, the average grade being C.

So there we were again, McCarthy arguing for explicit instruction, urging me to present models and identify criteria which distinguish philosophic writing from writing in other academic communities, and me, defensive and resistant, arguing that students should be allowed to invent their own strategies. I even told her how my few efforts to use my own finished work as models had, unfortunately, often resulted in my students becoming narrow imitators. I recalled that, in an essay I once shared with my students, I had examined the moral values behind a newspaper editorial. As a consequence, it seemed that for an entire semester all my students' papers focused on newspaper articles.

In addition, I worried that if I were too explicit about student writing, not allowing pupils to muddle their way to their own versions of the philosophic essay, they would miss the chance to develop their inner voices and the love of writing I claimed such personal discovery elicits. Sounding very much like the Bertoffian graduate of an NWP summer writing institute that I was, I argued strongly for something I called an internal standard of good writing. "I want students to write so often they finally let go of their fears, find their own natural rhythms, and discover they have written at least a few powerful sentences on their own. When this happens, they will know it. I will, too. Then I can point to those good sentences and say: 'See! You've done it! You can write well. You just have to keep writing more of these sentences.'"

Of course, to McCarthy, all this seemed romantic naivete. She urged me to read Bakhtin, to become familiar with social psychology's view that the language people speak—my so-called inner voice—is really language borrowed, as Bakhtin would have it, from the mouths of others (1981, pp. 293-294). McCarthy explained to me, "You may think language is just the expression of what's going on inside, but, really, what's happening inside is the expression of a community conversation." And to hammer home her point, McCarthy suggested I read theorists in sociolinguistics and the sociology of knowledge like Hymes (1974), Bazerman (1988), Becher (1987), and Myers (1985). I reluctantly agreed but, in turn, begged McCarthy to reexamine Berthoff (1979/1987a), Elbow (1973), and Murray (1968).

As readers will see in the next chapter, McCarthy's and my first collaborative study ultimately showed she was correct. I was indeed confusing and angering my students with my writing assignments. Particularly troublesome was the fact that, in Berhoffian fashion, I would ask them to write about a personally significant problem—one which, as I put it, "refused to go away." Many students warmed to this sort of assignment and wrote about heartfelt issues—broken homes, drug problems, troubles with boyfriends and girlfriends—only to feel tricked when I then asked for additional drafts focusing on the moral conflicts *behind* their personal problems. This student confusion and anger, which McCarthy soon uncovered, was influential in getting me to become more explicit in my approach to student essays. In subsequent semesters, at moments I deemed students ready for them, I offered both written and spoken suggestions about how to develop the philosophic essays I hoped they would write. (For more on implicit versus explicit writing instruction, see Delpit, 1995; Freedman, 1993; Nelson, 1995.)

However, my own teaching changes are not the whole story of our debate over student writing. Because of the democratic collaborative arrangement which McCarthy and I backed into—an arrangement which gradually showed us that alternation of insider and outsider roles can be mutually advantageous—our conversations about composition instruction affected McCarthy's teaching as well as my own. Although my role as outside observer of McCarthy's teaching never became part of any research report, it represented an important change in our collaborative relationship. This change from a clinical partnership to something more symmetrical began after my first visit to her composition class.

Insider and Outsider Alternate Roles

Not long after McCarthy and I started our work together, I sat in on one of her freshman composition classes, and it was my turn to be surprised. I took a seat in the back corner of the room and watched as McCarthy went to the board to outline the five-paragraph theme. "These are the things you'll be graded on," she told her students. "Good essays state the thesis in the first paragraph. In the second, third, and fourth, they develop that thesis and provide evidence. And please be sure that each paragraph begins with a clear transition from the preceding one and ends with a summary of what's been said."

As I looked on, I thought of the famous centipede who, when asked about his feet, found himself unable to walk. I wondered to myself how anyone could develop enthusiasm for a topic, much less appreciate the joys of writing, while keeping in mind a set of rules which seemed so externally imposed.

After completing her introduction to the five-paragraph theme and assigning students to bring in several thesis outlines, McCarthy asked students to talk about their homework. From my outsider point of view, it was a low-motivating, decontextualized exercise. The object of the game was to take an innocent sentence like "John went to the movies" and fill it with all sorts of extras, something like taking a plain potato and adding sour cream, onions, and tomatoes.

The first student, offering an expanded version of McCarthy's basic sentence, volunteered: "John, running from his shrewish wife, went to the movies." The second student had the task of adding further toppings to the first pupil's. A young woman named Karen said, "John, enveloped in a fearful sweat, running from his shrewish wife, went to the movies." This routine went on for a while until just before the end of class, when McCarthy concluded by asking students to use this sort of "multilevel" sentence from time to time as they developed their five-paragraph themes.

After class, as McCarthy and I walked to her office, it was my turn to be questioner. "Do you really expect students will be better writers by doing this sort of stuff? To me, the important thing is to help them enjoy writing, and even though you let them choose their own topics, it's the five-paragraph form, rather than the meaning, that's your main thing. Avoiding mistakes, as opposed to expressing oneself, is what this is all about."

At first, McCarthy did not take kindly to my comments. She pointed out that students very much enjoyed her class, that she repeatedly received excellent pupil evaluations, and that most of her students claimed they learned a lot about writing in her class. "And if you had just looked a little more closely today," she told me, "you could have seen students learning to complexify base sentences. This is important for pupils who write sentences as if they were composing telegrams. And don't snort at the five-paragraph theme; it may not be required in every university course, but it certainly is in some."

As we continued to argue, McCarthy told me she had successfully been teaching composition this way for a number of years. In her early days at Loyola College in Maryland, she had gotten used to the required textbook, one which featured the five-paragraph theme (Kerrigan, 1974). Because she had consistently gotten good results with her pedagogy, she saw no reason to change. I admitted I had no experience with freshman English, but I claimed to know something about the National Writing Project approach and the orientation of primary and secondary teachers I had gotten to know since attending my first WAC workshop. I desperately wanted McCarthy to hear that what had turned me on to writing was the opposite of her careful modeling. My appreciation of writing was the result of being encouraged to freewrite, to compose without the imposition of outside forms or objectives, to get going with so little restraint that my meaning and my writing became one.

As our interchanges continued, McCarthy started to take me seriously and, ultimately—as a result of our attempts to alternate insider and outsider roles—began experimenting with her courses. She ultimately offered her students the chance to work in those genres which most interested them, the ones they decided were most appropriate for their chosen topics. She also assigned more group work and—using her own social science background—asked students to interview classmates about their writing habits and techniques. The result was that she moved a little closer to my stance—just as I had moved a bit closer to hers—tempering her explicit modeling with some of my advice about allowing students the chance to muddle toward their own solutions, their own voices and texts.

Results of Our Mutual Questioning

In sum, McCarthy's initial questions to me—"What is philosophy?" and "What counts as good writing in your class?"—led me to ask about the philosophic tradition I was representing and the ways in which I was trying to initiate my students. In turn, my questions to McCarthy about her composition class got her asking about the purposes of writing instruction and the best ways to help students see writing as ally rather than onerous school task.

Although these specific consequences of what I call the first important event of Lucille McCarthy's and my work on "Boundary Conversations" point to interesting changes in our teaching, what is just as significant are their implications for our outsider-insider arrangement. Because McCarthy was open-minded enough to see the advantage of our switching roles, she did the remarkable thing of allowing me to make her teaching an object of our research lenses. This is a role for which her graduate training did not prepare her, nor was it one she witnessed in her collaboration with Walvoord. McCarthy's unusual openness—an attitude she maintained throughout of our work on "Boundary Conversations"— began to move our collaboration from a "clinical partnership" toward a more cooperative ideal. It is what Wagner (1997) calls a "co-learning arrangement" and what Ede and Lunsford (1990) refer to as "dialogic collaboration." Putting our own slant on it, since McCarthy and I see this arrangement as rooted in Dewey's (1927/1988) notion of democracy— people making their individualized contributions to a commonly valued goal—we call it "democratic collaboration."

EVENT 2: WHETHER TO WRITE NARRATIVE OR ANALYSIS
Steve Fishman

A second event which shaped McCarthy's and my collaboration—one which reflects disagreements in the teacher-research movement in general —concerned the writing of our report. Once data were collected, our questions were, What sort of genre should we employ to describe our research? and How should we do the writing? Being in separate cities, McCarthy and I knew we could not compose together. But we were unsure about who should take the lead. As already mentioned, McCarthy had previously published several classroom studies, one of which, "A Stranger in Strange Lands," appeared in *Research in the Teaching of English* (1987)—the same journal that published the articles criticized by Bissex and Ray as too academic and practitioner-unfriendly (see Chapter 1, above). For that study, McCarthy received the Promising Researcher

Award from the National Council of Teachers of English, and as a result, she wanted to publish in *RTE* again.

By contrast, I, as also already noted, had had minimal success with academic publications. However, I liked to write and did not want to sit on the sidelines or take a passive role in the reporting of our work. McCarthy finally decided on a minicompetition to see which of us was the better academic writer. She suggested we each compose our own version of an introduction to our report.

A week later we mailed our just-completed drafts to one another. McCarthy's introduction outlined her methodology and placed her questions about student composing in philosophy in the context of other analyses of discipline-based writing. By contrast, my own introduction was a first-person narrative of events leading up to our collaboration and an outline of what I thought the two of us had gained from our research.

As might be expected, I found McCarthy's draft almost unreadable. Every sentence, as I ungraciously put it in a phone conversation, hiccoughed at the end with citations. I complained to her that no one could get past the first three sentences without going to the library to begin some catch-up reading. I also worried that, with the absence of personal voice, McCarthy's draft would appear to have been written by a word processor rather than a live author.

McCarthy's reaction to my narrational and author-saturated introduction was equally vehement. My draft pretty much constituted final proof for her that I had no idea about academic writing, analysis, or the strategies required to get one's work published. She told me, "Really, if we ever submitted anything like this to Applebee and Langer [editors of *RTE*], we would be laughingstocks." By the end of the phone call, McCarthy had her way. What most convinced me was her claim that my narrative style would leave us with unpublishable work. My own failures to find takers for my earliest teacher stories were still fresh in my mind, and in the end, McCarthy was able to convince me of the superiority of her report approach.

These conversations about the appropriate report form—and our different predilections—reflected, like many of our other discussions, important debates within classroom research studies. My teacher reports were the result of my Writing Across the Curriculum and National Writing Project experiences. However, the sorts of writing these movements encouraged were insufficiently theorized and too unsystematic to successfully compete for academic journal space. Conversely, McCarthy's qualitative approach, although she called it nontraditional research, was really, by the early 1990s, a relatively well accepted form of investigation, one which enjoyed a peaceful co-existence with more traditional, experimental, and quantitative styles. However, as McCarthy and I negotiated our contrasting orientations toward research, we reflected opposing forces within a classroom inquiry field which was becoming somewhat uneasy about the ways in which theorists like Lincoln and Guba (1985) and Miles and Huberman (1984) had shaped qualitative research ("co-opted" it, some said) so it would be acceptable to traditional or orthodox researchers (Smith, 1997).

Following McCarthy's and my discussions about the appropriate report form for our work and our target journal, McCarthy took the lead. She organized our study around the classic American Psychological Association (APA) five-part scientific report, including Background, Objectives, Methods, Results, and Discussion. Although this genre is heavily indebted to experimental studies in psychology—research done with control groups and carefully isolated variables—McCarthy only sparingly used quantitative analysis. She did this when she coded my student think-aloud protocols. Further, McCarthy was nonexperimental insofar as she saw her primary task as presenting a rich description of my classroom and a triangulated account of two of my students' experiences.

In adopting this mix of quantitative and qualitative methods, McCarthy was within the spirit of Stenhouse's appeal for systematic, self-critical inquiry with careful documentation. She was engaging in a practice which ensured that her findings would at least seem to be trustworthy and transferable, although she could make no guarantees they were generalizable across contexts. She was also following, as I have indicated, a well-worked-out compromise between traditionalists who defend quantitative educational inquiry and nontraditionalists who disparage all pretense toward researcher objectivity and neutrality.

However, despite McCarthy's success with the detached, social science research she had been trained to do, she herself admired some of the more radical, personal approaches to qualitative classroom study. She was susceptible, therefore, to my challenges to the scientific sort of voice she was accustomed to adopting. Her openness to my reflections on her research, like her openness to my observations about her teaching, proved crucial in modifying our initial either/or positions regarding scientific report and narrative account. It also nudged our collaboration into new and more equitable territory. At one point, as we debated our report form, I protested that despite my desire to have our work published, I really just wanted to tell a good story. To my surprise, McCarthy agreed: "You may be right. When I find your classes interesting, it's really students' stories that strike me the most."

But how could we tell a good story when publication realities dictated an APA five-part report? McCarthy's first suggestion would have kept my hands off our classroom research and kept me in a subordinate position in our collaboration. She recommended I write a personal narrative of my teaching history, a background to the data-based accounts she herself would present. But I countered that my earlier efforts at similar writing had met with little publication success. After further negotiation, we decided I would adopt some of her student interview techniques and write my own account of my Intro course, an account focused on student talk rather than writing. As it turned out, I, unlike McCarthy, was more interested in studying successful class discussion than successful student papers.

Combining Narrative and Analysis in Our Report

After I began writing my part of our report—a first-person account of one class discussion—it became clear that McCarthy and I were developing a heteroglossic, or multivoiced, report genre (Clifford, 1983). We knew this broke with *RTE* tradition, but the more she and I worked at it, the more appropriate it seemed. The result was that we began to think of ourselves as innovators developing a more integrative text form, one that resembled *RTE* in some ways but was quite different in others. That is, the two of us decided we would maintain the formal APA five-part structure but within it use a more personal voice and employ narrative techniques. Our hope was that in McCarthy's sections, her snowstorm of citations and elaborate account of methodology would authorize our unorthodox reporting style.

A close look at the opening of "Boundary Conversations" reveals our struggle to reconcile the five-part scientific report with something more personal. We begin by pretending to roll the credits of a movie, introducing the featured characters, telling a little about them, and suggesting to our readers that our goal is close-ups of us and our student informants rather than findings separable from my local classroom context. We also include a "confessional tale" which, in narrative form, briefly tells our struggle to write our piece. McCarthy let me take primary responsibility for writing this section of our report, and this development not only helped us reconcile our very different writing skills but also added to the forces reshaping our collaborative relationship.

The APA genre we adopted, then, actually camouflages a structure familiar in the teacher-research literature. "Boundary Conversations" tells a tale of pupil struggle and achievement, of a number of students stumbling but eventually satisfying the demands of my class. It also focuses on the manners in which my students' "conflicting ways of knowing" mirror McCarthy's and mine as we conduct our classroom study. In this respect—as an exploration of pupil and teacher-researcher difficulty and triumph—our study, despite its APA disguise, fits into the same student-achievement narrative category as, for example, teacher-researcher Carol Avery's (1987) account of a first grader's difficulties and hard-won strategies to achieve school success. But having placed "Boundary Conversations" in a familiar teacher-research category, I alert readers that they will find our study's explanation of student achievement still draws heavily on McCarthy's social science background, on her sociolinguistic notion that learning means fitting into a discourse community, mastering its practices, ideas, and values.

Both McCarthy and I were pleased, of course, when *RTE* editors Applebee and Langer informed us they would publish our piece. In addition, to our amazement, "Boundary Conversations" received the 1993 James N. Britton Award for Inquiry within the English Language Arts. At the time, the two of us saw the acceptance of our heteroglossic text as a sign of increasing openness in the classroom inquiry field to new styles and forms of educational research. As I point out below, we were, in fact, adding to what would become a growing confusion about what constitutes legitimate classroom study and, in particular, what defines the parameters of bona fide teacher research (see Anderson & Herr, 1999; McCarthy & Fishman, 1996; Smith, 1997).

EVENT 3: BALANCING THEORY AND CLASSROOM DATA
Steve Fishman

Theory's role in teacher research seems to be a problem everyone talks about but no one quite solves. Berthoff (1987b, p. 76) tells her readers that swapping of classroom strategies should be prohibited unless there is also swapping of classroom theories. And Stenhouse (1981/1985a, p. 58) claims teacher research is worthwhile only if it contributes to the development of educational theory. But what is theory? How do you recognize it when it shows up, and how do you get it to emerge if it does not appear on its own?

Although theory is a vague term covering a multitude of contrasting examples (deductive theories in mathematics, for example, as opposed to probabilistic theories in sociology or history), I see it as the basis of explanation, a way of accounting for observed regularities. For example, if teachers find that students read more and with greater enthusiasm when they get to choose their own books, I might explain this correlation by appealing to a psychological theory of interest and effort. In other words, I might say we gain a fuller understanding of pupils' energetic reading of student-selected texts when we introduce the theory that people generally put forth more effort for tasks which interest them or serve important personal objectives.

If this example of an explanation of observed events can serve as a rough definition of theory, I am still left with the question of how to find an appropriate one if none shows up on its own. Hubbard and Power (1993) suggest that teacher-researchers who want to theorize their work should do literature reviews to find what they need. Offering quite different advice, McCarthy told me at the start of our first study that good qualitative researchers do not impose theory on data but, rather, let it emerge. Appealing to Glaser and Strauss (1967), she labeled this "grounded theory." But I resisted, thinking it sounded as if McCarthy were attempting to readopt her white-coated, scientific, neutral stance. "Like some immaculate conception," I protested, "you make it seem as if theory will arise simply from the facts as if researchers had nothing to with it."

Once again, McCarthy was open-minded. We agreed to state at the opening of our report our primary theoretical assumptions about learning, the ones at the heart of our research. McCarthy designated the approach of Bakhtin (1981), a theorist frequently cited in composition studies, to be our primary interpretive lens. Reflecting her graduate training, acutely aware of case study—à la Stenhouse—as uncovering local ways of writing, seeing, and knowing, McCarthy theorized that all learning is a form of imitation, the internalization of an ongoing communal conversation.

Taking a slightly different approach, I designated Dewey (1933/1960), a philosopher whose work I had long admired, as my prime theorist. Limited by my own trial-and-error undergraduate and graduate efforts, I saw learning—like a good Berthoffian—as dependent upon individual reflection and self-examination. I wanted to spotlight Dewey's ideas of intelligent thinking, of learning as dependent upon doubt, clarification of one's aims, and critical reconstruction of one's experiences.

These two theories—Bakhtinian and Deweyan—shaped McCarthy's initial interpretation of her data. She portrayed two focus students as having to set aside familiar disciplinary languages to learn the ways of writing philosophy. She also was sensitive to the impact of student differences and classroom debates upon closely held student beliefs. However, an unexpected thing happened as McCarthy worked to discover how students learned the nature of philosophy and how to do it.

From the start, the two of us exchanged numerous articles and books. At some point McCarthy sent me *Women's Ways of Knowing* by Mary Belenky and her colleagues (Belenky, Clinchy, Goldberger, & Tarule, 1986). This proved to be crucial for our study. At the time I was reexamining a number of class discussions in my Intro course which interested me. I chose these because I thought they were especially dramatic, although I was not sure why. Belenky et al. gave me a clue. While reading their accounts of interviews with women, I heard the voices of my own students, and I decided that one way to understand my more successful class discussions was to analyze them in terms of different categories of knowing. Alternatively put, Belenky and her associates' ideas of "separate knowing," "connected knowing," "received knowing," and "constructed knowing" all seemed to oscillate and riccochet in the class discussions I found most interesting. When I explained this to McCarthy, she was impressed, and she decided to add Belenky et al. to the Bakhtinian and Deweyan lenses she was wearing as she organized her data. The Belenkian categories proved most fruitful, as readers will see in the next chapter.

This third crucial event in McCarthy's and my initial study—our debates about theory and our reading of *Women's Ways of Knowing*—raised additional doubts for both of us about the view that theory emerges by itself from the data. Although it is true that I only noticed the relevance of Belenky et al. because I was familiar with our data, it was happenstance that McCarthy sent me *Women's Ways of Knowing* as we were completing our study. This suggests that theories already at the forefront of researchers' minds shape their classroom studies—the questions they pursue and the data they collect. It also suggests that surprises are possible, that the data can bring overlooked theory to the forefront in unanticipated ways.

This third event is not only instructive about integrating theory and data, it also, like each of the previous events, suggests something important about research collaboration. Although a researcher may set out to be fair to his or her informants—to share work, credit, and reward in fifty-fifty fashion—this only becomes practicable when both partners perceive each other as equally skilled and equally able to complete comparable parts of the joint study. Anecdotal evidence indicates that efforts at full cooperation fail whenever one partner begins to feel she or he is doing a disproportionate amount of the research work. As McCarthy's and my experience shows, despite her initial intention to make me a full partner, we did not truly move in this direction until she recognized that it was to her advantage to do so. That is, our collaboration did not begin to take on its co-learning, full-cooperation form until McCarthy saw that just as I needed her data-collection and APA report form skills, she needed my theoretical and narrative writing talents.

The shape McCarthy's and my collaboration takes in our initial classroom study suggests an alternative to the arrangements many theorists cite when they reject outsider-insider arrangements altogether. Our experience suggests that in cases where the researcher and practitioner find full sharing mutually advantageous, they are highly motivated to move from exploitive to more equitable types of collaboration. Our experience also shows that the researcher's open-mindedness and patience with the classroom practitioner is central to this transformation.

WHAT MCCARTHY AND I LEARNED FROM OUR INITIAL STUDY
Steve Fishman

Nearly all commentators on teacher research, as I explain in Chapter 1, name two justifications for it. First, teacher research, they say, promotes justice for teachers, empowering them by acknowledging the importance of their wisdom and privileging their position in the classroom "laboratory." It is they who should frame research questions and direct inquiry to construct answers. The second purpose of teacher research, according to commentators, is to improve teaching. Did McCarthy's and my first collaborative study empower me? Did it make me a better teacher? And what happened to McCarthy? How did our collaboration affect her research and her teaching?

Changes in Teaching: Integrating Academic and Personal Voice

As for Stenhouse's (1979/1985e; 1979/1985g) hope that teacher research will improve instruction by increasing professional judgment—that is, by increasing the keenness of our classroom observations and diagnoses of student problems and successes—McCarthy's and my experience offers only modest encouragement. Neither of us wants to claim that our initial study directly improved our teaching. Certainly, as a result of our application of Belenky et al. (1986), we were able to recognize more easily when a particular student was acting as a "constructed knower," for example, as opposed to a "received knower." But this did not necessarily mean that either of us could predict the appropriate stance for a student at any particular moment, and we only vaguely understood how we might bring about such a stance. This helps explain why McCarthy and I are uncertain about the degree to which our professional judgment has been sharpened by our first collaborative work.

However, both of us recognize that "Boundary Conversations" has at least changed our teaching, if not improved it. Now that I recognize philosophic writing as a distinct academic genre, I try to be more articulate with students about criteria for good writing in philosophy and about the sorts of knowing it requires. As for McCarthy, the role alternation which allowed me to question her neglect of personal writing in deference to the five-paragraph theme has led her to a more student-centered teaching style, one which encourages pupils to work in genres and organizations of their own choosing. Still, despite the fact that teaching changed for both of us, and our styles became more the product of expanded choice than single-minded habit, neither of us has evidence of more effective instruction.

Changes in Self-Image: Integrating Academic and Personal Knowledge

Although we do not want to claim we are better teachers, we both feel positive about the way our first study helped us articulate our notions of disciplinary communities, knowledge construction, and writing. In view of this result, Berthoff's (1979/1987a) conception of teacher research proved to be on target. Both McCarthy and I became more aware of what, in a tacit sense, we already knew. That is, our study forced us to bring into the open and contextualize our views of academic knowing, the function of writing, student initiation, and implicit versus explicit instruction. This happened as we questioned one another and exchanged relevant readings. It also happened because, while McCarthy and I were examining pupils in my Intro class, we discovered that the patterns these students displayed—their learning and writing, doubting and believing, resisting and opening—mirrored our own.

More specifically, in studying my own pupils, I developed a greater appreciation for myself as a student. I realized that, as an undergraduate, I was frequently frustrated and disappointed because my own disposition toward what Belenky et al. call "constructed knowing"—relating information about the world to oneself and speaking in one's own voice—was discouraged in favor of "separate knowing," or learning in which the self is weeded out (see Fishman & McCarthy, 1998, ch. 5). Prior to my first collaborative study, I had attributed my own school failures to lack of ability, but after reading Belenky et al. I began to see it as also a poor match between my own learning style and my teachers' instructional styles.

Whereas I gained understanding about my school failures, McCarthy, for her part, gained a better understanding of her school successes. She favored what Belenky and her colleagues identify as "separate" and "received knowing," that is, taking in what others present as well as standing back to achieve objective criticism. Belenky and her associates helped McCarthy see why she was usually able to figure out what others wanted her to know and what counted as an acceptable voice in the various academic disciplines in which she moved as an undergraduate and graduate student. These insights not only made both of us more conscious of our preferred ways of knowing, thus fulfilling Berthoff's (1979/1987a) promise for teacher research, they also helped us understand why the "boundary conversations" we experienced were not only between two people from different disciplines but also between two people whose fundamental ways of going at the world were often at odds.

Changes in Empowerment: Integrating Research and Teaching

With regard to questions about enhanced teacher empowerment, our answers are mixed—mine negative, McCarthy's positive. Because I teach in a philosophy department, I continue to meet resistance from my dean and peers about classroom research. They question whether an academic philosopher should be spending time studying classroom practice and pedagogical theory, especially when the results often appear in composition rather than philosophy journals. By contrast, McCarthy, who is seen by her English department as a composition specialist, receives considerable administrative and faculty support for her research. This is because her field values classroom studies and provides journal space for accounts of both student writing and learning.

Despite the markedly different responses by McCarthy's and my peers to our collaborative inquiries, I remain pleased with our work. No matter how it appears to my dean or department, I see our research as a chance to pursue philosophic theory by applying it in concrete classroom situations. Rather than abstract speculating—the sort of thinking philosophers frequently do but which has always made me uncomfortable—our research enables me to fulfill Dewey's (1916/1967) ideal that philosophizing should begin and end with concrete problems and that it should, in addition, lead to a philosophy of education (p. 328).

And what about McCarthy's attitude toward our collaboration? At this point, let me step aside to allow her to answer for herself.

A CHINK IN MY STENHOUSE ARMOR
Lucille McCarthy

Before I answer Steve Fishman's question about my attitude toward our collaboration, I want to return to two events he has just described. The first is the conflict over our research report form, whether to write narrative or analysis, and the second is the insider-outsider role exchange that occurred when Steve visited my class. Because these two events are highlights for me, I want to offer my perspective.

It is true, as Fishman has said, that the Stenhouse-Berthoff conflicts underlying our initial study were particularly obvious when it came time to write our research report. Steve, a National Writing Project enthusiast who took seriously its Berthoffian-expressivist message, was committed to personal narrative. I, by contrast, believed the future of composition studies belonged to Stenhousian social science analysis. The field was, in the late 1980s when Fishman and I met, a discipline trying to professionalize itself, and I was certain that the path to academic respectablity lay in scientific methods and language.

So the story Steve tells of our Berthoff-Stenhouse conflicts is a tale of two worlds within composition research at that time. In trying to get Steve to give up personal narrative and join me writing academic analysis, I was behaving toward him like Berkenkotter and Huckin (Berkenkotter et al., 1988) do toward Nate, the Carnegie Mellon graduate student they study. Berkenkotter and Huckin assume that Nate's personal expressive writing is somehow inferior to his academic writing, and the sooner he discards it the better off he will be. Like Berkenkotter and Huckin with Nate, I believed I could convince Steve it was time for him to put away childish things and join me in "real research."

Resisting Fishman's Pleas for Narrative and Personal Voice

But Steve did not easily let go. First, as he has recounted, we engaged in a minicompetition (*his* suggestion, as I recall) to determine who would write the introduction to our article. Steve produced an 8-page narrative that beautifully captured our voices and conflicts, and I wrote a 12-page argument, an author-evacuated analysis that set our work in the research literature. When we read each other's pieces, we were as tactful as but we were both disturbed. To accept my introduction, Steve felt, would be to erase himself completely. To accept his, I thought, meant we would never get published. Ultimately, I persuaded Steve, and he reluctantly consented to follow my social science lead.

Fishman's acquiescence on this Stenhousian point, however, set up his Berthoffian victory on the next. Three months later, when Steve told me he wanted to write his part of "Boundary Conversations," his study of class discussion, as a personal narrative, I agreed. I did so, first, because I believed that I had already adequately credentialed our work. That is, using my "sciency, white-coated researcher voice" (Fishman's terms), I had discussed our methodology and the related literature in ways I thought would open the *RTE* door. Second, it seemed only fair. The insider-teacher *should* get to choose his voice for his own section, I thought. So I gave Steve the green light and assumed that would be the end of it. As I saw it, I had already granted Fishman considerable research authority, far more than was the case in other clinical partnerships I had observed. Now, I thought, he ought to be satisfied.

But he wasn't. When he completed his classroom narrative and was waiting for me to finish my analysis of two of his students, he wrote yet another story. This time it was an account of his and my research relationship, our conflicts and decision making as collaborators. When he presented this five-page narrative to me, he argued that it too belonged in the article someplace. "Aren't our negotiations an important part of our research methods?" he asked. "They may be," I replied, "but you would never go public with this sort of thing."

Going against the Grain: Integrating Narrative and Analysis

However, when I read Steve's account of our research struggles, it was wonderful: insightful, funny, and self-parodying. He had gotten us right, I had to admit. The conversations he described had been central to our research. All right, I sighed, maybe, just maybe, we can get away with this too. But *RTE* editors and research justice were not the issues for me at this point. By now, to tell you the truth, I was simply fatigued with saying no to Steve. However, this latest plea for narrative was even more audacious than the others, and I just could not convince myself to go so deeply against the grain. That is, I could not, by myself, muster the authority to go against Berkenkotter, Huckin, Carnegie Mellon, and my own graduate training. Permission finally came from an unexpected source. It was Clifford Geertz.

I had recently read Geertz's new book, *Works and Lives: The Anthropologist as Author* (1988), in which he argues that anthropology is, at its heart, storytelling: particular accounts of field experiences constructed by fallible writers. Beneath every ethnography, no matter how placid and certain it appears on the surface, there is "a messy biographical affair." So here was a highly respected anthropologist challenging the notion that social life is simply gazed upon and described; rather, research and reporting, like all human activities, are shot through with power relations, negotiations, and compromise. Well, I thought, if Geertz can admit it, then so can we. I decided to sneak Steve's research story in at the end of our methods section, and before we were finished, I had even added a few details of my own. Shortly thereafter, we sent the article off to *RTE* and held our breath.

When *RTE* editors Applebee and Langer sent us the reviews six weeks later, one evaluator apparently saw the future of composition studies quite differently than I. In fact, he or she singled out Steve's research story for particular praise, commenting that it was a "relief" to finally hear about "the human side of scientific research." Then the reviewer dignified Steve's account by naming it. It was a "confessional tale," he or she said, and referred us to *Tales of the Field: On Writing Ethnography* by Van Maanen (1988). Furthermore, this reviewer continued, our confessional tale actually deserved greater prominence than we had given it. Instead of being buried in the methods section, it properly belonged with our findings. The researchers' ways of knowing—our own "boundary conversations"—resembled those we had identified in Steve's students.

Fishman, of course, was particularly gratified by this Berthoffian turn of events, but to his credit, he never once said, "I told you so." In fact, after polishing the confessional tale and moving it into the "Results and Discussion" section, he generously suggested we put both our names in the byline.

The Effects of Allowing Narrative In: A More Democratic Collaboration

This "confessional" event took place early in Fishman's and my 10-year collaboration, but it still remains strong in my memory. Why? Because for the first time, I was required to open a chink in my Stenhouse armor. Steve, who was unhappy with the balance of power in the collaboration, had been chipping away at my outsider's control, and when I realized that giving him his voice—mixing his Berthoffian narratives with my Stenhousian analysis—actually enriched our work, Steve, naturally, gained authority. His chutzpah, his refusal to take my word about what counted in composition research, required me to take risks, to defy the scientific conventions that I believed, until then, were sacrosanct. In fact, I was later to learn, Fishman and Geertz had plenty of company. Numerous other scholars in a variety of fields were, at that time, challenging the very positivist inquiry tenets I was working so hard to protect (see Clifford, 1983; Clifford & Marcus, 1986; Eisner & Peshkin, 1990; Guba 1990; Harding, 1986; Hesse, 1980). In sum, I wish I could claim that integrating narrative into our research report—now a widely accepted practice in the field—was the result of my own farsightedness. Obviously, I cannot. If I deserve any credit at all, it is for hearing Fishman's pleas for his own voice, for assenting to the justice of my teacher informant's request to articulate his own vision in his own way.

In any case, the success of "Boundary Conversations" and, in particular, Fishman's confessional tale marked a subtle shift in our collaboration. Steve and I had been, until then, in a "clinical partnership," an arrangement over which I, as outside-researcher, wielded primary control. But because my respect for Steve's theoretic and writing abilities had skyrocketed, as had my confidence in his academic instincts, it marked the beginning of a more democratic, "co-learning" relationship (Wagner, 1997). The success of the confessional tale explains, at least in part, why I was willing to take a chance on Fishman's next textual brain-storm, his proposal that we split our second research report in half. This is a story Steve tells in Chapter 5.

OUTSIDER AND INSIDER TRADE PLACES
Lucille McCarthy

My initial skirmishes with Steve Fishman suggest that Berthoff is justified in warning teachers to keep university researchers out of their classrooms (1979/1987a, p. 30). Outsiders dominate teachers, she says, grabbing control of research findings and language, and certainly Fishman's struggle to gain his voice in "Boundary Conversations" offers solid evidence for her claim. The second event I want to return to provides additional support. It is the time Fishman and I switched roles, when he asked to observe my teaching, a move that was intended, once again, to equalize our authority. However, Fishman's effort to balance power is not why I want to return to this event. Rather, what stands out in my mind is how hard it was for me to play teacher-insider. In order to fully under-stand Berthoff's caution about outside-researchers, I had to let one into my own classroom.

The Insider-Teacher Seeks Reciprocity

Fishman has already described his first visit to my composition class-room, one that occurred as we were finishing work on "Boundary Conversations." He recounts the story in a witty way, but when I recall it, nearly a decade later, I still feel a good deal of pain. I never invited him to come, actually, never imagined that a role reversal would be part of our clinical partnership bargain. None of the other teacher-insiders I had observed had ever asked for such reciprocity.

Furthermore, as Fishman and I worked together on our initial study, I was, as a good Stenhousian, quite content playing outside-researcher.

And no wonder. The observer has a powerful advantage over the observed (see Bleich, 1990; Burnett & Ewald, 1994; Keller, 1982; Lather, 1991). The implicit assumption in an arrangement like Fishman's and mine is that the outsider is an expert teacher, that I would never make the sort of mistakes we were uncovering in Steve's practice. But even if I ever did confuse or anger my students, it was, in any event, of no interest in this research situation. Steve, the insider, was the only vulnerable one, and this suited me fine. Looking back, I believe I especially appreciated my outsider advantage because I was, in nearly all other ways, Fishman's subordinate. I was a newly appointed assistant professor, he a long-time full professor. I was a female, he a male. My research role, then, along with some prior publishing success, was my only clear source of authority.

However, I was not aware of my outsider's privilege until the day Steve asked me to give it up. "Why don't I observe your class some time?" he inquired. I wanted to run from the room! I did not want to be watched! I would be exposed. He would discover I am not the perfect teacher. Although I was too embarrassed to say these things, I knew at some deep level that to relinquish my outsider role was to give up a lot. Still, to say no was like admitting I had something to hide or, equally damning, that I was a person who could not play fair. So, I murmured, "Sure, why not?" and agreed that Fishman could observe my composition classes—but only once or twice and only casually. No formal data collection.

In retrospect, I understand that Steve was asking for the sort of reciprocity between researcher and researched that feminists and others encourage (see Allen, Buchanan, Edelsky, & Norton, 1992; Harding, 1987; Keller, 1985; Lincoln, 1990; Mascia-Lees, Sharpe, & Cohen, 1989; Roman & Apple, 1990.) In my mind's eye, I see Ann Berthoff cheering him on. Berthoff, of course, would have advised Steve to keep me out of his classroom in the first place, but since I was already there, she certainly was sitting on his shoulder applauding. She would have supported his request not only to write about his own classroom in his own way but now, in addition, to mount the research horse himself.

Our Research Gaze Refocuses: My Composition Classroom in the Spotlight

Steve made several visits to my classroom in the early years of our collaboration, but I never felt comfortable being observed, despite the fact

I knew my teaching was profitting from his questioning. As Steve has explained, at the time of his first visit the five-paragraph theme was the centerpiece of my composition pedagogy. He was critical of that approach, and because he said so quite tactfully (more tactfully, as I recall, than he describes), I was able, gradually, to see it from his perspective. Increasingly, I found myself unable to defend such a teacher-defined genre, and over time, I edged slowly toward a more student-centered pedagogy.

After about 3 years of Fishman's occasional visits to my classroom—when I too was finally ready for a research role change—we agreed to a formal study. We would collect data for a semester in two of my composition classes in an effort to learn what shape a more democratic writing classroom might take. What teaching techniques, classroom arrangements, and writing assignments would help me construct more egalitarian, co-learning relationships among my students and between them and me? And how would this approach affect my pupils' writing attitudes and abilities? To answer these questions, Steve and I agreed we would videotape my classroom experiments, and he would interview students and analyze their writing. We would, in sum, adopt roles that were the mirror image of those we assumed in his classroom.

Although both Fishman and I kept our parts of the bargain and endured this role exchange for the entire semester, ultimately the project died. It had been a heroic effort, we agreed, but the fit was terrible: it was as if each of us spent 4 months walking around with our shoes on the wrong feet. Not only did I continue to feel uncomfortable and powerless in Fishman's research gaze, the thought of actually watching myself for hours on videotape was more than I could stomach. Likewise, Steve had little patience for the outsider's work, for collecting and organizing mountains of data. The very medley of student and teacher voices I so enjoy during data analysis alternately irritated, bored, or overwhelmed him. His interest, he told me, was in ideas, and data were all right when they illustrated a "theoretical story." But to have to sort through pages of irrelevant detail to get there was work for which, Steve said, he simply had "no heart." Furthermore, he admitted, he missed being in the research spotlight. The insider role which rendered me so ill at ease actually energized him, he claimed. When Steve was the object of our inquiry, he said, he was a better teacher, more excited about his work, more interested in his students.

About Outsiders: New Appreciation for Both Berthoff and Stenhouse

At semester's close, when Steve and I could finally reclaim our "natural" positions, we were both relieved, and in the half-dozen years since then, neither of us has ever suggested a repeat. As I returned to my outsider station and Steve to his insider role, we were resuming jobs that felt "right," ones for which our personalities, preferences, and academic training had prepared us. In addition, I believe we were resuming the only power relationship we could sustain. Insider-teachers, the objects of inquiry, are often female and lower in academic status than their observers, who are frequently male. I had stepped into that subordinate insider status, and it was hard for me. I experienced the sort of embarrassment, insecurity, and self-doubt that insider-teachers have described, feelings that I, as a safely positioned Stenhousian outsider, had not previously taken very seriously (see Cole & Knowles, 1993; Durst & Stanforth, 1996; Edelsky & Boyd, 1993; Ulichny & Schoener, 1996).

My New Respect for Berthoff's Warning about Outsiders
Fishman's and my role exchange gave me, then, new appreciation for Berthoff's advice to beware of university-based outsiders. I understood the danger she fears: in the presence of a powerful outsider, the teacher may never take research authority for herself. In my case, I seemed to be paralyzed by my mistakes. I suffered as Fishman and I watched videotaped evidence of missed opportunities in class discussion, off-target responses to students, and what I deemed overcontrol of the class, my eagerness to offer neat answers rather than let students muddle to their own solutions. In addition, I found it disconcerting to learn from Steve's interviews and other data sources what my students were actually thinking. I recall moaning midway throught the semester, "I *need* my illusions about my students!" and mounting a half-serious argument for the benefits of a single, coherent, hegemonic perspective on the classroom: my own.

From my stint as an insider, then, I learned that when outsiders are permitted into classrooms, they must work with teachers to find ways to support them and share power, to encourage and honor their visions and voices. Although Fishman had struggled to enlighten me in this regard with his persistent arguments for his insider rights, I now understood their importance from my own experience.

But if the insider role is so risky and potentially disempowering, why was Fishman so eager to take it back? The answer is complex. First, the insider role did not frighten Fishman, a male, full professor with 25 years college teaching experience, as it did me. In fact, after so long in the classroom, Steve says he welcomed the risk; it was part of the new energy for teaching he claimed our research fueled. Second, as Steve explains in Chapter 2, he had already followed Berthoff's advice to do solo teacher "re-search," and by the time he met me, he believed he had taken that approach as far as he could. Finally, Fishman is a man who hungers for integration. Being the insider allowed him to bring together in one setting his teaching, his research, and his writing. By contrast, our role exchange required Steve to prepare and teach his own classes and then study and write about mine. After a term as outside-researcher in my classroom, he longed to return to the feeling of wholeness, the singlemindedness he had enjoyed when we focused on him.

In sum, then, as I struggled to endure Fishman's research gaze, I gained new respect for Berthoff's warning about the dangers of outsider dominance. In addition, my admiration for teacher-researchers soared. It takes great courage, I learned, whether working under an outsider's scrutiny or by oneself, to inquire into one's own teaching. Instructors who investigate their classrooms have to be fearless, willing to pursue bad news as well as good, to explore classroom failure as well as success. Teacher-researchers are daring people. I take my hat off to them.

Stenhouse's Valuing of Outsiders

But let me now, having agreed with Berthoff about the dangers of outsiders, speak up for Stenhouse as well. In direct contrast to Berthoff, Stenhouse raises no warning flags, instead urging teachers to solicit outsiders' perspectives for triangulation purposes (1980/1985c, pp. 107, 109). From my insider experience, I learned that Stenhouse, like Berthoff, is also correct. Outsiders can, in a trusting relationship, help instructors see their classes in ways they cannot do alone. Just as I helped Fishman make the familiar become strange in his classroom, awakening him to student difficulties he had been blind to by himself, he helped me see the limits of my five-paragraph theme approach. Although it was a genre about which I had had some doubts, it was only as a result of Steve's observations and our ongoing conversations that I was able to see its limitations more clearly and figure out ways to change. During that semester I borrowed several of Steve's expressivist activities, ones I had watched succeed with his students, and equally important, I started to reconstruct my philosophy of composition, reading under Steve's guidance the educational theories of John Dewey (1902/1990), who urges teachers to integrate "child and curriculum." Without Steve's outsider viewpoint, I would not have had the insight or courage to make what have turned out to be revolutionary and enduring changes in my teaching.

So, as Stenhouse promises, the outsider perspective can be very valuable. And, equally true, as Berthoff promises, it is fraught with peril. The challenge Fishman and I have faced for a decade is to believe both theorists and, using our best research and negotiating skills, figure out ways to avoid the dangers while holding onto the benefits. To this end, as we show in this book, we have tried to shape our research roles and responsibilities to allow our unique strengths to come forward and to create jointly authored reports in which we make space for both our voices.

Conclusion

Let me return, finally, to the question Fishman was asking when he concluded his section 10 pages ago: What did McCarthy learn from "Boundary Conversations?" Specifically, what was her attitude toward our collaboration at the close of our initial study? My response is that by moving toward a more reciprocal arrangement with Fishman, I felt I had made a significant advance, taken a step beyond my previous data-extraction and clinical partnership agreements. Although in "Boundary Conversations" I was still primarily the outsider, that role felt quite different than it had in my previous work. In my efforts to honor Fishman's voice—ultimately encouraging him to explore his own questions and report on them in his own way—I was no longer the detached observer, working alone to construct findings about the teacher. Instead, I was now engaged in the more difficult (and also more symmetrical) task of constructing findings with Fishman about both his classroom and mine, of working with him to understand the relation of our research to our teaching in both settings. In short, I felt I was moving into more integrated research territory.

In the chapter that follows, Fishman and I temporarily leave the private tapes of our work to reprint their first public outcome: "Boundary Conversations: Conflicting Ways of Knowing in Philosophy and Interdisciplinary Research."

CHAPTER FOUR | *Reprint 1*

BOUNDARY CONVERSATIONS: CONFLICTING WAYS OF KNOWING IN PHILOSOPHY AND INTERDISCIPLINARY RESEARCH

Lucille McCarthy and Steve Fishman

Abstract. This naturalistic study, coauthored by a composition specialist and a philosopher, explores the learning experiences of college students in an Introduction to Philosophy course and the learning experiences of the research collaborators themselves. The researchers identify conflicting ways of knowing in class discussion, student writing, and within their own interdisciplinary collaboration. They then ask questions about how these ways of knowing interact and with what effects. In order to answer these questions the researchers draw upon student data they collected in two consecutive semesters as well as the close records they kept of their own collaborative work. Four research methods were used: observation, interviews, composing-aloud protocols, and text analysis. Conclusions are drawn from the data regarding the benefits for students and researchers of juxtaposing multiple epistemological perspectives. Also presented are conclusions about the learning contexts that promote epistemic growth. The textual form of this study is "heteroglossic," that is, certain sections are written by the composition researcher, certain sections by the teacher-researcher, and others are coauthored by both.

This article first appeared in *Research in the Teaching of English, 25* (December 1991), 419-468. Copyright 1991 by the National Council of Teachers of English. Reprinted with permission.

Note: The Works Cited list for this reprint, as for the other three, appears at its conclusion.

INTRODUCTION

We offer our readers a twin study. In it we examine students' initiation in two Introduction to Philosophy classes and our own interdisciplinary research collaboration. Both parts of our study begin in the fall of 1989 when a composition specialist and a philosopher agreed to a year-long naturalistic study of two of the latter's Introduction to Philosophy classes. In each semester 25 students enrolled, their majors covering the full spectrum of undergraduate offerings. Our four principal characters are Ginny Lewis, a 21 year old junior English major, who took philosophy as a humanities option; David Kaiser, a 27 year old junior business major, who enrolled to fulfill a general degree requirement; Lucille McCarthy, 46, an assistant professor of English at the University of Maryland Baltimore County, who was the composition researcher; and Steve Fishman, 52, a full professor of philosophy at the University of North Carolina Charlotte, who was the teacher-researcher. A number of other philosophy students appear in lesser, but still significant, roles. Fishman undertook the study in order to improve his teaching. McCarthy wanted a collaborative project in which she could share equal authority with a discipline-based teacher.

Theoretical Assumptions

Three theories of learning are central to our twin study. First is the Deweyan assumption that learning involves conflict and reconstruction of the self (1934). There is, writes Dewey, "an element of undergoing, of suffering in its large sense, in every experience. For 'taking in' in any vital experience is something more than placing something on the top of consciousness over what was previously known. It involves reconstruction which may be painful" (p. 41). The tension Dewey speaks about reflects his view that learning is practical, a form of evolutionary adjustment in which the organism struggles with the environment to achieve momentary harmonies.

The second theory we draw upon is Bakhtin's notion that learning is the struggle for new language (1981). According to Bakhtin, we take words from the mouths of others to see how they fit in our own. Like Dewey, Bakhtin highlights the struggle involved, although Bakhtin describes it in political rather than biological terms. The acquisition of discourse is like the colonialization of another's property, for words are never unclaimed lands awaiting our discovery. They are always owned by someone. Struggle occurs because some discourse resists our annexation. Bakhtin writes,

Prior to this moment of appropriation, the word does not exist in a neutral and impersonal language (it is not, after all, out of a dictionary that the speaker gets his words!), but rather it exists in other people's mouths . . . : it is from there that one must take the word, and make it one's own. And not all words for just anyone submit equally easily to this appropriation, to this seizure and transformation into private property; many words stubbornly resist, others remain alien . . . ; they cannot be assimilated into the context and fall out of it (pp. 293-294).

What appeals to us about Bakhtin's theory is the idea that learning includes trying on new language. It is a social rehearsal in which practice with someone else's speech leads us to someone else's internal dispositions or ways of thought. Changing our language is part of the process of changing the way we think.

Still, by themselves, Dewey and Bakhtin do not give us the central image of learning we have adopted for our twin study. For further refinement we turned to Belenky and colleagues (1986) who describe learning as reconstruction of the self in less combative terms. Introducing their own theory of "constructed knowledge," Belenky and her coauthors stress the integration of several ways of knowing. They write that the "constructed knowers" they interviewed

> told us that their current way of knowing and viewing the world . . . began as an effort to reclaim the self by attempting to integrate . . . personally important knowledge with knowledge they had learned from others. They told us of weaving together strands of rational and emotive thought and of integrating objective and subjective knowledge (p. 134).

This passage speaks of "weaving" different ways of knowing, "rational and emotive," "objective and subjective." Instead of struggle and appropriation, Belenky and her associates present an image of neutral threads binding together a variety of epistemologies. We do not take this to mean that these investigators underestimate the importance of resistance and struggle in learning. But the change in tone and imagery is significant. Dewey and Bakhtin give us moments of harmony when one point of view or manner of speaking dominates and brings others into order. These harmonies do not endure, however, and give way to fresh conflicts and renewed struggles. By contrast, we stress that learning requires what Belenky and her associates call a "tolerance for internal contradiction and ambiguity." As they put it, constructed knowers abandon completely the either/or thinking....They recognize the inevitability of conflict and stress, and although they may hope to achieve some respite, they also, as one woman explained, 'learn to live with conflict rather than talking or acting it away' (p. 137).

Although we agree with Dewey and Bakhtin that learning involves struggle and reconstruction of the self, we follow Belenky and her colleagues in seeing learning not so much as a cycle of conflict, domination, and momentary harmony but as a process of increasing openness and tolerance for divergent ways of knowing.

Our Study's Central Image

Boundary conversations is the image we have adopted for learning. In boundary conversations we envision ourselves and our students encountering unfamiliar languages or opposing approaches to the world. These engage our attention and, at first, invite our scrutiny from across the border. We may, however, at some point, decide to step gradually into the unfamiliar neighborhood, at first listening closely, then perhaps deciding to try some phrases of the new language, first mimicking them, then examining them critically. As we open ourselves more fully to the strange neighborhood, holding longer conversations and trying out new roles, we learn more about how people in this neighborhood think. But it is not in abandoning our old ways of knowing and points of view that learning occurs. Rather it is in preserving and contrasting our various discourses, moving back and forth among them, clarifying and repositioning them, that we create conflict and force reconstruction of ourselves. Our home neighborhood is changed. Our familiar ways of knowing and speaking, our comfortable points of view, our old roles all feel different. Just as we understand English better for having learned French, so we see our home countries and borders more clearly, with new significance, because we have engaged in boundary conversations.

This Study's Relation to Previous Research

It is now common in composition studies and education to assume that meaning is constructed as participants, texts, and settings interact (Applebee, 1984; Bartholomae, 1985; Bazerman, 1998; Bazerman & Paradis, 1991; Bizzell, 1982; Brodkey, 1987; Bruffee, 1984; Cooper & Holzman, 1989; Faigley, 1985; Langer, 1987; McDermott, 1977; Mishler,

1979.) Although much previous writing across the curriculum research has shared this assumption, it has focused primarily on only one of the players in classroom studies, the student, saying relatively little about the teacher and outside researcher (Berkenkotter, Huckin, & Ackerman, 1988; Herrington, 1985; North, 1986; McCarthy, 1987). In this study we examine students, two in particular. But in addition we focus on the teacher and the researcher. The philosophy teacher provides his view of his discipline and his research findings about his classroom. The composition researcher's perspective, in turn, is revealed as we report on crucial aspects of her dialogue with the teacher during this project.

In this collaborative study we agree with those who argue that teaching is rooted in the teacher's own interpretive frame and tacit sense of mission. Thus we believe that educational research has too long focused on teachers' supposedly reproducible behaviors while excluding their voices (Apple 1986; McDonald, 1988; Fenstermacher, 1986). In addition, we agree teachers should be seen not only as consumers of research but also as agents of research with their own unique expertise (Cochran-Smith & Lytle, 1990).

Recent theoretical scholarship has explored the ways in which conflict promotes the sort of learning we have called boundary conversations. First, theorists have argued that in collaborative learning the goal is not the elimination of differences but, rather, their identification, maintenance, and explanation (Trimbur, 1989). A second sort of conflict has been explored by theorists who argue that reintroducing narrative into the classroom alongside exposition sets up productive tensions. Having students integrate their own stories into otherwise expository texts will, these theorists believe, help students dialogue with abstract material (DiPardo, 1990; Rosen, 1985). A third type of conflict has been the focus of theorists interested in problem-solving. They argue that students should be asked to solve more "ill-defined" problems, that is, problems which grow out of actual conflicts among values, beliefs, and experiences (Carter, 1988). Finally, Hill (1990), a composition theorist, argues that learning and writing require dissonance, turbulence, and even fear. New ways of thinking are born, Hill says, when we face "the feared other," that is, when we explore opposing points of view and move back and forth between teaching and learning, emotion and cognition, mind and body, female and male, and between one discipline and another (p. 149).

There is, thus, theoretical support from several quarters for the value of conflict in learning. What has not yet been done, however, is to examine how various sorts of conflict actually work in particular classrooms and for particular students. Our study offers information about the nature and functions of boundary conversations in one college classroom as well as in our interdisciplinary research collaboration. Specifically, in our study we answer Lyons' (1990) call for research which describes the interaction among students' and teachers' conflicting ways of knowing.

The ultimate aim of this study is twofold: First, to contribute to our understanding of how students learn and, second, to provide a model for sharing authority in collaborative classroom research. Findings from this study corroborate the notion that learning involves not only resolving conflicts but also promoting and nurturing them.

METHODS

Our Inquiry Paradigm and Choice of Research Report Form

We chose the naturalistic paradigm because it best suited our inquiry situation. Our questions, as we began the study, were broad ones about students' and teachers' ways of knowing. They were the general questions that Geertz says are traditionally asked by ethnographers entering new research scenes: "What's going on here?" and "What the devil do these people think they're up to?" (1976, p. 224). Thus we began with no hypotheses to test and no specially devised tasks. (For a contrast of the naturalistic and scientific paradigms, see Lincoln & Guba, 1985). Because the assumptions underlying the naturalistic research paradigm shaped our methodological and reportorial decisions, we describe them briefly here.

Naturalistic researchers assume that realities are multiple and evolving and are constructed by participants as they interact in social settings. Further, naturalists assume that the investigator and the object of study cannot be separated and that inquiry is never value-free. Research is, rather, an interactive process which aims for insights into particular situations. Naturalistic researchers use both qualitative and quantitative methods, and research design, as well as explanatory theory, emerges as salient features are identified and explored. Researchers in this tradition understand themselves as instruments of inquiry and acknowledge that both tacit and explicit assumptions influence their work.

In writing our naturalistic study, we have heeded recent calls for research report forms which are consistent with the assumptions of the naturalistic paradigm. Theorists have argued that in order to accurately render the complex relationships of social life, naturalistic studies must be, "multi-voiced," that is, they must replay the range of unmerged voices, legitimated and nonlegitimated, which created the original scene (Anderson, 1989; Quantz & O'Connor, 1988; Zeller, 1987). Thus new textual forms must be developed which foreground the multiple realities of researcher and informants, describe their negotiations and mutual influence, and represent all their voices. It is our understanding, then, that textual forms are not neutral but, rather, embody assumptions about the world. As Bazerman puts it, certain features of text reveal "the author as an individual statement-maker coming to terms with reality from a distinctive perspective" (1988, p. 26).

Although there are as yet few examples of alternative textual forms in the composition or education literature, they might include staged dialogues (see Lewis & Simon, 1986), oral histories (see Weiler, 1988), dramas (see Brodkey, 1987), multiple interpretations of the same data (see Clark & Doheny-Farina, 1990), reflexive monologues (see Woolgar, 1988), and informant and researcher narratives, as in the present study. (Arguments for including narrative in academic discourse are found in Bleich, 1989; Bruner, 1985; and Mitchell, 1980. In particular, discussions of narrative's role in ethnographic texts are found in Atkinson, 1990; Brodkey, 1987; Geertz, 1988; and Van Maanen, 1988.)

We thus report our study in what Clifford (1983) calls a "polyphonic" or "heteroglossic" text, a form in which researcher and informant both speak in their own voices and in which narrative as well as exposition is employed. This heteroglossic form preserves our differences, empowers us equally, and assumes that we are in a dynamic and mutually shaping relationship (Gergen, 1988; Woolgar, 1988). We believe that we create with our multivoiced text a fuller picture of classroom interactions and inter-disciplinary research than we could by using a single, blended voice.

Our Data Collection and Analysis

To answer our questions about conflicting ways of knowing, we used a naturalistic design that employed three sorts of triangulation: among sources, among methods, and between the two investigators (Denzin, 1978; Lincoln & Guba, 1985; Mathison, 1988; Miles & Huberman, 1984). We reasoned that this multimodal approach, in which data generated by one method adds to and crosschecks data generated by others, would help us construct a rich portrait of Fishman's classroom. We could, in short, view the participants' boundary conversations through several windows and then share with each other what we'd seen. Our design assumes that just as the strengths of one method compensate for another's limitations, so one researcher's interpretations enrich and refine the other's. This triangulation process has been compared to that of a fisherman who uses multiple nets, "each with a complement of holes, but placed together so the holes in one net are covered by intact portions of other nets" (Lincoln & Guba, 1985, p. 306).

We collected data from September, 1989, through May, 1990, focusing on five fall semester students, including Ginny Lewis and David Kaiser, and, to a lesser extent, on five spring semester students. We chose these students because we already had, or believed we could get, rich data about them and because we found their boundary conversations particularly interesting. These students all contributed to our understanding of Fishman's classroom and provided a context for the stories of Ginny and David which McCarthy reports below. A detailed summary of our data collection is reported in Table 1.

Observation

Though McCarthy and Fishman observed the classroom from very different perspectives and for very different periods of time, each focused on the interactions among participants and their ways of knowing during class discussion. McCarthy wrote her field notes during and after her class visits in December, and Fishman wrote his self-reports after each class in letters to McCarthy. These letters, in which Fishman also discussed theoretical and research issues, then evoked further written and oral exchanges between the investigators.

Interviews

McCarthy interviewed the five fall semester students three times—in October, December, and April—in order to elicit their interpretations of writing in Fishman's class. She conducted the first of these hour-long interviews on the phone before she met the students. The second interviews, in December, were conducted in person with two students together at one interview session and three together at another. McCarthy reasoned that the interaction among students who, by that point in thesemester, knew each other quite well would produce richer data than shecould get in one-on-one sessions. The final interviews, follow-ups with the five students in April, were again conducted by phone. McCarthy also audiotaped four, hour-long interviews with Fishman to determine

Table 1
Data Collection Record: September 1989–May 1990

Observation
 McCarthy
  observation of two class sessions, fall semester
 Fishman
  teacher-observation in all classes
 (Both researchers drew upon all observation data.)

Interviews
 McCarthy audiotaped
  three hour-long interviews with each of the five fall semester students
  four hour-long interviews with Fishman
 Fishman audiotaped
  five hour-long interviews, one with each of five spring semester students
  four 30-minute conversations with students about revising their papers
 (Both researchers drew upon all interview data.)

Class documents
 Fishman collected
  Students' "classnotes" recording all class discussions
  All other class documents (including questionnaires)
 (Both researchers drew upon all class documents.)

Students' Texts with the Teacher's Responses
 McCarthy collected
  The two or three required drafts of both essays for the five fall semester students along with Fishman's response letters
  Numerous other students' drafts with Fishman's responses
 (Both researchers drew upon these textual data.)

Protocols with Retrospective Interviews
 McCarthy audiotaped
  One 30-minute protocol and 30-minute retrospective interview with each of the five fall semester students as they composed the final draft of their second (last) paper
 (Only McCarthy drew directly upon the protocol data.)

Letters from Fishman to McCarthy
 Both researchers drew upon data in some 80 letters Fishman sent to McCarthy between September 1989 and May 1990.

his views of philosophy, his personal history and relation to his discipline, his goals for students' learning and writing, and his perceptions of classroom events. These interviews took place in November, December, February, and March.

Fishman recorded a total of nine interviews and conversations with students, including Ginny and David, who came to his office of their own volition for help with revising their papers. These conferences provided rich information about these students' boundary conversations, that is, about the interaction among Fishman's and their various ways of knowing. In addition, Fishman interviewed five spring semester students in May, after grades had been turned in, questioning them about what and how they learned in his course. All interviews took place in Fishman's office or classroom.

Both investigators' interview questions were suggested by the students' earlier comments or by emerging patterns in the data which we wanted to pursue. All interviews were transcribed for later analysis.

Analysis of Observations and Interviews

Both investigators drew upon all observation and interview data. We read and reread field notes, letters, and interview transcripts looking for patterns and themes. McCarthy began theme and pattern analysis as soon as she collected her first interview data in October 1989. During the early months of the project McCarthy focused on emerging categories of disciplinary ways of knowing. As students worked to use philosophic discourse, McCarthy noted instances of conflict, blending, substituting, and mixing of students' already familiar discourses with the new language of philosophy. These categories emerged from the data for McCarthy, but as Glaser and Strauss remind us, "the researcher does not approach reality as a *tabula rasa*. He must have a perspective that will help him see relevant data and abstract significant categories from his scrutiny of the data" (1967, p. 3). McCarthy's earlier research in students' disciplinary initiation had, no doubt, readied her to see these categories.

By March, McCarthy, now aided by Fishman, had begun to identify categories of knowing that appeared to transcend disciplinary differences. As we heard students speak about their broad attitudes toward knowledge, learning, truth, and expertise, Fishman's philosophic perspective became important. He began distinguishing epistemological stances, first identifying the two categories we have come to call separate and connected knowing. Separate knowing appeared to emphasize disengagement and objectification, whereas in connected knowing a central image was hearing, proximity between subject and object, the sympathetic placing of oneself in the position of others, positions which initially may seem strange or abhorrent.

At this time both researchers recognized similarities between the epistemological categories we were developing and those we had recently read in *Women's Ways of Knowing* by Belenky, Clinchy, Goldberger, and Tarule (1986). We were particularly struck by the similarity of Fishman's students' language and the language of women questioned by Belenky and her co-investigators, especially in light of the gender and age difference among participants in the two studies. Ultimately we decided to use Belenky and her associates' epistemological scheme because it helped us organize and explain what we were seeing. Moreover, we could compare our data and findings with those generated by Belenky and her colleagues.

In deciding to use a theoretical frame grounded in data other than our own, we knew we were taking risks. Such a procedure is fruitful, according to Glaser and Strauss, only when the theory fits the data and works to explain the behavior in the new situation (pp. 3-6). Belenky and her associates' system proved fruitful for us. Although for McCarthy, conflicting disciplinary discourses and Bakhtin's theory of learning as trying out new language continued to be important, and although, for both McCarthy and Fishman, Dewey's theory of learning as conflict still had a central place, the epistemological categories of Belenky and her associates gave both researchers a powerful way of exploring their data. (For the use of an earlier generation of epistemic categories—W. G. Perry's—in a study of undergraduate philosophy students, see North, 1986.)

We summarize the five ways of knowing proposed by Belenky and her colleagues as follows:

1. *Silence:* At this position women experience themselves as mindless, voiceless, and subject to the whims of external authority.
2. *Received Knowledge:* In this perspective women believe they can receive and reproduce knowledge from all-knowing external authorities but are not capable of creating knowledge of their own.
3. *Subjective Knowledge:* Women in this perspective conceive truth as personal, private, and intuitive.
4. *Procedural Knowledge:* In this "developmental moment" (p. 103) women are invested in learning and applying objective procedures for obtaining and communicating knowledge. There are two types of procedural knowing:
   a. *Separate knowing* involves taking an impersonal and skeptical stance toward the external object and applying methods that promise objectivity. The knower distances herself in order to "doubt" (p. 104). "Separate

knowers learn through explicit formal instruction how to adopt a different lens...that of a discipline" (p. 115).

"Separate knowers bring to their group propositions they have developed as fully as possible and that they hope to sell in the market place of ideas. Members must know the rules, but they need not know each other" (p. 118).

b. *Connected knowing,* by contrast, involves empathizing with others' ideas, stepping into their shoes, and "believing" them (p. 113). "Connected knowers learn through empathy...to get out from behind their own eyes and use a different lens...the lens of another person" (p. 115).

"In connected knowing groups people utter half-baked truths and ask others to nurture them. Since no one would entrust one's fragile infant to a stranger, members of the group must learn to know and trust each other" (p. 118).

5. *Constructed Knowledge:* In this position women view themselves as creators of knowledge, working to weave together subjective and objective strategies for knowing, to connect personal knowledge with knowledge learned from others.

These five epistemological perspectives were generated by Belenky and her colleagues as they examined transcripts of interviews with 135 women of differing ages and backgrounds. These investigators admit that their abstract categories are not fixed or universal, that not all women pass through all positions, and that similar categories can be found in men's thinking (p. 15). (For recent scholarship which specifically relates feminist theories of knowledge to the teaching of writing see Ashton-Jones & Thomas, 1990; Bleich, 1989; Caywood & Overing, 1987; Cooper, 1989; and Flynn, 1988.)

During our analysis of the observation and interview data, *classnotes* from Fishman's philosophy class provided a valuable source of information. These were a teaching device Fishman had used for several years in which a different student took notes each class session and then prepared a report of 2-4 pages for distribution and presentation at the beginning of the next class. Because these notes were "published," that is, photocopied by the student recorder for the entire class and read aloud, students took great care to make them both accurate and entertaining. Notetakers often recreated large chunks of classroom discussions which we used to add to, refine, and crosscheck our observation and interview data. Other class documents—syllabi, the teacher's model essay, essay guidelines, etc.— were also useful in this regard. In addition, we consulted data generated by two brief questionnaires which we had distributed to Fishman's students at midterm and semester's end eliciting their views of philosophy. We were guided in our analysis of observations and interviews by the work of Miles and Huberman (1984) and Spradley (1979, 1980).

Analysis of Students' Written Texts and Teacher's Responses

Another window through which we viewed the interactions among Fishman and his students was text analysis. Fishman assigned two essays, the first with three required drafts, the second with two. He responded to each student's five drafts with page-long, typed letters in which he suggested various ways a philosopher might "explore" or "push further" the conflicts underlying their chosen topics. McCarthy collected all five drafts from the five fall semester students along with Fishman's response letters. In addition she examined numerous other students' drafts and Fishman's responses throughout the project.

McCarthy and Fishman relied on close readings of these texts, continuously discussing them as we worked to reconstruct students' thinking and learning. We viewed the written interaction between student and teacher as a two-person conversation set within the larger classroom context where similar multiperson discussions took place. We understood student writing as shaped by and, at the same time, shaping the ways of knowing and speaking in the classroom. Further, we viewed students' and teacher's writing for each other as a cooperative endeavor in which meaning is negotiated socially to reach a mutually defined goal. Our work with students' texts and teacher's responses was influenced by Freedman (1985), Sperling and Freedman (1987), and by our own previous work (Fishman, 1985, 1989; McCarthy & Braffman, 1985).

Protocols and Retrospective Interviews

To add to and crosscheck information from interviews and text analysis McCarthy audiotaped a 30-minute protocol as each of the five fall semester students composed their final drafts of the second paper in early December. Each protocol was followed by a 30-minute retrospective interview in which McCarthy asked students to tell her more about the process they had just been through. McCarthy reasoned that in this interview students' major concerns would be reemphasized, whereas the smaller issues that may have occupied them during composing would be forgotten. Students wrote at a desk in a small library study room while McCarthy sat nearby in a position from which she could observe and make notes about their behaviors. She also jotted questions she wanted to pursue in the retrospective interview. Because McCarthy followed these five students across the semester, she could interpret the protocol data in light of what she knew of their thinking and writing across time.

The information provided by the protocols generally corroborated and fleshed out information provided by interviews and text analysis. Of particular interest, however, were the points at which the protocol data contradicted interview or textual data, that is, when what students actually did during composing differed from their metacognitive descriptions of their processes or texts. These points spurred further inquiry. Although composing-aloud was not a comfortable process for any of the five students, they did all produce usable sections of their final draft during the composing session.

Analysis and Scoring of the Protocols and Retrospective Interviews

Stage 1. In the first stage of our analysis of the protocol and retrospective interview transcripts, McCarthy classified and counted what she called the *writer's conscious concerns*. She identified these concerns as anything the writer paid attention to during composing as expressed by (a) remarks about a thought or behavior or (b) observed behaviors. McCarthy's analysis of the transcripts was carried out in a two-part process. First, McCarthy read them several times and drew from them general categories of writer's concerns, along with a number of subcategories. Then, using this scheme, she classified and counted the writer's remarks and behaviors. McCarthy worked alone during the first stage because she viewed her knowledge of students' writing over the semester as essential to this process. This approach fit with our overall design in which we were working for confirmability among sources and methods rather than agreement among raters (Lincoln & Guba, 1985, pp. 299-301). McCarthy was guided in her analysis of the protocol data by the work of Berkenkotter (1983), Bridwell (1980), Flower & Hayes (1981), and Flower, Ackerman, Kantz, McCormick, Peck, & Stein (1990).

Stage 2. In the second stage of protocol analysis McCarthy and Fishman worked together, inferring the epistemological perspectives associated with each of the writers' concerns McCarthy had identified in Stage 1. As we discussed the transcripts, we worked to take on the writers' perspectives, often placing their statements and behaviors in the context of what we knew about them from other data sources. Collaboration between the two investigators was important in this stage as we reconstructed students' stances.

Ensuring the Trustworthiness and Transferability of Our Findings

To ensure the trustworthiness of our findings and interpretations we used several other techniques in addition to triangulation: (a) Extended periods of engagement with our informants during which salient features were identified for more detailed inquiry; (b) credibility checks in which we shared drafts of our findings with several of our informants who responded orally and in writing; (c) an ongoing search for "negative cases," that is, cases or events which lay outside our tentative categories and findings; and (d) external checks on our inquiry process and emerging interpretations by established researchers who knew nothing about Fishman's classroom. (See Lincoln & Guba, 1985, for a discussion of validity and reliability in naturalistic research.)

In addition, we have provided specific details about participants and setting in our study so that readers may judge the transferability of our findings to their own situations.

RESULTS AND DISCUSSION

Information from all data sources supports two conclusions, one concerning the interaction among multiple ways of knowing in Fishman's classroom and the other concerning Ginny's and David's experiences with these ways of knowing in their writing. First, although students in Fishman's class appeared to favor a particular epistemological perspective, they were able to move back and forth among various stances. This moving back and forth among epistemologies—in particular the juxtaposition of strong subjective knowing with procedural and constructed knowing—led students to new ways of seeing in what we call boundary conversations.

Second, although Ginny and David differed in age, gender, and prior academic experience, both preferred separate knowing, and both had difficulty writing constructed knowledge, that is, weaving together personally important knowledge with philosophic research. Both Ginny and David succeeded as constructed knowers, however, and this success was tied to what each ultimately learned from the class. Findings about Ginny and David are supported by protocol, interview, and textual data.

We report our results in three voices. First, Fishman describes his classroom and his research findings. He focuses on the ways students juxtapose different epistemological perspectives in class discussion. McCarthy then follows with her findings about two students and their writing experiences in the class. Finally, Fishman and McCarthy coauthor the story of their research collaboration.

Introduction to Philosophy: When Upside Down Is Right Side Up *(by Steve Fishman)*

Course Goals and Requirements

My class is an effort to connect student concerns and broader cultural ones, to relate ordinary undergraduate talk and the language of philosophy. This means the heart of my class is motivating students to explore their own views in relation to the views of others. Thus my primary teaching task is to make my classroom safe for different voices and to help my students hear them.

Let me begin this description of my Intro to Philosophy class by discussing the course requirements and arrangements. I ask students to attend all sessions, take all the short quizzes, and complete two five-to-ten page essays. Students choose their own essay topics, but I strongly urge them to explore problems both personal and compelling. As for texts, we normally read five or six pieces from the traditional literature. My list usually includes a couple of Platonic dialogues, Descartes' *Meditations*, chapters from Dewey's *Reconstruction in Philosophy*, Russell's *Marriage and Morals*, and essays by John Stuart Mill and Harriet Taylor. To encourage timely completion of these texts, I give a series of ten-minute quizzes on the readings.

What is upside-down about my classroom is that the quizzes are graded but do not count while the essay drafts count but are not graded. Since student and teacher voices are the class focus, philosophic texts are not introduced until midterm. In addition, we sit in a circle with me choosing a different desk each day, and, instead of all students taking notes, one is designated to record the discussion and make copies for everyone to read at the start of the next class session. My reasons for proceeding this way? To upset the normal distribution of authority in the classroom, to change the roles student and teacher are expected to play, and to honor student narratives. All of these goals are grounded in my view of philosophy.

The Instructor's View of Philosophy

In graduate school one of my professors said that when our future Intro students ask about the nature of philosophy, we should tell them, "That's the last question to ask, not the first." I suppose philosophers are leery of such questions because the discipline's history is so varied. There is the old standby, "Philosophy is love of wisdom," but unless you say this very fast, you are left with new questions about the nature of both love and wisdom. However, one definition has stayed with me over the years— that philosophy is reflection on cultural conflict. This definition comes out of the Deweyan tradition, and it determines the goals and structure of my class.

Dewey's view of philosophy is tied to his view of thinking. Only when our habits are interrupted, when we encounter detours, do we stop and ask what has gone wrong. This forces reevaluation, reexamination of our goals and plans for action. Without obstacles, thought is unnecessary (1916/1967, pp. 139-151). For example, when my trip from work is smooth, I find myself in the driveway without any recollection of the drive home. In contrast, my recollections are vivid when I face road construction or heavy traffic. It is in this spirit that Dewey says philosophy is reflection upon cultural conflict (1920/1962, p. 26). Thought is functional. It begins with friction amongst our beliefs, an incongruity which forces us to question our assumptions.

As applied to my Intro class, asking students right off to reflect on conflicting values within our culture would be too vague, too intimidating an assignment. Instead, I ask for a narrative about any problem which "refuses to go away," which demands attention. A few students claim they have no problems. Some say they cannot talk about themselves and retreat to topics like capital punishment. But most students come up with personal subjects, like leaving home, troubles with studying and dating, consequences of family divorce. I respond to these drafts by letter, explaining how a philosopher might develop the essay they have started. My first task is to help bring forward the conflicting values embedded in each narrative. This is not easy since most student problems come in forms quite different from those in standard philosophy anthologies. However, my thinking is that, if I work hard enough with my students, at the core of each of their problems we will find the reflection of cultural tensions. In this way, I introduce students to philosophic thinking by encouraging them to connect their own conflicts with broader, cultural ones.

How do I help my students find their conflicts? Matt Cashion, a senior English major in my Spring 1990 Intro course, was one of five students I interviewed at the end of the semester. He reminded me that on the first day of class I had said, "This is a course in which you will find your own voice." I was not after anything esoteric. Certainly I don't believe each of my students will invent their own language or express themselves in entirely unique ways. I simply want them to hear themselves, to attend their own experiences, searching them, dissecting them. This requires restudying their lives through narration, being more alert to patterns, assumptions, and consequences they might have missed the first go round. Most important is helping students find their multiple selves, their multiple voices, for in this way they find the center of their conflicts. Taffy Davies, a junior sociology major, wrote about feeling guilty when she left home to pursue a career. In my response-letter I suggested she listen to the different voices within herself—the childhood admonitions to put family first versus the schoolroom demands to compete for herself.

What I most want my students to avoid is what Dewey would have called "irresponsible" thinking, stockpiling of information in a helter-skelter fashion, experiencing their courses as unrelated to one another, seeing their lives as unconnected episodes (1933, pp. 32-33). It is not easy, however, for students to find connections between their personal and their academic languages, to be constructed knowers. Initially, when I ask what they think about an issue, they seem insulted, as if I've violated a rule. Why do they respond this way? In my view, it goes back to finding their own voices. They do not know how to work their opinions into school conversations, how to profit from close study of themselves. My students want desperately to look things up, appeal to a book, keep *themselves* out of their work. When I say, "These essays demand thinking research rather than library research," they become uneasy. (This will be seen when McCarthy reports the stories of Ginny and David below.)

Juxtaposing Ways of Knowing in a Classroom Discussion

I want to describe a class in which students succeeded in finding connections between their personal and academic languages, a class in which they juxtaposed a variety of ways of knowing. It was my Intro to Philosophy class of Tuesday, February 6, 1990. The previous period I had introduced a moral dilemma, an updated version of one Plato presents in the *Euthyphro* (1953, pp. 3-4). "If you discovered your parents were dealing drugs," I asked, "would you turn them in?" At this point we were 4 weeks into the semester and had not yet read any assigned texts. A draft of the first required essay had already been turned in and a second draft was due the following week. My purpose was to get students talking about the ideas behind their ethical judgments. I wanted them to find general foundations from which their views might be defended. On the face of it, my assignment was very much an exercise in logical analysis or separate knowing. Phrases like "defense of their view" sound adversarial rather than nurturing. And looking for "general foundations" suggests distance rather than proximity to different points of view. However, a careful look at the classnotes shows subjective knowing was just as central to our discussion, and that, at a fulcrum point, a variety of types of knowing led the class to new discoveries.

When I first introduced the moral dilemma, two distinct camps developed—those who would turn their parents in and those who would not. The principal spokespeople for each position were also clear. Diana Roldan, 26, a junior creative arts major from Colombia, South America, spoke forcefully for going to the police about parents, and Vickie Fowler, 22, a former dance student who now was a senior business major, argued for leaving parents alone. But rather than placing a single label on the knowing these students employed, I find it more appropriate to describe them as employing multiple ways of knowing. Although neither Diana nor Vickie displayed the classic subjectivist stance by saying, "I don't know why I believe what I do, I just believe it," the dose of intuitive judgment in their positions was as strong if not stronger than their reliance on specifiable procedures. Certainly they both gave reasons for their views—and this suggests procedural rather than subjective knowing—but my hunch is a "still small voice" was also working as they developed their arguments during class discussion. My hunch is based on the unusual vehemence with which they presented their positions. Over the years I have noticed that most students are reluctant to champion a point of view before their peers. It is not that college students lack sufficient procedural knowing to argue in front of their classmates. What I find is that, for most of them, their inner voices are insufficiently provoked and, therefore, they cannot commit their procedural knowing in the service of a single point of view. Diana and Vickie were exceptions to this general pattern, each of them showing strong commitment to the position she had adopted.

Randy Hollandsworth took the classnotes during our first discussion of the drug issue. He is a 35 year old railroad investigator who was not working toward a degree but taking the course as a special student.

Randy's notes indicate that three-quarters of my students did not make a clear choice. He writes,

> At this time Steve said to think about whether we would turn our parents in for drug dealing. To get clear on our thoughts he asked us to begin with a 10-minute freewrite. Ginger read her freewrite first and expressed how she would do everything to stop her parents, but she would not turn them in. Richard stated that he would seek outside help but could not turn them in. Mary stated the she would be shocked and would still love and stand behind them but would not condone their activities. Wendy added that she had a different view of the drug war issue and that she would not infringe on her parents' rights. Vickie Fowler agreed with Wendy that she would leave her parents alone, and Melissa questioned them on the dangers involved.
>
> Diana Roldan said it would be difficult, but she would turn them in to save them. David and Adrian both hit on the idea of the seriousness of the actions either way and the strength of the bonding with parents. Michelle said that if you grew up watching this, then you would be more accepting of it. Amy said she hated drugs but that the average dealer is not like television portrays them with shootouts, etc. . . . Kelley stated she would just leave, and Diana ended, stating in strong terms that the easier way out might not be best.

According to Randy's notes, 12 students (25 were present) responded in class to my question. Only three, Diana, Vickie, and Wendy, committed themselves to one alternative over the other. Ginger, Richard, Mary, and Taffy hunted for a middle ground. They said they would try to stop their parents, admitting that what their parents were doing was wrong, but they wouldn't turn them in. David, Adrian, Michelle, and Amy sidestepped the dilemma by offering tangential comments, calling it a serious stress on the parent-child bond, noting that decisions depend upon circumstance, saying real and TV drug dealers are different. One student, Kelley, indicated her frustration by saying she would leave home.

At the conclusion of our first discussion, I thought there was more we could do with this dilemma, but I wasn't sure students would continue their initial enthusiasm for a second period. Still, I thought it was worth a try. I began the second period by restating the controversy. Fortunately, Diana and Vickie took up their earlier positions and developed them further. Taffy was notetaker for this class, and her record of the class discussion which she later circulated captures some of the arguments

Diana and Vickie employed. Her notes also show the entire class moving back and forth between different types of knowing. Taffy writes,

> A tad reluctantly we took a few steps backwards to our discussion of a moral dilemma: "Whether or not to put our parents away for dealing drugs." Steve started the battle off by restating Vickie's view versus Diana's view. Vickie wouldn't interfere in her parents' life over drugs because she feels that drugs are a constant in today's society, and turning her parents in wouldn't change the scheme of things. Diana would do everything in her power to bring them to their senses, but if it didn't work, she would have no choice but to turn them over to the Law
>
> ... Vickie said that she could not morally "judge" her parents because, after all, they do not judge her.

As her choice of words reveals, Taffy saw this as a "battle," as Vickie "versus" Diana. And verbal battles in classrooms usually employ the methods of separate knowing—detection of inconsistency, reliance on disinterested reason, detachment from the issues. Vickie's side used arguments of this type. I, in my letter to my co-researcher, recorded three: drugs aren't wrong—it's just a bad law; turning in parents would not be effective as a way of stopping the drug problem, so why do it?; and I don't have the right to judge anyone else. Except for Vickie's claim that she wouldn't judge her parents because they don't judge her, her arguments could have been voiced by anyone. They do not appeal to any special circumstances in Vickie's life. I call these "separate knower arguments" because they stand by themselves. The assumption is that any reasonable person would assent to them, regardless of what they knew about Vickie.

In contrast, Diana's arguments relied on classmates knowing her story, that is, on connected knowing. She tried to put the class in her shoes by describing her experiences. Again, appealing to my own letter, I record Diana as saying, "I was about the only one who said they would turn their parents in. Maybe it's because I'm from Colombia, and I have had relatives killed and heard shooting on the streets all the time." She also said she would want someone to stop her if she were doing drugs, another way of drawing closer to the dilemma rather than stepping back. For Diana to be persuasive, the class had to know Diana's background, had to imagine how her childhood differed from theirs. Diana's thinking asked the students to step closer, whereas Vickie's asked them to step back.

At this point during the class I was excited by the commitment Vickie and Diana were showing. Their passion caused other students to attend more closely, to listen up, to hear the boundary conversations between two opposing views. This sort of development was a dream for me because of my view that philosophy is exploration of conflict. It was, as Dewey might say, classroom thinking as functional, a conflict of values forcing everyone to reflect on his or her own views. After a number of exchanges I sensed the two sides were repeating themselves, or maybe I caught whiffs of anxiety from the class. A few students were laughing nervously, and I took this to mean I had to do something, like sensing a player has been center-stage too long and a new character must come on. "Let's hold for a second," I said. "Can someone describe the basic values at stake here?" We all moved back in our chairs as if to rest. My seat was in the circle near the windows, and I was watching for a hand to go up when I realized Michael Howard, sitting three desks to my right, was waiting for me to call on him. "It is the right to privacy versus the need to protect one's family," he said. Michael's remark changed the tone in the room. Everyone became quiet. We were no longer listening to an argument between Vickie and Diana. We were participating in something larger. We were now talking about whether or not we had the right to interfere when we saw others doing harm to themselves. Vickie was saying hands-off, and Diana was saying hands-on. Finding the general foundations behind these two positions was like a click, a sudden switch from one way of knowing to another.

Michael had managed to step away, to become an outsider to the disagreement—should parents be reported or not—to find the differing assumptions about responsibility behind these positions. By logically analyzing the opposing views, Michael was doing separate knowing. He had asked himself, "What basic difference between Diana and Vickie leads one to interfere with parents and the other to leave them alone?" This was classic philosophic thinking, a search for general principles, for the universal form embedded in the particular. It was not surprising that Michael made this contribution. Of all the students in Intro to Philosophy that semester, he was the most fluent in academic speech, the most capable of separate and abstract ways of thinking. When Michael stepped away from the disagreement between Diana and Vickie, he took the entire class with him.

But, if I leave it at that, my account of what occurred would be too simple. In fact, we were not just stepping away. We were moving back and forth, identifying with either Diana or Vickie, then separating again to retry their views. In her classnotes Taffy reports Todd Williams's comment about this alternation of ways of knowing. Todd was a third year architecture student. Taffy writes, "Todd suggested it might be viewed as a macro versus micro way of looking at the situation." Todd went on to give an example about understanding an architectural principle very differently after seeing it illustrated on a field trip. "On the blackboard in architecture class, the principle was removed," Todd said, "but seeing it in an actual building changed my view of both the principle and the building." By analogy, the moral principle—different views of responsibility toward others—put the opposition between Diana and Vickie in a different light. The axiom and the concrete example ricocheted off each other. The moral principle was not something debated by founding fathers off in the blue; it applied to our approach toward our parents— what we say to them, what we hold back. And the disagreement between Diana and Vickie was not just about family loyalty; it was about rights and responsibilities, about what prices we are willing to pay for which freedoms. At this point, as if to illustrate Todd's comments, Vickie said, "It just jumped out at me. I can really see the differences between Diana and me."

Although the period was almost over, I couldn't keep still. I had been doing my own version of back and forth, connecting our class discussion with ones in Mill's *On Liberty* which were sounding in my ear (1947, pp. 77-85). Strangely, I started talking about Mill as if everyone knew him— but it felt that real, that close to me. I said, "John Stuart Mill writes about the same issues. He recognizes that no one is entirely isolated. So, if we harm ourselves, we automatically harm others. But, on the other hand, Mill also recognizes the value of independence. If we never risk harming ourselves, we'll never stand on our own two feet." I was speaking quickly, waving my arms, offering a mini-lecture. I was putting my students in the position of received knowers who had little clue about the identity of John Stuart Mill. But it was in the spirit of connected knowing that I offered my comments. I wanted to tie our discussion to one of philosophy's luminaries, to suggest we had been mixing some of Mill's language with ours, working through moral tangles similar to the ones he faced. Taffy uses one of my favorite words when she concludes her classnotes. She records, "Right before we left, we started to discuss Mill and what his opinion would be in this context." In class I use the word "context" a lot. I was, as Taffy says, bringing Mill in. My intention, however, was also to carry us out to Mill, to suggest we had found our own way into the center of a classic philosophic debate. Taffy was taking notes at the desk immediately to the left of mine. She stopped. "Yeah," she said, "Steve's right. Mill even thinks it's okay to get drunk." Just then the bell rang, and chairs scraped as everyone packed to leave. I said nothing more, wanting to end the period without closure, to let our differences simmer.

During our discussion the class moved to a higher level of abstraction, perhaps a new, more powerful level of separate knowing, but it was not the move to the higher level itself which was important. It was the juxtaposition of different ways of knowing which allowed the class to click. Vickie saw herself differently in relation to Diana, the whole class saw Diana and Vickie differently, and everyone heard connections between what they had been thinking and Mill's theories of liberty. My suspicion is that various ways of knowing should only loosely be understood as developmental, that is, it may not be desirable to become constructed knowers—and remain constructed knowers—all the time. Although constructed knowing, making connections between student and cultural problems, is the core of my course goals, I believe this comes about by juxtaposing a variety of epistemic stances. I believe it is in the tensions among these conflicting stances, our sensitivity to the boundary conversations between them, that learning occurs. (The value of juxtaposing multiple ways of knowing recalls Elbow's arguments for juxtaposing different "modes or textures" of writing, 1986, pp. 44-45).

Lessons from Research

What do I learn from this analysis of my classroom discussion? It made my tacit insights about teaching more explicit. During the actual drug-class I sensed intuitively that the session was good. What I now understand more fully is that a climate of trust allowed students to do the attentive listening and open exploration I witnessed. It also made clearer to me that what I ask of my students is complex. I learned I want them to become connected knowers in a way which does not exclude separate knowing. As they approach other students—as well as their own previously-silenced positions—I want them to be nonjudgmental, sympathetic, connected knowers. But when studying their own majority or most centered views, I want them to be separate knowers, to be detached and skeptical, alert to inconsistency and self-serving rationalization. My analysis helped me articulate my intention that students treat their own positions as outsiders and unfamiliar positions as insiders, that they be strict with themselves and liberal with others.

The significance of a trusting environment, of how this helps students shift to open listening and exploration, was also supported by my semester-end student interviews. On May 3, 1990, I spoke with Todd Williams, the junior architecture major. His comments suggest that, at some point during the course, he began to approach his classmates as a more sympathetic or connected knower. At first Todd was concerned about the impression he made and took extra precautions with his responses. But some time during the second half of the semester he changed strategies:

> At the beginning you want to make a big bold impact. When the barriers of worrying what people are going to think are broken, you mumble on and see if maybe somebody else can pick out what you mean by what you're saying. . . . So the last few weeks I said, well, I just need to get it out. So I'd just throw it out there, and sometimes I'd find myself fumbling a lot, and I'd say, I don't know what I mean, but someone might be able to help me. It was okay for people to see I wasn't polished.

Todd believed his classmates cared enough to help him develop his position. He assumed they could step into his shoes, understand his point of view, and try out his language and habits of mind. I identify Todd's connected knowing with an environment of trust and openness.

Studying my classes helped me see that the nurturing community which Todd describes developed because students were given space to share their stories. Instead of just hearing differences amongst their classmates, students got to know each other well enough to respect and account for these differences. Taffy Davies told me,

> Everybody got to the point where I did, where they were going to say what they were going to say, and it didn't matter to them what people thought about it. If you're not scared to say things in front of people, you're not scared to approach them. You're not scared to say Hi. Just the fact that you are talking in a open forum and expressing your own ideas, you have sort of an understanding of where they're coming from, and they are a person and not just this face in this body that has no soul, no life, no personality.

Both Todd and Taffy talk about the safety to speak out. Both indicate they try to understand other students on their own terms, and that this comes about when they get to know other members of the class. As Taffy says, she doesn't just hear words, she hears words coming from particular students.

Analysis of my classes and my semester-end interviews also brought home to me the patience required to do philosophy in the Deweyan tradition. Since the goal is not consensus but greater sensitivity to conflict, I have to nurture the plurality of voices within each student as well as within the class. That's how I justify beginning the period with ten minutes of writing. Once we had time to tune to our own voices, we could tune to the voices of others. Since my purpose was not to overthrow old values but to place them in context, I was moving my students back and forth between different types of listening, between favored and less favored languages, between close-up and more distant examination of the issues. As a result, the drug discussion taught me that my teaching requires community, the kind which encourages communication and shared experiences for all members. It helped me see that my teaching depends upon students feeling safe enough to try out new voices and to hear the boundary conversations among them.

My analysis also led me to ask what I had done, at least on that day, to bring about a supportive environment. I discovered my strategy focused on making students' texts the center of class discussion, casting the traditional canon in a supporting role and reversing the usual relationship between student work and classical pieces. I discovered that asking a different student to record class discussion each day—to be read the following period—let classmates find out how other students understood their voices. It shared some of my authority, allowing student emphases and languages to contribute to the direction of class. And I realized that changing my position in the circle each period helped me blend better with the crowd, helped students talk to each other rather than just to me. Like the other strategies, it was a way of encouraging students to value their ordinary languages, their everyday experiences. Ultimately, because of my study, it became clearer to me that my first task is not to help students find the discourse of philosophy, but to help them find their own. It became clearer to me why I turn my classroom upside down.

Two Students Writing in Intro to Philosophy
(by Lucille McCarthy)

Ginny Lewis, a 21 year old junior English major, and David Kaiser, a 27 year old junior business major, both enrolled in Fishman's "upside down" course in the fall of 1989. Ginny attended Catholic high school in

Winston-Salem, North Carolina. Although neither of her parents has completed a college degree, both have taken college courses and both read and write at home and in their work. Ginny's mother is an executive secretary, and her father is employed by an engineering company. David graduated from a public high school in Charleston, West Virginia, and when we met, he had been a college student for 10 years. He had completed an Associate of Science degree in nursing at West Virginia Institute of Technology and was now working for a degree in business administration. David is married (no children) and works in a local hospital on weekends. David's mother is an elementary school teacher, and his father, who has a 2-year degree, is an insurance salesman. Ginny's grade point average as she began her junior year was C+; David's was B+. Both students are white.

Information from all data sources supports the conclusion that both Ginny and David preferred separate knowing, and both had difficulty developing constructed knowledge, that is, weaving together personally important knowledge with philosophic research. Both succeeded as constructed knowers, however, and this success was tied to what each ultimately learned from the class. The reason I found Ginny's and David's boundary conversations interesting was that although their general epistemological profiles were similar, their particular stories— their conflicts, their resistances, and their insights—were quite different. These dissimilarities resulted, in part, from the fact that Ginny was a newcomer to separate knowing, whereas David was a veteran. Ginny had only recently learned disciplinary procedures in literary studies, and she clung to these, describing herself as a "struggling English student trying to make the conversion to philosophy." In late October she described her writing in philosophy:

> I can't circle around in the neat pattern I'm used to in English because in philosophy there are no right answers. It seems like an endless conversation where they are always asking more questions, always opening other doors. I've never asked so many questions in my life as I have in this class. I can just hear Steve at the dinner table. His daughter says something, and he asks, "How do you know that? What makes you think that?"
>
> ... And you can't just go to the book to get examples to back up your claim like in English. In philosophy "research" means making up your own examples—and not only for your own viewpoint but for other positions as well.... It's hard.

Writing in philosophy differed significantly from the formula Ginny had developed for constructing successful English papers, and she reacted at first with fear and then with resolution. She told me that in mid-October, when she had gotten Fishman's ungraded response to the second of three drafts of her first paper, she was "scared to death." Fishman had asked her to combine her narrative—a six-page story of a "terrible" flying experience she'd had the previous summer—with philosophic research. He had identified two value conflicts underlying Ginny's story and suggested three philosophic techniques she might choose to explore one or the other of these. She told me,

> I didn't think I could do it. He was asking too much, I thought. I was used to getting a grade, not a long response asking for big changes. It's hard for me to know what my views are. This may sound strange, but I've never thought much about my ideas. I usually just accept things; I say that's just the way it is. . . . The hardest part was trying to put myself in positions opposite my own.
> . . . I was frustrated. But it was a good frustration. I decided to stick with it. I went to talk with him, and he helped me a lot.

Ginny had only just begun to feel secure with separate knowing procedures in English, and now Fishman was asking her to write constructed knowledge, to use philosophic methods to explore her own and opposing values. No wonder Ginny was scared.

Whereas Ginny was at the early stages of separate knowing, just learning there are a variety of disciplinary procedures, David Kaiser was an expert. He was a student who could use procedural knowledge for his own purposes, a student who had successfully employed the methods of several disciplines and who was comfortable with skeptical thinking. He told me in late October, "I enjoy writing, and I've been around long enough to do it in the teacher's way." Separate knowing was not only a classroom stance for David; he also used it outside school. He told me he had always been interested in politics and was "a current events junkie," reading the local newspaper and the *Wall Street Journal* every day. He and his friends debated about political situations, such as the Soviet presence in Afghanistan, arguing for opposing positions and speculating about their consequences. Such debates were, he said, "a game you can play if you know enough." In addition, David described his mother as a questioner. He remembered her being skeptical, for example, about TV commercials, "picking them apart to see what they were really saying to you... I'm a conscious questioner too. I enjoy playing the devil's advocate."

I knew David would be interesting to study when I saw a note he had scrawled, apparently to himself, on the bottom of Fishman's response to his second draft in mid-October. This was the same response round which had scared Ginny to death, and David too appeared to be resisting Fishman. However, David's resistance sounded very different from Ginny's. He was clearly angry. In large letters he wrote, "The feeling I got when we started this was that it was going to be a very personal paper, but now I feel like we are being asked to do a research paper without any research."

David was angry because Fishman was upsetting the teacher-student relationship that David was so comfortable with as a separate knower. Fishman was asking David to develop constructed knowledge, and that meant David had to listen to his own voice as well as the teacher's. When Fishman assigned the paper in mid-September, he told students, "Write about something you care about, a problem that won't go away." David did just that, tracing his inability to converse with his father back to his parents' divorce when he was 7 and to the Sunday afternoons his father failed to pick him up for their scheduled visits. In his response Fishman asked David to leave his narrative to focus on a value conflict underlying the story. Fishman then asked him to analyze the conflict with one or more of the philosophic techniques he suggested. David told me,

> It was like breaking the contract. I'm used to teachers telling me what they want. That's why I scrawled the note. In my other courses—in science and business, even in another Intro to Philosophy course I once took—the teacher gives set criteria and specific guidelines for papers. But Steve seemed to be playing dumb, not telling us at first what he wanted. I guess he thought we'd learn as we wrote. But it seemed like a game, like he was plotting, and I didn't like having something pulled over on me. I felt sort of betrayed.

David could not so efficiently adopt Fishman's methods and language as he apparently did in his other classes for three reasons. First, Fishman did not lay out "set criteria in specific guidelines" in advance. In fact, Fishman said that he purposely didn't describe the final form of the paper or offer a model until students had finished their own first papers. He feared they wouldn't listen to themselves, would try to mimic him or pick topics to which they weren't personally committed. Fishman explained,

I tell my students, "You give me your projects, and I'll help you explore them philosophically." Students must figure out what's important to them, what they care about. In my responses I listen carefully, trying to seize the conflicts among values or viewpoints that are at the heart of their story. But I keep asking them if what I've said is helpful. It's up to them to decide. It's their experience, their conflict, and they must articulate and explore it. They are empowered in that way, empowered about something I can't know ahead of time because I've read more books than they have. When they have created a context in familiar language, then I introduce disciplinary language, and together the students and I work to find intersections.

David was right; Fishman was plotting. He wanted David to share the authority for shaping his paper. (For research concerning the pros and cons of explicit instructions for students' processes and text forms, see Applebee, 1981, 1984; Durst, 1984; and Nelson, 1990.)

David's frustration, however, resulted not only from his inability to "figure Steve out," his suspicion that Fishman really did "have an agenda" despite appearing "nondirective." There was a second reason. David was also confused, he said, because Fishman was asking him to do a crazy kind of "research without research." David told me,

> I think the part that confused me most was that Steve asked us to explore our views and where they were coming from without outside research. That's hard: you have no facts. Research to me means going to the library and getting stacks of books, taking loads of notes, and building a paper. I don't think of research as going into my own mind to take stock of my feelings and asking what in my environment shaped my assumptions, what influenced my perceptions of what a good father-son relationship should be. It's a new thing to seek out your own meaning rather than having it given to you. It's mind research rather than book research.

Finally, a third reason for David's frustration was Fishman's unusual classroom persona, another factor upsetting David's expectations about student and teacher roles. David told me that "from day one Steve's humor and self-deprecation have reminded me of Woody Allen. It's even the same New York accent." Not only was Fishman refusing to set guidelines and asking for unorthodox research, he was also subverting the traditional professorial posture. (David's comparing the professor to the clown brings to mind Bakhtin's (1984) notion of carnival, moments in communal life when festive humor challenges the social order and permits, even encourages, the expression of nonlegitimated voices.)

Thus, Fishman by mid-October had engaged Ginny and David in boundary conversations that scared Ginny to death and frustrated David to the point of anger. The unfamiliar drafting process, the unusual authority situation, and Fishman's requirement that students combine personal concerns with philosophic techniques of analysis all contributed to these students' resistances. Both Ginny and David preferred separate knowing, and separate knowing is, after all, what students in most college classrooms are expected to employ. However, successful writing in this class—"mind research," as David called it—required juxtaposing separate knowing with several other ways of knowing as well.

Developing Constructed Knowledge or Doing "Mind Research"

What exactly constituted successful writing in Fishman's Intro class? What sorts of thinking, what textual features, were students required to produce in order to be deemed "communicatively competent" (Hymes, 1972, pp. xxxvi)? Drawing upon all data sources, I identified three characteristics of successful writing in this setting: (a) competent use of at least one of five techniques of philosophic analysis, (b) evidence of ownership of the topic ("integration"), and (c) evidence of independent thought ("progress").

Requirement A: Five Techniques of Philosophic Analysis. "Philosophers are like poets," Fishman told me. "They're always working for new ways of seeing." The five methods, which Fishman teaches implicitly in class and explicitly in his responses to students' writing, are, he explained, "all context supplying techniques. All are efforts to get clearer about our beliefs and values, to see them in new ways." Fishman chooses among these techniques depending on which one(s) will "give us the best clarification" in each student's case. As Ginny and David explored value conflicts in their second papers, Ginny used two of these techniques, and David used four, as we'll see in the protocol data below. The five techniques are presented here along with the epistemological stance(s) associated with each:

1. *Conceptual clarification* in which philosophers clarify or enrich the definitions of abstract concepts, such as racism or materialism, by exploring many "ordinary" examples of the concept (separate knowing).

2. *Justificatory context* in which philosophers argue for or against the conflicting values at stake (separate and connected knowing).
3. *Cultural context* in which philosophers attempt to locate the "roots" of the conflicting values in such contemporary cultural practices as advertising, the media, literature, music, politics, and popular behaviors and myths (separate and connected knowing).
4. *Historical context* in which philosophers attempt to locate the "roots" of the conflicting values in historical events or movements (separate and connected knowing).
5. *Belief or value context* in which philosophers attempt to provide a "belief map," speculating about assumptions which precede the belief, consequences which follow it, and other beliefs likely to be associated with it (separate and connected knowing).

My questioning of Fishman about the nature of philosophy in his class had pushed him to articulate these techniques more and more explicitly. In the middle of spring semester he gave students a handout defining them, persuaded by my argument that such a list might help separate knowers like Ginny and David. Fishman said he felt a bit nervous about these techniques:

> Some other philosopher might come in here and say I'm not doing philosophy. Though these methods are very much in the Deweyan spirit, they aren't ones he ever discussed explicitly, and I never read in any text that this is what philosophers do. Probably only the first of my techniques, conceptual clarification, has ever been discussed; lots of twentieth century language philosophers, like Russell and Wittgenstein, have spoken about conceptual clarification. But the other four techniques represent *my* conception of philosophy, a very slippery area.
>
> ...In defining my own techniques, I'm hoisting a big chunk of responsibility up on my shoulders, and it feels a little odd because, as teachers, I think we believe we're not really passing on something of ourselves but rather something more neutral, more scientific and universal. Still, I'm confident these methods reflect the patient sifting of ideas that we know from Socratic dialogue as well as from the British and American analytic traditions.

Requirement B: Ownership or "Integration." Fishman said that his "standard of evaluation" for student writing was not based solely on mastery of philosophic method. At the heart of doing well was caring about the enterprise. "I want to know that the paper is integrated into students' lives, that they have conducted this exploration because it means a lot to them. How can you keep going back to revise and rethink and ponder and revise again if you don't care about the problem?" (For further discussion of the importance of student ownership, see Langer & Applebee, 1987, and Spellmeyer, 1989.)

Requirement C: Independent Thought or "Progress." Fishman also looked for evidence that students had gone beyond his questions and suggestions and made discoveries on their own. He explained, "Two students can say similar things, but one knew it from the start. The other pushed in her drafts and discovered it in her own way. That's progress."

When I pressed Fishman to tell me how he judged these two criteria —ownership and independent thought—he told me he knew students very well from class discussion and the drafting process. He knew what they cared about, and he could distinguish independent thinking from thinking they had heard in class or in his response letters. I pushed him still further. What about textual features? "What do you see in students' texts that tells you they are engaged with the topic and have discovered new insights?" Fishman thought a minute and replied, "I think the examples students choose are an important part of my analysis and evaluation." He explained that as students use the five techniques to explore the value conflicts within their papers, they must move back and forth between general and particular. The general principle is a tool for learning about the particular example, and the particular example is a tool for modifying the principle. If students explore the value conflict Fishman has identified with their own fresh examples, he knows "they're trying to make the bridge," to integrate their communities with his. And students who use examples from their own experience and knowledge to explore principles are likely to make the new discoveries, the progress he rewards. Fishman concluded, "I want my students to change, and that won't happen if they say, 'I'll just stay out of this and do what he tells me.'" Rather, students must own the problem they're exploring and make some independent discoveries about it.

Thus, in order to be deemed competent writers in Fishman's class students must develop constructed knowledge, weaving a complicated tapestry of various types of knowing. Not only must they move in a dialectic between particular and general, they must also move back and forth between personal and disciplinary perspectives. Furthermore, Fishman's five disciplinary techniques require students to alternate between separate knowing and the far less familiar procedure of connected knowing. And, as Ginny and David lamented, Fishman requires students to do all this without using books as their primary source of information. Although both Ginny and David longed for the separate knowing situations with which they were familiar, both understood that Fishman was asking them, as David put it, "to research ourselves." Both admitted this was an important project, and in their second papers, both students succeeded in doing it. (For research concerning students' various relationships to assigned course texts, see Flower, Ackerman, Kantz, McCormick, Peck, & Stein, 1990, and Walvoord & McCarthy, 1991.)

Ginny Lewis: On the Cusp of Epistemic Change

In early December, as Ginny composed aloud the third and final draft of her second paper, she was no longer the fledgling separate knower she'd been seven weeks earlier. At times she still wished for right answers and invoked external authorities, nervous that what she was saying was "just my opinion." However, she was beginning to respect her own voice and to see that answers are multiple and often ambiguous. In class and in her writing she'd stepped into unfamiliar or opposing viewpoints and realized "there can be more than one way to approach things, and a lot of times it is not cut and dry whether they are good or bad." Ginny was also "playing with ideas," questioning "why things are the way they are and how they got there in the first place." Authorities, she was beginning to see, could be challenged. Ginny, in early December, was a young woman developing a new sense of herself. Like constructed knowers, she was starting to understand that knowledge is an achievement and truth a matter of the context in which it is embedded.

The protocol data (Table 2) give insight into Ginny's emerging ability to move back and forth among several epistemologies. As she composed her final draft, 56 percent of her expressed concerns were for creating historical context and clarifying concepts, the two philosophic methods she used to explore the value conflict behind her narrative. She kept Fishman's response suggestions close at hand, rereading them twice during the protocol as if to make his words her own.

In the initial draft of this second paper in early November, Ginny had narrated a painful experience she'd recently had when taking a visiting high school friend, John, a young black man, to a local restaurant. The evening had been ruined for them when the hostess and the all-white clientele made clear their disapproval of an interracial couple.

One man snickered and hit the guy in the plaid shirt next to him....An older couple stared at us and whispered to each other, and another young couple seemed nervous because they kept staring intently at their food.

Ginny was certainly engaged with this topic. She was angry, embarrassed, hurt, confused, and worried about John. Fishman suggested that in her next two drafts she explore the conflict between her attitude toward blacks and the attitude of the restaurant patrons. In her second draft in late November, Ginny chose from among Fishman's suggestions and created a justificatory context for both racist and nonracist positions. Although it was not easy for her, Ginny was able to get beneath the surface of her own view and, in addition, to imagine the reasons racists might give for their position.

Table 2
Ginny's Concerns Expressed During Composing-Aloud Protocol and Retrospective Interview

	Percent of Comments
Cognition: Using philosophic method to explore narrative (Constructed knowing)	
Historical context (Separate knowing)	
Developing historical examples of racism	20
Concept clarification (Connected knowing)	
Inferring reasons for/types of racism in examples	18
Investigating personal narrative	
(Subjective, separate, and connected knowing)	18
Metacognition: Describing philosophic inquiry (Separate knowing)	
As back and forth between general and particular, personal and shared knowledge, questions and answers	6
As inferring assumptions behind positions	3
As "backing up my claim"	6
As open-ended exploration with "no right answers"	7
As different from literary criticism	12
Reflections on composing process (Separate and Subjective knowing)	
Describing/planning organizational structures (Separate knowing)	4
Editing words and sentences (Separate knowing)	2
Expressing feelings about on-going process (Subjective and Separate knowing)	4
Total	100
Number of Comments	72

As Ginny composed aloud her third draft, she followed Fishman's response suggestion and created a historical context, developing four historical examples of racism, three of which she took from literature. As she described these examples, she adopted a separate knowing stance, quoting frequently from the literary texts she'd chosen ("Othello," Alan Paton's *Too Late the Phalarope*, and Sharon Olds' "On the Subway.") Ginny then became a connected knower, stepping into each historical/literary situation to discover the racists' underlying assumptions, identifying in each example a quite different type or "level" of discrimination. During the protocol Ginny returned 13 times (18 percent) to her restaurant experience, using the types of racism she had just identified as "investigatory tools." Her purpose was to see if they would give her insight into what had happened to John and her. As she reimagined the restaurant experience, she used connected knowing to adopt and explore the views of the racist patrons and subjective and separate knowing to examine her own.

As I watched Ginny compose, I was aware that she was engaged in a complex boundary conversation, juxtaposing conflicting ways of knowing, stepping into and out of positions she found foreign and uncomfortable, modifying her understanding of racism while reliving John's and her experience from several vantage points. Late in the retrospective interview, as Ginny struggled to make sense of the restaurant experience, she spoke of seeing it in new ways: "This is the most challenging writing I've ever done. I never thought there could be so many levels of racism. It never occurred to me. If I went back to the restaurant now, I'd probably see it all differently." And instead of the inexperienced separate knower, unable to use disciplinary procedures to come to her own conclusions, Ginny now challenged the patron's views and began to listen to herself.

> At first I thought maybe I should have made the atmosphere more comfortable by telling them that John and I are just friends and not romantically involved. But now I'm wondering what right did they have to demand an explanation of us or show their disapproval? What right did they have to be so condescending?

During the protocol and retrospective interview Ginny made frequent metacognitive statements describing the thinking she was doing and how it felt to her (34 percent of her expressed concerns). She spoke of the back and forth movement between concepts and examples, between personal and publicly shared knowledge, and between questions and answers. She commented on philosophy's openendedness, twice comparing it to play dough where "you keep stretching and pushing and questioning." Nine times (12 percent) she contrasted the writing she was doing to her English papers. She told me, "In philosophy one thing leads to another; you're never finished. In English, it's different. You sum up. You say Sylvia Plath did such and such in her poems. You document it, and it's done. It's over."

That Ginny speaks so often about the methods she's using suggests she was learning she could choose among disciplinary systems and that she could employ such systems to explore questions she herself had posed. Furthermore, she had seen that for certain kinds of questions simple and final answers do not exist.

Fishman responded to Ginny's final draft in his usual typed-letter format, beginning "Dear Ginny." After complimenting her analysis and use of the four historical examples "to probe different reasons for racism" and questioning her briefly on her application of these to her own experience, he concluded:

> All in all this version of your paper is a big improvement and jump forward from your earlier drafts. You should be proud!!! A

Ginny had indeed changed since mid-October when she thought Fishman "was asking too much" and feared she couldn't do it. When, at that time, she'd gone to see Fishman to get help with the final draft of her first paper, she was still struggling to understand that value conflicts might underlie her experiences and that these could be worthy of study. Furthermore, she didn't yet believe she could generate knowledge herself; she thought it all originated outside her.

In that mid-October conference, which we audiotaped, Fishman was clearly excited about Ginny's first draft narrative and the "bigger things at work here, the different views and the roots in the culture that lead people to take these views." Ginny had, in the initial draft of her first paper, described the difficulties she encountered flying alone for the first time. She detailed delays and missed connections, tearful calls home, and conversations with rude airline employees as she flew from Winston-Salem to Toronto to see her boyfriend. As Fishman and Ginny spoke together, Fishman reiterated the value conflict he saw between Ginny's and the employees' views of airlines' responsibilities to travellers. He then modelled how she might get into the employees' heads to explore their thinking and the origins of their values. This sort of connected knowing was foreign to Ginny, and she protested, "I can't tell what the employees' views are or what shaped them. I've never been one." Furthermore, Ginny's own values and their roots seemed equally mysterious to her. Fishman seemed to realize this, and he questioned her about them, helping her articulate and explore them. Near the end of the 30-minute session Ginny was making progress when she apparently lost her confidence and asked Fishman, "Do you think I should trash this whole idea? Maybe my trip isn't too deep. Other kids are writing about death." Fishman reassured her, and in the third draft of her first paper Ginny was able not only to articulate the conflicting values embedded in her narrative, she also was able to create some cultural context for each. Fishman rewarded her progress with a B, and Ginny was vastly relieved.

When I asked Ginny in an interview on the last day of the semester what had been most helpful to her in learning to write philosophy, she remembered her mid-October conference with Fishman, saying he'd been very supportive and had helped her understand better "how philosophers ask questions." But what had helped her most with her writing, she said, was class discussion. "In class we were doing philosophy." Listening to other students had helped her realize just how numerous and diverse the viewpoints on an issue can be, and this had, in addition, helped her articulate and examine her own positions. The class provided a safe atmosphere in which to speak up and to disagree with others, Ginny explained, "because no answer was ever wrong."

> We all faced each other in the circle, and that gave the impression that we were all teachers learning from each other. I wasn't used to hearing others' viewpoints, and they'd state their view, and it would be the last thing I'd have thought of. I'd say in my mind "definitely not," but then they'd give their reasons, and I'd say, "Yeah, that *is* another possibility." We were always following a line of thinking in class that made me state my convictions and think deeper about them. We listened and questioned and stated opposing positions or exceptions.
>
> ...I'm usually too shy to speak up in class, but in this class it became difficult *not* to participate when I agreed or disagreed strongly with a classmate or Steve.

Class discussions, then, were boundary conversations in which Ginny practiced juxtaposing conflicting ways of knowing: subjective, separate, and connected. And as she reevaluated her own position in light of class discussion, she was practicing constructed knowing.

What Ginny Took from Intro to Philosophy

What did Ginny's experiences in philosophy ultimately mean to her? I asked her to speculate about this in an interview 4 months after the course was finished. She had forgotten specific aspects of philosophic method, such as how, exactly, philosophers use examples. However, she had, she told me, taken some of her new attitudes with her. First, she said, she was more "daring" in her writing: "I think that in my English papers I now go more in depth and play with ideas to see how far I can go with them." Second, she was more confident about her own ideas; she was no longer afraid to voice her opinions in class. "Because of the relaxed atmosphere in Steve's class and the interest of the students, I now feel comfortable speaking up when I have an opinion or strong conviction. I'm not so afraid people will laugh at me." Finally, she said, she's less likely to take things for granted.

> It's no fun being an inanimate object in life, going along with everything, never questioning the way things are. Like when I wrote about racism. It was something I felt strongly about, and I tried to figure out how it came about. I took on other people's perspectives, and I think the transformations I went through were important. I felt like Socrates, questioning authority.

Ginny's comments show that what she took from Introduction to Philosophy was not particular information or disciplinary methods, but a new attitude about herself as a knower. Ginny learned in philosophy that she could do more than reproduce what others had said. She could question their pronouncements and their methods, state and explore her own views, and pose her own questions. Ginny learned she could construct knowledge that integrated her concerns with what she'd learned, knowledge which, as she said, "starts out being an interesting journey to find out about people around me but ends up being about myself."

David Kaiser: Discovering New Sources of Authority

In early December as David composed aloud the second and final draft of his second paper, he had discovered a new source of authority: himself. Because Fishman, in requiring constructed knowledge, could not tell David exactly what to put in his papers, David had had to "dig stuff out of my own head." He realized, he told me, "There are things you can pull out of yourself if you work hard enough. I like seeing this paper coming out of my own mind." David's granting authority to himself was tied up with his discovery of a second new source of knowledge: other students. David told me that in 10 years of school, he had never listened so attentively to other students. "You have to listen carefully to their positions," he said, "because you can't know what they may be. And you can't know what others have been through." By the end of the semester David had adopted the stance of connected knowing with his classmates and, in a sense, with himself. This was important in his transformation from a separate to constructed knower.

The protocol data (Table 3) give insight into David's constructed knowing. As he composed, he skillfully moved "back and forth, question to answer," using four philosophic techniques to explore his value conflict: "What do I want to give my children? What do we owe to future generations?" This developing of constructed knowledge constituted 51 percent of David's expressed concerns. Unlike Ginny, who reread Fishman's response suggestions several times during her protocol, David never referred to any notes at all. Rather, he spoke about the organization he was creating, comparing it to other philosophic texts, including Fishman's own writing, a model he had shared with students at midsemester. These comments about textual structure and features constituted 21 percent of David's expressed concerns.

A particularly important moment in the drafting of David's second paper came in mid-November when, after receiving Fishman's response to his first draft narrative, David once again resisted Fishman. This resistance was, however, almost the opposite of David's frustration at the same point in drafting his first paper. At that time, in mid-October, David had been angry because Fishman hadn't taken enough authority, hadn't told the class exactly what their final paper should look like. David's anger had dissolved, however, when he had successfully completed his first paper, making an A and finally understanding Fishman's requirements. David told me at the end of October that he had to admit that Fishman's approach "did get me exploring my own thoughts rather than a ready-made issue you can take either side of without getting very involved." He explained,

> Even though I was frustrated with Steve, he was probably right about making us start with our own feelings and experiences and *not* telling us he was going to use those as a springboard to help us find a philosophic conflict to explore. If he'd have asked us to start with our second drafts rather than

our first, students would have chosen the easy way and written about abortion or capital punishment.

. . . My three drafts of my first paper did give me some insights into my relationship with Dad, although I'm not sure any paper I could write would make it easier for us to talk. As I wrote my second and third drafts, looking at my own view of father-son relationships and stepping outward to other views, I always kept looking back at Dad's and my experiences. I realize I could be wrong about them. There are other ways to see it. It's made me think about things a bit differently.

Table 3
David's Concerns Expressed During Composing-Aloud Protocol and Retrospective Interview

	Percent of Comments
Cognition: Using philosophic method to explore narrative	
(Constructed knowing)	
Concept clarification (Separate knowing)	
Developing examples of children "having it better" than parents	21
Historical context (Separate knowing)	
Developing historical examples of progress	7
Cultural context (Separate and connected knowing)	
Developing cultural examples and inferring assumptions	6
Justificatory context (Separate and connected knowing)	
Stating alternate view and inferring assumptions	6
Investigating personal narrative	
(Subjective, separate, & connected knowing)	11
Metacognition: Describing philosophic inquiry (Separate knowing)	
As questioning "what you mean" by a concept	7
As finding historical and cultural roots, "where your views are coming from"	6
As conflict among views, values, beliefs	4
As compared to four others of David's discourses	7
Reflections on composing process (Separate knowing)	
Describing/planning organizational structures	10
Commenting on words and "style"	4
Comparing emerging text to model texts	11
Total	100
Number of Comments	54

If David was frustrated in mid-October because Fishman hadn't taken enough authority, in mid-November David was frustrated because Fishman had taken too much. In Fishman's response to the initial draft of

David's second paper, he had identified a value conflict and made suggestions that were not consistent with David's own intentions. David had written about the bicycle he'd had to go without as a child and his determination to give his children better. He also discussed the depleted and polluted environment his children would inherit. Fishman responded,

> As I read your paper, I tried to find the central conflict. At first I thought it had to do with children's being better off each succeeding generation. But then you shifted to ecological issues, and now I think the central issue is how should we behave toward the environment. If I am correct, then I make the following recommendations.

Fishman was not correct, however, and David, now comfortable with philosophic "mind research" and pleased by the authority Fishman gave him for defining his topic, arranged a conference with Fishman. David told me later,

> I wasn't as frustrated as I'd been in the first paper when I was deep into my feelings about my father and Steve unexpectedly asked me to look at my conflicts in a bigger context. In Steve's response to this draft, he was trying to help me, but he just wasn't seeing it right. I didn't want to go where he thought I did. So I went to see him.

In their 30-minute, tape-recorded conversation, Fishman admitted he'd felt bad about his response because "deep in [his] bones" he had thought David might be more interested in the idea of what we owe to future generations than he was in ecology. The two men then began to dialogue in connected knowing ways, much like in class, where one threw out an idea and together they worked to develop it. Fishman was both modelling and midwifing as he and David worked to clarify the concept of children "having it better" than their parents.

They next worked to create a historical context for David's value conflict. David suggested Darwin and evolution, and Fishman was excited by this. However, a minute later, David said, "I don't have the historical background for this."

> *Fishman:*   But you came up with Darwin on your own! That's a B+ or A
>   right there! Try it, and if you don't feel you're making progress
>   and getting some good clarification going, just let it go.

David:	Well, there's also the Horatio Alger myth and Abraham Lincoln versus the feudal system.
Fishman:	Yes! (Getting excited) That's another view of life and history that may underlie your assumption that your kids should have it better than you.

At this point in the conference, David began to understand he *was* an authority; he brought knowledge to this class that he could draw upon. Two weeks later, as David described this session to me, he spoke of the connected knowing that helped him realize this:

> Steve helped me pull things out of myself I didn't even know were there. He helped me bring out ideas that were inside me that I couldn't bring out alone. As we talked, he'd strike an idea and come to me with that, and I'd go to work with it for a second and come up with some other angle. In the first paper I felt uncomfortable with no outside research. It wasn't right... where were you supposed to come up with your information? But now I'm more comfortable with it; I'm more comfortable with thinking. It's enjoyable to watch it come out of my own mind.

After Fishman and David had speculated about the historical roots of David's view, they moved on, still dialoguing in connected knowing fashion, to consider alternative positions. At this point in the conference David engaged in what appeared to be a boundary conversation with Bertrand Russell. A "click" of discovery resulted from David's juxtaposing conflicting ways of knowing, first approaching Russell as a separate knower, then stepping into Russell's position using connected knowing. Finally, David was able to become a connected knower to himself, to get inside his own position and see it in new ways.

Fishman began the discussion of alternate views by reminding David of the prologue to Russell's *Autobiography*: "Remember Russell said he'd live his life over again if he could. He was a satisfied man. Wouldn't a person like that want to give his kids the *same* life?" David replied that he hadn't thought about that. He'd not really considered *why* you'd want to give your kids something better. He mused, "If you want better for your kids, it must mean there was something wrong with your life. If you were satisfied, you'd try to give them the same, no better, no worse." David told me in our conversation two weeks later,

> Steve got me to talk about the other side—that some people want the same life for their kids. Russell didn't say this exactly, but I think he would have felt it.
>
> ... That got me thinking. Why *do* I want my kids to have it better than I did? Was my own life so miserable? No. I actually want my kids to have the same values I had. What *do* I mean by "having it better?" Steve's bringing up opposing view points gave me somewhere to work from. It's hard to step outside your own assumptions because your own views are so easy and safe.

This conference with Fishman helped David see himself as an authority. In early December as he composed aloud the final draft of his second essay, he confidently drew upon his own experiences and ideas. He integrated these with philosophic techniques of analysis as he successfully developed constructed knowledge. Fishman responded with an A.

The second new source of authority David discovered was other students. His learning to listen to himself and "give validity to my own thoughts" was bound up with the connected knowing stance he was learning to take with others. In an interview four months after the course ended, David described the class discussion that helped him give authority to other students, helped him realize they too knew a great deal. It was the same drug-dealing-parents discussion that Fishman describes above, although a semester earlier. David told me,

> Steve began class by asking, "Would you turn your father in if you found him dealing cocaine?" When he asked us to write our answer for 10 minutes, the girl next to me said, "I can't write this. It's my story."
>
> That got me thinking how much baggage people carry around. I think I'm so smart sometimes, but that gave me pause. In a later class, when people got heated up giving their views of rape, I wondered, did they go through that?

David told me that prior to this class he had felt superior to other students when he heard the naivete of their statements or the holes in their arguments. This class, however, led him to appreciate other students' experiences as sources of knowledge. It's not only what people say, David realized, but also the contexts from which they speak. He told me, "I was never required to change my viewpoint in class, but often in the process of hearing others, I did." David's willingness to change his position after hearing other students signaled his changing view of authority. Instead of listening only to the teacher, he was now listening to himself and other students as well.

What David Took from Intro to Philosophy

In my postcourse interview in April, I asked David what his experiences in philosophy meant to him. What, in particular, had he learned from his writing in that course? David answered by contrasting Philosophy to the Business Communication course he was currently taking. He said, "It's back to reality this semester." That is, he had returned to the writing situation he had wished for in the early weeks of Fishman's course. He was once again developing separate knowledge according to teacher-set guidelines. And now he missed the kind of writing he had done in philosophy. David explained that though Fishman did expect certain things,

> he left me alone to structure the piece, to create my own points as I needed them. And in the draft process Steve helped me see what *I* might want to get out of the writing.
>
> ...This semester in Business Communication I wanted to put more of myself in, so on the first paper I did. No! I got my wings clipped! The teacher wants it *his* way. He tells you exactly how to think: "Your organization should look like this. Your points come here and should be developed in this way." He has worked in business, so he must know what he's talking about.

David was back in his old position, defining the professor as expert, himself as apprentice, and producing writing according to preannounced guidelines. But it felt different to him. In Fishman's class David had been an authority, and other students, by virtue of their life experiences as well as their arguments, were authorities as well. In Business Communication David had to surrender this authority, and he was disappointed. In spite of this, he told me, he still "tried to hang on to the idea of the examined life. I try to look at how I'm living and ask if it's what I want it to be. And when possible, I try not to allow someone else to set my criteria."

David's comments show he learned in philosophy that he didn't always have to play the role of apprentice to the teacher-expert. He too could be an expert. He could integrate his own ideas and experiences with procedures he learned from a teacher. He could, in school, generate personally important knowledge.

On the last day of the semester, David once again scrawled a note, this time to Fishman, which he attached to the front of his second paper.

It shows in a light-hearted way that David knew his interactions with Fishman all semester had been about sharing authority. "Dear Steve," David wrote,

> Thanks for the enjoyable class. I will recommend it highly to anyone who wants to learn what philosophy is without having to hear from the prof. everything they ever wanted to know about Plato (or is that Pluto?), Aristotle, and Socrates in 24 easy lectures.... I never knew and still don't know when you were orchestrating the flow of the conversation in class and when you were just letting it gallop along unbridled. It did seem sponta- neous, as if *we* really were in control. Keep up your enthusiasm, and some day Woody Allen may come to be compared to you! With warmest regards for a happy holiday season, David Kaiser.

The Researchers' Boundary Conversation
(by Steve Fishman and Lucille McCarthy)

This narrative of our research collaboration is what anthropologists call a "confessional tale" (Van Maanen, 1988, p. 73). Confessional tales are highly personalized accounts of how the fieldworker came to understand the studied scene and how the ethnography came into being. These tales stand beside the ethnography itself, and in them the authoritative tone of the research report gives way to the "modest, unassuming style of one struggling to piece together something reasonably coherent out of displays of initial disorder, doubt, and difficulty." The confessional tale shows the human qualities of the fieldworker and how his or her life "was lived upriver among the natives" (p. 75).

We describe our collaboration here for two reasons. First, our bound- ary conversations resemble those of our students. We, like they, learned as we articulated and positioned our differences, as we listened carefully to one another, and as we were able to redistribute authority. Our self-reflection thus fills out and illuminates our findings about our students. Second, the difficulties we encountered during our research are not unique. Although the details may change from one interdisciplinary collaboration to another, the three problems we discuss here are, we believe, likely to generate the most difficult challenges faced by other such research teams. Our three problems were (1) conflicting assump- tions about students' disciplinary initiation, (2) differing views of authority over the project, and (3) misunderstandings about methodology resulting from our different disciplinary practices. (For further discussion of collaborative research see Brodkey, 1987, and McCarthy & Walvoord, 1988.)

Our first difficulty concerned our conflicting assumptions about students' disciplinary initiation. McCarthy originally took the view that students in introductory philosophy should be treated as apprentice-philosophers. Her initial research design called for close examination of how these students produced satisfactory texts in Fishman's course. However, this required a clear picture from him of what constitutes philo-sophic writing. But Fishman couldn't supply such a picture, nor could he provide a straightforward definition of philosophy. To make things worse, he responded with hostility to the idea that he was master to a classroom of apprentices. Apparently little interested in training junior philosophers, Fishman told McCarthy he wanted to "help students find themselves and their own voices." Very quickly McCarthy began to see her key informant as a romantic with little sensitivity to the social aspects of learning. In turn, Fishman began to see his collaborator as following a cookie-cutter view of education, wanting him to employ a template of philosophy upon blank-tablet minds.

Our second difficulty had to do with control over the project—the roles each of us would play in data collection, analysis, and writing. From the start, in September 1989, when McCarthy first presented the idea of this study to Fishman, McCarthy wanted to incorporate the teacher's unalloyed voice in the study's final report. She was also convinced that what happens in a classroom is strongly influenced by the instructor's relationship to his or her discipline, although traditional writing across the curriculum research offered little about this aspect of the teaching equation. Wanting to address this lack in the research, McCarthy offered Fishman equal responsibility for the project. Their earliest plan divided the study into two parts. In the first, Fishman would present his teaching autobiography and include details about his own academic initiation. In the second part, McCarthy would describe how several of Fishman's students satisfied the writing requirements in his class. Trouble developed, however, when Fishman became unhappy with his role, complaining that his function as autobiographer/informant was inferior to McCarthy's. He protested that composition and education specialists would not be interested in reading a teaching autobiography. McCarthy disagreed but could not assuage Fishman's anxiety.

At the close of their second semester of research, McCarthy presented a conference paper about her struggles with her collaborator. We quote at length from her presentation because it captures our boundary conversations: our initial attempts to grapple with our different views of student initiation, our conflicts over issues of authority, and our different disciplinary backgrounds. McCarthy began,

> Let me tell you about an event where Steve's and my ability to deal with difference was tested. This event shows, first, how hard it was for us to articulate our differences because so much of what we know is tacit, and, second, how hard it was for us to make each other's way of knowing our own. This event occurred in early January 1990, when Steve and I exchanged drafts of possible introductions to our article.
>
> All fall we had been collecting data from students and conversing frequently, I questioning Steve in various ways about what constituted philosophy in his classroom and what counted as successful student writing there. At one point I asked him point-blank: "What *is* philosophy anyway?" He replied, "I'm not sure I know. In any case I don't care so much that my students learn the conventions of philosophy as I do that they learn to celebrate their own voices, learn that they have beliefs and values that are worth exploring." "But Steve," I responded, "I know you're working with students' own conflicts and questions, but you're using philosophic methods on them. I can hear that your methods are different from those of literary criticism or business or biology."
>
> Just as it was hard for Steve at first to articulate his disciplinary ways of knowing, so was it hard for both of us to articulate our tacitly held views of disciplinary initiation. What helped us eventually clarify our views was common reading we did. Steve sent me sections from the *Encyclopedia of Philosophy* and various textbooks as well as passages from philosophers he admired, such as John Dewey, and we discussed these. I sent him David Bartholomae's article, "Inventing the University," to explain my view that students must learn to speak the language of the professor, and he shot back with sections from Peter Elbow's work, saying that good writing of any sort must come out of personal commitment. We were, during the fall, working to articulate our positions, identify our disagreements, and create a common language for talking about them. I was getting his perspective, I thought, and he mine.
>
> I should have been alerted that this was not going to be so easy when I heard Steve's response to a manuscript I sent him in December. The manuscript reported a collaborative, coauthored study like our own, and it seemed fine to me, a naturalistic study in which the researcher, after a careful description of his methods, worked to construct the teacher's reality. But Steve hated it. "This sounds like a treaty," he said, "Where are the conflicts?

They've all been leveled. Sure, I hear the teacher's voice, but only as quoted by the researcher. And why all this talk about methods?"

Nonetheless, in early January we thought we could speak for each other and agreed we'd each draft an introduction to our article, which we hoped to place in a composition journal. Steve's eight-page draft arrived at my house first, and I said to myself after reading it, "Oh no, this will never get published." It was a beautifully written narrative that captured our voices and our conflicts, but it didn't fill out the methods or the issues, nor did it set the piece in the ongoing disciplinary conversation.

And Steve's objections to my 12-page draft echoed those he'd made to the manuscript I'd sent him the month before. He told me as tactfully as he could that I had not represented his views of writing fairly and that he found my tone too "sciency." I was, he said, keeping myself too much outside the piece, playing too much the role of white-coated, objective researcher. By contrast, in our report, he said, he would be fully exposed. "Besides," he said, "you're *not* neutral. You influenced my teaching in the fall." And then Steve raised the issue of authority, saying that by citing my own work and referring to myself by my last name and to him by his first, I was making "an implicit statement of who's in charge and whose voice counts."

As McCarthy's talk shows, the co-researchers conflicted over issues of power, and, at the start of their work, they spoke very differently about student initiation, a concept at the heart of their research. McCarthy held that instructors should teach students the language conventions of their fields. Fishman, on the other hand, held that instructors should relate the conventions of their fields to students' other languages. In time we came to realize that this conflict was rooted in our own experiences as students.

Fishman's view of disciplinary initiation was shaped by his sense that as a student he had been silenced. He recalled that as a college sophomore he enrolled with high expectations in a Shakespeare class. Shakespeare taught the language of love, Fishman believed, and if there was anything he thought he needed as an undergraduate, it was advice about love. But he was quickly disappointed. Andrew Chiappe, his professor, used each period to recite sonnets he had memorized, and his 100-item identification tests terrorized every member of the class. Fishman remembered staring at him as he paced the front of the room and thinking, "Why can't he say something about real life?" It was that same semester that Fishman came upon sections in Dewey which talked about the episodic quality of modern living. Dewey wrote:

...an individual as a member of different groups may be divided within himself, and in a true sense have conflicting selves, or be a relatively disintegrated individual. A man may be one thing as a church member and another thing as a member of a business community. The difference may be carried as if in watertight compartments, or it may become such a division as to entail internal conflict (1927, p. 191).

What Dewey described was exactly what Fishman believed he was experiencing. It was as if there were several conversations going on in his life which never met: constant inner dialogue, approval-seeking conversations with friends, family chats in roles which no longer fit, and struggles in the classroom to reach the melody line of the instructor. Fishman believed he was playing roles which hid many of his other selves, only part of him working at any one time.

In sharp contrast to Fishman, McCarthy's introduction to academia was smooth. She had been successful throughout her undergraduate and graduate careers, easily understanding her professors' methods and languages and easily making these her own. In contrast, Fishman, as we have just seen, viewed himself as an outsider, unable to find relationships between his student and his more private roles. It was little wonder that McCarthy originally viewed initiation as adoption of disciplinary language, whereas Fishman stressed development of student voices. McCarthy's hunch—that a teacher's autobiography is important—was correct: people's own experiences as students deeply affect their visions of teaching and learning.

As McCarthy mentions, in the months following our first conflicts over the nature of disciplinary initiation, we exchanged numerous articles. McCarthy taught Fishman enough composition theory so that he could identify himself as a member of what Faigley (1986) and Berlin (1988) call the "expressionist" rhetorical camp. And Fishman presented McCarthy with enough examples of philosophy so that she could appreciate the diverse character of its conventions. These exchanges gave us a shared language with which we could more clearly define our differences. But not only were our exchanges of disciplinary texts enlightening our disagreements, they were also influencing the way we saw our closely held beliefs. Fishman became convinced he should be more explicit with his students about the nature of philosophic method. And McCarthy came to see that her view of the classroom researcher as outsider was inconsistent with her own view that meaning is socially constructed.

Our second difficulty, Fishman's anxiety about his role as co-researcher, was resolved when we agreed he would, on his own, collect and analyze data. It also helped when we agreed we would report our research in a heteroglossic form in which each of us could speak for ourselves. These events occurred halfway through the second semester as we realized that our primary research interests had diverged. Whereas McCarthy wanted to focus on students' writing experiences, Fishman wanted to study his classroom discussions—why some classes were marked by active student participation and why others were silent. At the same time, Fishman, having listened to McCarthy's taped interviews with students and having read transcripts of her interviews with him, was expressing signs of what he called "data envy." To change the "balance of power," he interviewed five students in his spring semester class. These interviews were approximately an hour in length, with Fishman imitating McCarthy's style of questioning. When Fishman sent these tapes to McCarthy, she was impressed and suggested a new plan for our research together. Again, we would divide our report into two parts, but this time Fishman would take responsibility for describing and analyzing his classroom community while McCarthy would retain her focus on student writing. In May she urged him to review the data he had available, including transcripts of her four interviews with him, transcripts of his own interviews with Intro students, and copies of over 80 letters he had sent McCarthy describing and commenting on his class. This was crucial for settling our conflicts over authority. Not only had we each agreed to write our own findings, we were now both responsible for data collection and for answering our own questions. Like his student, David Kaiser, Fishman needed to see himself as an authority, as someone capable of generating his own ethnographic knowledge, before he could define himself as an equal partner in research with McCarthy.

Our third and last problem concerned methodology and was rooted in our disciplinary differences. Specifically, it involved the different relationship between data and theory in our two fields. As Fishman conducted data analysis and began drafting his research report in July of 1990, this problem came to a head. Philosophers, as Ginny Lewis understood early on, make up examples, and they use them to explore or modify generalizations and theory. In fact, a single hypothetical example, McCarthy realized as she read Dewey, might serve for three or four pages of philosophic theorizing. Thus, Fishman found focusing on piles of empirical data during theme and pattern analysis an unfamiliar and tedious job. He was as restless with pages of data as McCarthy had been with pages of unsupported theory. Initially, then, Fishman's disciplinary tendency as he drafted led him to write extended discussions of the epistemological categories of the students and of Belenky and her associates. McCarthy admired these, but she argued they overshadowed the local participants' stories. Eventually, Fishman was able to honor our data in new ways. McCarthy's approach to the data, in turn, was enriched by Fishman's discussions of theory.

Finally, in November 1990, we completed our manuscript. It was a process accompanied by the refinement of our collaboration, a refinement which continued until the very end.

CONCLUSIONS

How are we the wiser for this study? Our most important conclusion is that learning involves juxtaposing conflicting ways of knowing. We found that learning occurs when authority for knowledge is redistributed. Such redistribution leads to closer listening and, in turn, promotes our ability to juxtapose conflicting ways of knowing.

Redistribution of authority was central in both the student learning we studied and in our own collaboration. Todd told Fishman about his willingness to throw out "half-baked" ideas so other classmates could interpret and develop them. Ginny told McCarthy about how she and her fellow students all became teachers, how they learned from one another, and David said he paid closer attention in philosophy when he realized it was important to understand his classmates' experiences as well as their arguments. In each case, students were granting new authority for generating knowledge to themselves and to other students. And with this shift in authority came a new form of listening, a willingness to engage in a different sort of conversation, a boundary conversation with themselves and the multiple voices of others. Fishman's efforts to turn things upside down meant a redistribution, however slight, of responsibility for learning. It encouraged students to take different roles—to be teachers, students, and observers—sometimes alternatively, sometimes simultaneously. And it was in moments when their new listening was most keen, when students could juxtapose a variety of epistemic approaches, that learning occurred.

In McCarthy's and Fishman's collaboration learning was marked by a similar connection between new distributions of authority and new sorts of listening. Initially, what seemed equal sharing of responsibility to McCarthy was taken to be inequitable by Fishman. To understand our conflicts we discovered we had to listen closely not only to our disciplinary differences, but also to our experiences as students. Our own initiations and preferred epistemological stances were as important as our membership in different academic fields. Our study suggests that to understand an academic's approach to instruction and research means knowing more than his or her discipline. Just as important to Fishman's research assumptions as his commitment to philosophy are his student experiences as an outsider, experiences connected to his preference for constructed knowing. Although McCarthy's background is revealed in less detail in our study, we learn that her research posture is also a product of her student experiences. They influence her preference for separate knowing. Satisfactory assignment of authority over our project meant finding ways to step into each other's shoes to discover the roots of each other's remarks. Fishman's efforts to wrest more authority from McCarthy could only be understood and acted upon when we both realized that Fishman's commitment to constructed knowing made it imperative that he own his research questions and data.

The new listening which facilitated the redistribution of authority was also central to students' and researchers' learning, to those boundary conversations when we moved back and forth among different epistemic stances so they could inform one another. Fishman's students, in writing and class discussion, employed a variety of epistemologies in a short period of time. For example, in the drug-discussion class students expressed strong subjective knowing. Concurrently, they stepped outside themselves to hear their classmates respond to them. They could respect and understand these responses because, as Taffy Davies put it, they knew where other students "were coming from." In other words, the subjective knowing involved separate and connected knowing. Then, as students returned to their original positions, reseeing and at times reshaping them, they were engaged in constructed knowing.

Likewise, Fishman and McCarthy employed a variety of epistemologies during their research. Both drew upon connected and separate knowing, sometimes doubting one another, sometimes suspending their questions in order to get inside the other's point of view. There were also moments when McCarthy and Fishman, as subjective knowers, insisted that they knew just because they knew, and there were other moments, especially at the start of their project, when they played received knowers to one another. Our finding that learning occurs as people juxtapose conflicting ways of knowing poses questions about developmental epistemological schemes. It may be oversimple to view people as inhabiting single epistemic positions or to assume that our role as teachers is to transform students from one epistemic posture to another. Our data suggest that serious intellectual work requires a full repertoire of epistemological stances.

In addition to clarifying how learning occurs through boundary conversations, our study suggests that student-teacher conflicts may be understood in terms of epistemic differences. These differences help account, for example, for Ginny's and David's resistances, their initial reactions of fear and anger. Understanding student-teacher conflicts in these terms may help reduce the emotional charge as well as clarify the underlying sources of these resistances.

Furthermore, David's writing experience in the semester following Introduction to Philosophy raises questions about the desirability and appropriateness of constructed knowing in academia. Was Fishman really helping David succeed at the university by encouraging him to integrate personal and disciplinary knowledge? Although many university-level teachers see themselves as constructed knowers, in fact, most of us have to produce separate knowledge in order to publish and gain tenure. As a result, we are likely to privilege separate knowing in our university courses.

As we analyzed our data, we also found that epistemological stances were equally useful in describing the ways both women and men approach knowledge. Our data suggest that some categories which have been characterized as especially comfortable for one gender as opposed to the other were equally comfortable or uncomfortable for both. For example, although connected knowing is sometimes said to be more attractive to women, in our study, David became at least as good at connected knowing as Ginny. And at the beginning of the course, both students appeared equally inexperienced and uneasy with this stance. Conversely, although men are sometimes assumed to prefer separate knowing, where the self is weeded out, Fishman was far more dissatisfied with separate knowing than McCarthy.

Finally, our study brings into question the mechanism for increasing students' epistemological repertoires. The contexts in which Fishman's students worked were characterized by trust and shared authority.

Fishman's students testify that his classroom made it safe for them to try on new roles and views of expertise. Although we as teachers may believe that we can extend our students' epistemic perspectives by presenting increasingly complex tasks, our study suggests that epistemic growth also requires changes in the educational context. It is necessary to increase the chances for students to listen closely to themselves and to their classmates. It is also necessary to give students authority to generate knowledge as well as to possess it.

References

Anderson, G. L. (1989). Critical ethnography in education: Origins, current status, and new directions. *Review of Educational Research, 59*, 249-270.

Apple, M. (1986). *Teachers and texts: A political economy of class and gender relations in education*. New York: Routledge and Kegan Paul.

Applebee, A. (1981). *Writing in the secondary school: English and the content areas.* Urbana, IL: National Council of Teachers of English.

Applebee, A. (1984). *Contexts for learning to write: Studies of secondary school instruction*. Norwood, NJ: Ablex.

Ashton-Jones, E., & Thomas, D. K. (1990). Composition, collaboration, and women's ways of knowing: A conversation with Mary Belenky. *Journal of Advanced Composition, 10*(2), 275-292.

Atkinson, P. (1990). *The ethnographic imagination*. London: Routledge.

Bakhtin, M. (1981). *The dialogic imagination*. Austin: University of Texas Press.

Bakhtin, M. (1984). *Rabelais and his world*. Bloomington: Indiana University Press.

Bartholomae, D. (1985). Inventing the university. In M. Rose (Ed.), *When a writer can't write: Studies in writer's block and other composing-process problems* (pp. 134-165). New York: Guilford.

Bazerman, C. (1988). *Shaping written knowledge: The genre and activity of the experimental article in science*. Madison: University of Wisconsin Press.

Bazerman, C., & Paradis, J. (1991). *Textual dynamics of the professions: Historical and contemporary studies in writing in professional communities*. Madison: University of Wisconsin Press.

Belenky, M. F., Clinchy, B. M., Goldberger, N. R., & Tarule, J. M. (1986). *Women's ways of knowing: The development of self, voice, and mind*. New York: Basic Books.

Berkenkotter, C. (1983). Decisions and revisions: The planning strategies of a publishing writer. *College Composition and Communication, 34*, 156-169.

Berkenkotter, C., Huckin, T. N., & Ackerman, J. (1988). Conversations, conventions, and the writer: Case study of a student in a rhetoric Ph.D. program. *Research in the Teaching of English, 22*, 9-44.

Berlin, J. (1988). Rhetoric and ideology in the writing class. *College English, 50*, 477-494.

Bizzell, P. (1982). Cognition, convention, and certainty: What we need to know about writing. *PRE/TEXT, 3*, 213-243.

Bleich, D. (1989). Genders of writing. *Journal of Advanced Composition, 9*, 10-25.

Bridwell, L. (1980). Revising strategies in twelfth grade students' transactional writing. *Research in the Teaching of English, 14,* 197-222.

Brodkey, L. (1987). *Academic writing as social practice.* Philadelphia: Temple University Press.

Bruffee, K. (1984). Collaborative learning and the "conversation of mankind." *College English, 46,* 635-652.

Bruner, J. (1985). Narrative and paradigmatic modes of thought. In E. Eisner (Ed.), *Learning and teaching the ways of knowing* (pp. 97-115). Chicago: University of Chicago Press.

Carter, M. (1988). Problem solving reconsidered: A pluralistic theory of problems. *College English, 50,* 551-565.

Caywood, C. L., & Overing, G.R. (1987). *Teaching writing: Pedagogy, gender, and equity.* Albany: State University of New York Press.

Clark, G., & Doheny-Farina, S. (1990). Public discourse and personal expression: A case in theory-building. *Written Communication, 7,* 456-481.

Clifford, J. (1983). On ethnographic authority. *Representations, 1,* 118-146.

Cochran-Smith, M., & Lytle, S. L. (1990). Research on teaching and teacher research: The issues that divide. *Educational Researcher, 19,* 2-11.

Cooper, M. M. (1989). Women's ways of writing. In M. M. Cooper & M. Holzman (Eds.), *Writing as social action.* Portsmouth, NH: Heinemann.

Cooper, M. M., & Holzman, M. (1989) *Writing as social action.* Portsmouth, NH: Heinemann.

Denzin, N. K. (1978). *Sociological methods.* New York: McGraw-Hill.

Dewey, J. (1927). *The public and its problems.* New York: Henry Holt and Company.

Dewey, J. (1933). *How we think.* Chicago: Henry Regnery Co.

Dewey, J. (1934). *Art as experience.* New York: Capricorn Books.

Dewey, J. (1920/1962). *Reconstruction in philosophy.* Boston: Beacon Press.

Dewey, J. (1916/1967). *Democracy and education.* New York: Macmillan.

DiPardo, A. (1990). Narrative knowers, expository knowledge: Discourse as dialectic. *Written Communication, 7,* 59-95.

Durst, R. K. (1984). The development of analytic writing. In A. Applebee (Ed.), *Contexts for learning to write: Studies of secondary school instruction.* Norwood, NJ: Ablex.

Elbow, P. (1986). *Embracing contraries: Explorations in learning and teaching.* New York: Oxford University Press.

Faigley, L. (1985). Nonacademic writing: The social perspective. In L. Odell & D. Goswami (Eds.), *Writing in nonacademic settings* (pp. 231-248). New York: Guilford.

Faigley, L. (1986). Competing theories of process: A critique and a proposal. *College English, 48,* 527-542.

Fenstermacher, G. D. (1986). Philosophy of research on teaching: Three aspects. In M. C. Wittrock (Ed.), *Handbook of research on teaching; Third edition* (pp. 37-49). New York: Macmillan.

Fishman, S. (1985). Writing-to-learn in philosophy: A before and after story. *Teaching Philosophy, 8,* 331-334.

Fishman, S. (1989). Writing and philosophy. *Teaching Philosophy, 12,* 361-374.

Flower, L., Ackerman, J., Kantz, M. J., McCormick, K., Peck, W. C., & Stein, V. (1990). *Reading to write: Exploring a social and cognitive process.* New York: Oxford University Press.

Flower, L., & Hayes, J. (1981). The pregnant pause: An inquiry into the nature of planning. *Research in the Teaching of English, 15,* 229-244.

Flynn, E. A. (1988). Composing as a woman. *College Composition and Communication, 39,* 423-435.

Freedman, S. W. (1985). *The acquisition of written language: Response and revision.* Norwood, NJ: Ablex.

Geertz, C. (1976). From the native's point of view: On the nature of anthropological understanding. In K. H. Basso and H. A. Selby (Eds.), *Meaning in anthropology* (pp. 221-237). Albuquerque: University of New Mexico Press.

Geertz, C. (1988). *Works and lives: The anthropologist as author.* Stanford, CA: Stanford University Press.

Gergen, M. M. (1988). Toward a feminist metatheory and methodology in the social sciences. In M. M. Gergen (Ed.), *Feminist thought and the structure of knowledge* (pp. 87-104). New York: New York University Press.

Glaser, B., & Strauss, A. (1967). *The discovery of grounded theory: Strategies for qualitative research.* New York: Aldine De Gruyter.

Herrington, A. (1985). Writing in academic settings: A study of the contexts for writing in two college chemical engineering courses. *Research in the Teaching of English, 19,* 331-359.

Hill, C. E. (1990). *Writing from the margin: Power and pedagogy for teachers of composition.* New York: Oxford University Press.

Hymes, D. (1972). Introduction. In C. Cazden, V. P. John, & D. Hymes (Eds.), *Functions of language in the classroom* (pp. xi- lxii). New York: Teachers College Press.

Langer, J. A. (1987). *Language, literacy, and culture: Issues of society and schooling.* Norwood, NJ: Ablex.

Langer, J. A., & Applebee, A. N. (1987). *How writing shapes thinking: A study of teaching and learning.* Urbana, IL: National Council of Teachers of English.

Lewis, M., & Simon, R. (1986). A discourse not intended for her: Learning and teaching within patriarchy. *Harvard Educational Review, 56,* 457-472.

Lincoln, Y., & Guba, E. (1985). *Naturalistic inquiry.* Beverly Hills, CA: Sage Publications.

Lyons, N. (1990). Dilemmas of knowing: Ethical and epistemological dimensions of teachers' work and development. *Harvard Educational Review, 60,* 159-180.

Mathison, S. (1988). Why triangulate? *Educational Researcher, 17,* 13-17.

McCarthy, L. P. (1987). A stranger in strange lands: A college student writing across the curriculum. *Research in the Teaching of English, 21,* 233-265.

McCarthy, L. P., & Braffman, E. J. (1985). Creating Victorian Philadelphia: Children reading and writing the world. *Curriculum Inquiry, 15,* 121-152.

McCarthy, L. P., & Walvoord, B. E. (1988). Models for collaborative research in writing across the curriculum. In S. McLeod (Ed.), *Strengthening programs for writing across the curriculum* (pp. 77-90). San Francisco: Jossey-Bass.

McDermott, R. P. (1977). Social relations as contexts for learning in school. *Harvard Educational Review, 47,* 198-213.

McDonald, J. P. (1988). The emergence of the teacher's voice: Implications for the new reform. *Teachers College Record, 89,* 471-486.

Mitchell, W. J. T. (1980). *On narrative.* Chicago: University of Chicago Press.

Miles, M. B., & Huberman, A. M. (1984). *Qualitative data analysis.* Beverly Hills, CA: Sage Publications.

Mill, J. S. (1947). *On Liberty.* Arlington Heights, IL: Harlan Davidson, Inc.

Mill, J. S. (1969). *Autobiography.* Boston: Houghton Mifflin.

Mishler, E. (1979). Meaning in context: Is there any other kind? *Harvard Educational Review, 49*, 1-19.

Nelson, J. (1990). This was an easy assignment: Examining how students interpret academic writing tasks. *Research in the Teaching of English, 24*, 362-396.

North, S. (1986). Writing in a philosophy class: Three case studies. *Research in the Teaching of English, 20*, 225-262.

Plato. (1953). *Euthyphro, crito, apology, and symposium.* Jowett translation, M. Hadas (Ed.). Chicago: Henry Regnery Co.

Quantz, R. A., & O'Connor, T. W. (1988). Writing critical ethnography: Dialogue, multivoicedness, and carnival in cultural texts. *Educational Theory, 38*, 95-109.

Rosen, H. (1985). *Stories and meanings.* Sheffield, England: National Association for the Teaching of English.

Spellmeyer, K. (1989) A common ground: The essay in the academy. *College English, 51*, 262-276.

Sperling, M., & Freedman, S. W. (1987). A good girl writes like a good girl: Written responses to student writing. *Written Communication, 9*, 343-369.

Spradley, J. (1979). *The ethnographic interview.* New York: Holt, Rinehart and Winston.

Spradley, J. (1980). *Participant observation.* New York: Holt, Rinehart and Winston.

Trimbur, J. (1989). Consensus and difference in collaborative learning. *College English, 51*, 602-616.

Van Maanen, J. (1988). *Tales of the field: On writing ethnography.* Chicago: University of Chicago Press.

Walvoord, B. E., & McCarthy, L. P. (1991). *Thinking and writing in college: A naturalistic study of students in four disciplines.* Urbana, IL: National Council of Teachers of English.

Weiler, K. (1988). *Women teaching for change: Gender, class & power.* South Hadley, MA: Bergin & Garvey.

Woolgar, S. (1988). *Knowledge and reflexivity: New frontiers in the sociology of knowledge.* Beverly Hills, CA: Sage Publications.

Zeller, N. (1987). *A rhetoric for naturalistic inquiry.* Unpublished dissertation, Indiana University.

Using Stenhousian Research to Defend Berthoffian-Expressivist Pedagogy

Steve Fishman with Lucille McCarthy

B oundary Conversations" allowed me to step into Lucille
McCarthy's world, and among discoveries I made, one of the most
surprising was that the Berthoffian-expressivist approach to the
teaching of writing was under academic attack. Until McCarthy and I
hooked up, I thought that the Berthoff-Britton-Elbow axis presented
instructors with teaching techniques which were a tonic for every classroom need. But McCarthy, as I indicated in Chapter 3, quickly showed me
that things were not quite so simple in the world of teacher research and
composition studies.

Criticisms of Berthoffian-Expressivist Pedagogy

It took us a while, but I finally learned from McCarthy how to distinguish
social constructionists from cultural critics from critical pedagogues.
Everyone with theoretical sophistication seemed to be disappointed with
the Berthoff emphasis on personal writing. David Bartholomae (1985), for
example, charged that asking students—as I was now proudly doing in
my Intro to Philosophy class—to start with their own problems and their
own voices was to do them a disservice. In his famous "Inventing the

University" article, Bartholomae argues that successful writing is mastering the conventions of a particular community, and with regard to the university, this means each instructor should, properly, help students focus not on personal voices but on communal and disciplinary ones.

James Berlin (1988), I found, criticized the Berthoff-Elbow approach on political rather than pragmatic grounds. He charged that teachers like me were unwitting dupes of capitalist ideology. Berlin's point was that to emphasize personal writing is to reinforce the capitalist myth that we are all self-sufficient, self-interested individuals, our words and compositions private artifacts, and we are incapable of working in concert with or understanding others. This sort of atomizing, according to Berlin, played into mainstream, capitalist hands, isolating individuals and making conjoint action against the status quo conceptually impossible.

Further, my adoption of expressivist pedagogy was, according to such critics, epistemologically bankrupt. In asking my students to dig deep inside, telling them—as I so often did—that when they found what was most peculiarly their own, they had found the universal, I was sticking my head in Cartesian sand or, alternatively, closing my eyes to the postmodern turn. In other words, when I assured my students they really had something to say, I risked encouraging the belief that knowledge is a personal construction, and, of course, to do this was to promote a self-centered epistemology and to reinforce political isolation. Understandably, as I read theorists like Bartholomae and Berlin, I knew they were talking about me. That is, I was chagrined to learn that the pedagogy which had been so generative in my own life was potentially a professional, political, and epistemological disaster.

But there was more to the nightmarish discoveries I made when I stepped across my boundary into McCarthy's world. In addition to social constructionists like Bartholomae and Berlin, there were cultural critics like Bizzell (1992) and Shor (1992). The focus of their attack on expressivist classrooms like mine was, once again, political. However, this time it was not so much that I was isolating my students but that I was missing opportunities to work real reform. In asking my students to find their voices, I was encouraging a false sense of freedom, a flawed, up-by-your-bootstraps grand narrative. I was saying to them, "Once you set aside the demands of your teacher, textbook, and parents, you will be free. You will find what is truly yours." But my critics claimed this was linguistically naive. Whatever rhythms and styles my students discovered in their personal writing carried just as insidious a political cargo as did teacher, textbook, and parent talk. In thus turning my back on postmodern scholars' deconstruction of language, critics argued, I was failing to give my students the tools they needed to become reflective about their own language. Such self-consciousness is crucial, according to expressivism's critics, if students are to have a chance to intelligently choose a language, to adopt speech whose ideological cargo they truly accept.

Obviously, then, I saw these criticisms by Bartholomae, Berlin, Bizzell, and Shor as important ones—ones since continued, in fact, by a second generation of expressivism's critics, including Flinders (1997), Lensmire (1994), and Wilhelm (1997). I wanted to be open to these charges, and, at first, felt bad that unwittingly I was misleading my students and missing opportunities to help them become agents of social reform—something I desperately wanted to do. But even worse, my asking them to write about events or issues in their own lives which "refused to go away" was to perpetuate capitalist values and strengthen the chains into which my students had been born.

RESPONDING TO CRITICISMS OF BERTHOFFIAN-EXPRESSIVIST PEDAGOGY

But then I got my back up. And it was not because I could do some fancy theoretical footwork to show that these thinkers were sloppy or inconsistent, that postmodernism was a false step, or that deconstruction was simply an interesting form of 20th-century nonfoundationalism. It was really Berthoff again. She and Britton and Elbow had taught me to value personal experience, to trust my tacit knowledge, to trust, that is, what I felt but could not fully explain. Further, I suspected I was not the only person to have experienced the energy of personal writing, of the mapping and brainstorming and small group work featured by expressivist pedagogy. Surely, it seemed, whatever the shortcomings of the expressivist classroom, if it could turn students on to the joys of self-discovery, to the power of what Coleridge calls "coming to know what we know," then it would be foolhardy to turn it out because the theory underlying it was insufficiently developed. And this gave Lucille McCarthy and me the focus of our second study.

But where to begin? How could I defend myself if I did not have ready answers to these very serious criticisms from across the postmodern spectrum? My first breakthrough occurred while having lunch with Lucille and Peter Elbow. In outlining to us the many attacks to which his own work had been subject, Elbow commented that he was frequently called a romantic. And I, without much thought, asked, "What's wrong with romanticism?" The long and the short of it was that Peter did not know what was wrong with romanticism, but he did acknowledge there was a close connection between Berthoff's notion that writing is a creative process and the romantic view that creativity, truth, and insight are intimates. These questions about romanticism and its relationship to the expressivist classroom led me to explore the romantic tradition.

Tracing Expressivism to Its Romantic Roots

In the end, my exploration took the form of a comparison and contrast between the view of writing of Peter Elbow and the view of language of Johann Gottfried Herder, the 18th-century German Romantic. In particular, my research showed me that romanticism was a protest against the harsh uniformity and mechanical quality of industrial life. Romanticism's search for uniqueness can, surely, be egocentric, but it can also, as Herder intended it, be a way of sharing with others, of transcending the competitive barriers and isolation of modern life. Put differently, it occurred to me that Herder's claim (1770/1966) that to understand another person is to imaginatively step into their world, that we cannot judge another's perspective while remaining in our own, is very much akin to Elbow's believing game (1973, pp. 145-191). That is, the point of personal writing is not simply to learn about oneself. The point is to help another person step into your world so he or she can see where you are coming from, so your world can truly make sense to someone else.

These comparisons between Herder and Elbow presented a way to complexify expressivist theory, suggesting to me that at least one strand of romanticism was an effort to use idiosyncrasies not to isolate people but to connect them through understanding. Although it is true that all language has a social and ideological function, my examination of expressivism's romantic roots showed me that it is also true that important aspects of language can be grasped only in a personal context. My growing understanding that romanticism is complex, that it has communitarian as well as isolating dimensions, presented me with a thread I thought I could follow in defending Berthoffian pedagogy against its many critics.

Using Classroom Data to Test Critics' Charges against Expressivism

However, my efforts to answer expressivism's critics by appealing to the history of romanticism is only half the story of McCarthy's and my second classroom study. Fighting this battle solely on theoretical turf felt unsatisfying to me. Having long been unhappy with philosophers' seemingly endless abstract debates, I was appreciative of Stenhouse's insistence that issues of classroom practice should not be settled in the theoretical forum. To the contrary, he counsels teachers to test theories in their own classrooms to determine which are most effective.

And loud in my ears were data McCarthy collected in our first project. These provided evidence, I thought, of the value of personal voice in students' development of academic competence. I remembered my student David Kaiser saying that when he learned more about the personal backgrounds of his classmates in Intro to Philosophy, he had to pay better attention to what they said. In interviews with McCarthy, this 27-year-old business major said that if a student who had been raped spoke about rape, he would attend to her quite differently than to a student who had not had that experience. This suggested to me that pupils who bring personal experience and language into the classroom do not necessarily end up isolated or talking to themselves or believing that knowledge is an individual construction.

Fortunately, McCarthy's and my collaborative arrangement presented us with an opportunity to follow Stenhouse's lead. With McCarthy's social science skills, we could look more closely at my Intro students to see if charges by expressivism's critics were on target. From what we could tell, these critics had never actually studied expressivist classrooms to see if students were indeed discouraged from self-criticism, collaborative conversation, and successful entry into academic communities. After considerable discussion, McCarthy agreed to go back to the classroom data with these questions in mind in order to evaluate my students' experiences. Thus we found ourselves, at the start of our second classroom study, in the odd position of using Stenhouse's approach to teacher research to try to support Berthoff's approach to pedagogy.

OUR REPORT FORM

Two Parts Rather Than Five

Having set our task, McCarthy and I faced an additional challenge. If I were to focus on theory and she on the classroom, what would our report form look like, and where would we publish it?

In our first study, we followed, at least on the surface, the five-part APA format. In addition, at the outset of "Boundary Conversations" we determined to send it to *Research in the Teaching of English*, a journal noted for quantitative studies but open to qualitative research reflective of the scientific paradigm. As our conversation continued about the shape of our second report, we concluded that it needed to be quite different. And it seemed natural to us, given our emerging fifty-fifty collaboration, to divide our second report down the middle.

This was a radical departure from "Boundary Conversations" since I would now take full responsibility for the half of our report devoted to theory, and McCarthy would take control of the entire classroom study. This meant that our second article was truly an experiment in fashioning a qualitative report form reflective of our working relationship and the way in which we carried out our study.

Credentialing Our Second Study with Theory

In addition to being a two-part report with two separate authorships, "Is Expressivism Dead?" varied from "Boundary Conversations" in a second way. Although in both we attempted to present a detailed classroom account which would be, in Stenhouse's terms, "illuminative" (1979/1985e, p. 31), in the two articles we credential ourselves in starkly different manners.

For "Boundary Conversations," as I have explained, McCarthy wrote an elaborate methodology section, outlining our data sources and analytic procedures in order to gain credibility with *RTE* readers. In our second study, however, we eliminate the methods section altogether. Having seen the way in which theory increased the significance of our first project, our second study is very much a product of our growing realization that when properly theorized, classroom studies have potential interest for a larger audience than they normally attract. Put another way, "Boundary Conversations" appealed primarily to a readership that was interested in how students succeed with their writing in disciplinary courses. Although, as I outline in Chapter 3, we used Belenky et al., Dewey, and Bakhtin to help explain my students' behavior, these theorists' work was not featured but simply interwoven into our report. In our second study, however, by devoting the first half of our report to an exploration of the theoretical roots of my Berthoff-Elbow pedagogy, we hoped to attract a larger readership.

Developing Unique Strengths within Collaboration

A third and final major difference between the report forms of our first two collaborations was that in the second, I, as a teacher-researcher, said nothing about my own classroom. On the surface it might appear that I left this entirely up to McCarthy. A casual reading might also suggest that, in the absence of my voice, McCarthy risked exploiting me, using our project to simply extract my data for her own purposes. But a closer look reveals that she was actually giving me far more responsibility in the second project than the first and therefore, whereas she was first author of "Boundary Conversations," we agreed that I should be first author on our second study.

Further, the second piece was even more of a boundary conversation than the first. I was much less McCarthy's assistant in the second piece. She realized that, since theory was so important for classroom work, my using my philosophic skills to set the focus for our second study would make it more valuable to her field. That is, the second study made even better use of our different disciplinary backgrounds and skills than our first. And dividing our report in half was in no way a sign that we were going our separate ways. To the contrary, we had to listen quite closely to one another since our new arrangement required that McCarthy use theoretical lenses which I developed in my portion of the study. That is, she had to pay careful attention to my theoretical work since she needed it for her analyses of classroom data, and I, in turn, had to be attentive to her data in order to fine-tune the theory so she could make maximum use of it.

What stands out from this experience reinforces comments I made earlier about the ingredients which have allowed both McCarthy and me to feel positive about our collaborative arrangement. Responsibility for our second study felt equally distributed. But this does not mean I can say McCarthy was doing precisely 50% of the work and I was doing the other 50%. This would be misleading. When I say our collaborative work was shared equally, I do not have a number in mind. McCarthy and I had no idea if the work each of us did was equally difficult or took the same amount of time. What did matter was that we had different things to contribute, each of us doing the best we could at tasks we knew were especially suitable to our different skills and interests. This meant, simply, that we truly needed each other. I recognized that I could not do this study of my own students as well as McCarthy could, and such a study was vital to successful completion of our project. By the same token, McCarthy informed me she could not work with theory as well as I, and theory was equally crucial to successful completion of our study.

As this project moved forward, then, the report form we developed represented much more clearly than our *RTE* piece the actual division of labor of our work. In addition, by dividing our report into two sections—mine focused on theory and McCarthy's on classroom data—we could show the significance of theory for teacher research as well as the need for practitioner inquirers to maintain a constant theory-data interplay.

PERSONAL VOICE AND COLLABORATIVE WORK: RECONCILING INDIVIDUAL AND GROUP NEEDS

Although we did not understand it at the time, the challenges that McCarthy and I faced as we managed our individual roles within our conjoint work paralleled the problem I faced with my Intro students: how to encourage students' personal voices while also helping them participate in the particular form of collaboration called academic conversation. Put most broadly, it is the 300-year debate about the work-ings of democracy, about which communal arrangements best develop the idiosyncratic potential of each individual while, at the same time, satisfying the collaborative needs of the group.

Within composition studies and education in the 1980s and 1990s, the idea of collaboration has received considerable attention (see Burnett & Ewald, 1994; Ede & Lunsford, 1990; Hafernik, Messerschmitt, & Vandrick, 1997; Reagan, Fox, & Bleich, 1994; Roen & Mittan, 1992; Yancey & Spooner, 1998). Numerous researchers have pointed out the bankruptcy of an individualism rooted in 18th-century notions of the self-actualizing citizen (see Miller, 1994; Sullivan, 1994). That is, many have pointed out that the social contract myth about each of us being autonomous, requiring only the proper political and social space to realize our potential, is unrealistic. And some have extended this argument against autonomous self-determination to the individual writer, contending that individual scholarship is a contradiction in terms, that all so-called individual work is really a collective construction (Brodkey, 1987; Entes, 1994). In this way, critics of individual scholarship join social constructionists like Bartholomae (1985) and Berlin (1988) in questioning personal voice and authorship. In sum, both social constructionist and collaborationist criticisms of the independent author have their taproot in the effort to dislodge the ideal of the self-sufficient individual.

However, one shortcoming of this promotion of collaborative authorship at the expense of the autonomous writer is that it leaves unclear what to do with the undeniable differences among people. Granted that, as Ede and Lunsford (1990) and Sullivan (1994) point out, our ideas and language are social achievements, it is equally undeniable that each one of us reflects our social environment in very special and unique colors. McCarthy and I believe that the ways in which we have divided our work, and the variety of bylines we have adopted—sometimes co-authoring, sometimes single authoring, sometimes, as in the present chapter, one of us leading with the other consulting—illustrate a collaboration that attempts to honor both what we have in common as well as what we have apart.

In other words, although criticisms of independence and self-sufficiency are well taken, it is shortsighted to go to the other extreme and deny the individual author altogether. McCarthy's and my collaborative arrangement—and our classroom research findings, as we will show—suggest that just as overemphasis on our individuality is dangerous, so too is overemphasis on our commonalities. Just as there can be no effective writing that is not social, so too there can be no vibrant collaborations without the input of different and individualized voices.

I say this despite the fact that a number of collaborators have recently claimed that the success of their conjoint work has led them to a blended voice, to such sharing of writing responsibilities that the order in which their names are listed is totally arbitrary (see Hafernik et al., 1997; Lu & Horner, 1998; Orner, Miller, & Ellsworth, 1996; Thompson & Gitlin, 1995). Their blended voice is so much a surrender of individual authorship, they claim, that they cannot (or will not) distinguish their unique contributions to their cooperative project. In fact, Lisa Ede and Andrea Lunsford (1990) felt this blending to such a degree they even considered mixing their names (e.g. Annalisa Edesford) in an effort to show the merging of their separate identities (p. x).

McCarthy and I do not deny the effectiveness of a collective voice as the expression of shared work; in fact, we ourselves have frequently employed such a "we" voice. However, the ideal underlying our joint projects is quite different from that underlying collaborations in which authors strive for a collective identity. In our case, we envision our collaboration as an opportunity to recognize and more fully develop our contrasting strengths. In fact, rather than seeing our cooperative work as overcoming the limitations of individual authorship, we see it as one of the best places for our personal voices to develop. And this parallels the claims we make for the expressivist classroom in our second piece. We find that just as our own voices have strengthened as we have collaborated, the development of students' personalized voices goes hand in hand with their entry into and understanding of conversations within a discipline. Our research and classroom experiences, then, suggest that an individual's personal fulfillment depends upon rich and committed associations just as surely as fruitful community depends upon unique and individualized contributions.

In short, McCarthy and I now realize in retrospect that the point of collaborating—for us as well as for my students—is not to suppress our differences but to promote them, because when we share a common objective, our differences are a valuable strength rather than a weakness. In other words, when working alone, our eccentricities can be dangerous, leading us into unchecked extremes, whereas these same idiosyncracies, balanced by the reactions of collaborating others, can be a source of fresh insight and discovery. Thus, as Lucille's and my work developed, she was no longer asking me to give up my Berthoffian zealousness or my theoretical bent, nor was I requiring her to relinquish her Stenhousian positivism and interest in classroom data. Instead, we were, more and more, seeing our joint work as a chance to sharpen our differences, to develop what each of us does best in order to better achieve what we both wanted: enhanced understanding of classroom teaching, learning, and research.

GETTING OUR SECOND STUDY INTO PRINT

Because we had abandoned the five-part APA scientific report style, the standard configuration of *RTE* articles, McCarthy and I both realized we had to find another journal for our second piece. We decided to submit it to *College English (CE)*, not because that journal normally prints classroom studies, but because of its wide readership. McCarthy and I reasoned that the Berthoff-Elbow pedagogy still had broad appeal even if postmodern criticisms of its theoretical underpinnings seemed to have swept away its respectability. By proceeding this way, McCarthy was putting aside what she knew was a successful formula with *RTE* editors to devote considerable time to a new sort of qualitative report that might not earn academic journal space. And this was especially risky for her because she was, at the time, an untenured assistant professor. I, by contrast, had received tenure many years before.

To add to McCarthy's worries, when the two of us discussed our new report style with her colleague Barbara Walvoord, Walvoord's judgment was that we really had two articles and that any effort to splice a classroom study onto a purely theoretical discussion would surely take away from both. And when we discussed this same project with Peter Elbow, he confided that there was no way to predict what editors might do with such a hybrid work.

After submitting the manuscript to James Raymond, *CE*'s editor at the time, several months went by. Finally, in mid-fall of 1991, I called the *CE* office and was informed by Raymond's secretary that the piece had been rejected, although notification had not yet been mailed. Understandably, when I relayed the information to McCarthy, she was disappointed and expressed uncertainty about the wisdom of our continued collaboration. The rejection of our second study reawakened her earlier suspicion that my Berthoffian zeal and theoretical skills were no substitute for the Stenhousian skill so helpful for making one's way in the world of academic publication. I too was disappointed but had no satisfactory reply other than my weak mumble that "it seemed like a good idea at the time."

But McCarthy is not one to leave stones unturned. When the referees' reviews arrived in the mail, along with Raymond's rejection, and they proved to be highly laudatory—both of them recommending that our piece be published—she quickly got on the phone to Raymond. He told her that despite the positive reviews, he did not want to publish it because it was too much a classroom study, and besides, a philosophy class was of little interest to teachers of English. McCarthy and I were now facing together what I had often faced alone: the difficulty of convincing academics in the disciplines that classroom research is worthy and interesting enough to receive their attention.

Ultimately, however, McCarthy was persuasive in her phone conversation with Raymond. Using our two positive reviews as leverage, she convinced Raymond, who was about to make way for a new *CE* editor, Louise Smith, to pass our second study on to Smith for fresh consideration. Several months later, after completing her own evaluation of the piece, Smith wrote McCarthy to say she would publish it, giving it, in fact, the lead position in the October 1992 issue.

In our musings about why Louise Smith took "Is Expressivism Dead?" McCarthy, who was much more familiar with *College English* than I, confessed that she had always believed the odds were against our classroom work ever appearing in *CE*. It was a journal, she reminded me, that had traditionally been devoted to literary theory and criticism and had given only modest space to classroom practice. Although McCarthy speculated that Smith was far more sympathetic than Raymond to classroom studies, McCarthy concluded that it was the theoretical section, the ways in which I had traced expressivist pedagogy to Herder and romantic roots, which turned the tide in our favor.

This development reinforced our view that theory is crucial for teacher research because of the ways it expands the relevance of classroom studies. What readers of our article were getting was not just an account of students in a local setting, they were also seeing my students through the lenses of theories of language, specifically, the relationship between personal and communal discourse.

WHAT DID WE LEARN FROM OUR SECOND COLLABORATIVE PROJECT?

The Value of Theory for Teacher Research

First, with regard to the nature of teacher research, both our pieces, but especially the second, showed us that theory is an excellent way to give our classroom studies wide relevance. As McCarthy speculated at the time of Louise Smith's acceptance of "Is Expressivism Dead?" Smith was more open than Raymond to the value of classroom research. But neither of us believed Smith would have accepted our study without the theoretical section which gave it a broad context. Just as Belenky et al. (1986)

turned our students in "Boundary Conversations" from just plain Ginny Lewis and David Kaiser to "separate knowers" faced with the challenge of being "constructed knowers," likewise, Laurie Wilson in "Is Expressivism Dead?" was not simply a first-generation college student trying to get along in a foreign academic environment. She was also a counterexample to social constructionist and cultural critics who charge that expressivism is incapable of generating disciplinary competence and student change in the classroom.

The fact that theory—and its vivid interplay with classroom data— was apparently getting us a readership as large as *CE*'s 18,000 subscribers was especially significant, given the problems I had had with my first teacher-researcher stories and the stand James Raymond took toward "Is Expressivism Dead?" In my own look at anthologies of teacher research, the studies that gain my attention do so because of their ability to generate drama and present a picture rich enough to make me care about the main characters. However, McCarthy's and my *CE* experience suggests that if, in addition to telling a dramatic story, teacher-researchers would show that the issues they and their students face have implications for theories of learning, say, or social reform, or disciplinary initiation—and not just for pedagogy—they might enter larger conversations and generate greater academic respectability. For example, teachers who present successful practice accounts might enrich their work by discussing the psychological theories about knowledge acquisition which lie behind their practices. Similarly, teachers who tell stories of their conversions from one classroom approach to another might gain larger readership if they explored the implication of these changes for their views, say, of what constitutes a just society and the responsible, moral citizen.

In playing up the significance of theory for increased teacher-research respectability, our work leads us to integrate rather than oppose Stenhouse and Berthoff. As I mentioned in the opening chapter, both of these writers argue that theory is central to classroom research. Just as Stenhouse sees the classroom as the testing ground for different approaches to teaching and learning, so Berthoff highlights the importance of theory when she urges teachers that their exchanges of instructional recipes or techniques should be accompanied by similar exchanges of theoretical visions.

Effects upon Our Teaching

With regard to the effects upon our teaching of our second classroom study, we were in the same situation as at the end of our first: we could not with assurance say, as Stenhouse would have wished, that we were better teachers. However, on reflection, it became clear that although neither of us could claim our teaching was more effective, our classroom research was affecting my teaching in two important ways.

Understanding My Own Pedagogy

First, "Is Expressivism Dead?" helped me understand better what I was already doing. And thus, once again, it seemed that Berthoff was correct to claim that the real value of teacher research is its ability to help practitioners articulate what they, in some sense, already know. The story we tell in our second study about Laurie Wilson and the way she subjected her own beliefs to a type of scrutiny which allowed her to reappraise them made me more comfortable about the expressivist pedagogy I was practicing. In other words, our data indicated that, at least in the setting of my Intro class, encouraging students to talk about their own beliefs in personal language did not, as theorists like Bartholomae and Berlin predicted, prevent them from opening to alternative ways of going at the world. Instead, Laurie was able to use philosophic techniques and felt comfortable enough in the Intro environment to listen to others, engage in self-criticism, and take the difficult step of reorganizing her initial point of view. In short, McCarthy and I were able to use Stenhousian research to quell our fears that Berthoff-Elbow pedagogy was too conservative, likely to inhibit student reappraisal and change.

Redirecting My Teaching Gaze

"Is Expressivism Dead?" also had a second effect upon my teaching which was not at first obvious. It led me, eventually, to redirect my focus from individual student learning to student interaction and the social structures of my classroom. This emerging sensitivity to student associations was spurred by my recognition that Laurie Wilson's particular experiences and language were important to others besides herself. As she expressed these in the class, she was not only rethinking and developing them for herself, she was also helping her classmates reflect on the differences between her world and theirs.

Effects upon Our Research

My developing concern for student-to-student relationships and classroom structures was stimulated not only by our second study but also by changes taking place in McCarthy's and my collaboration. Once I realized that Herder was an ancestor of Berthoff and Elbow, and that Herder claimed we only understand ourselves when we adopt the perspectives of others, I was able to connect a number of important theorists who are seminal in my teaching life. As I have already indicated, I had long been a fan of John Dewey (see Fishman, 1993). When I realized that Herder saw language and self-expression as primarily a social tool, I sensed that Dewey (1916/1967) was saying much the same thing a century and a half later. In 1916, when Dewey tells us—as I quote in Chapter 1—that all communication involves stepping outside oneself to make one's ideas plain to another, I hear Herder. I hear the same romantic protest against the isolating forces of modern life. To communicate, according to Dewey, requires like-mindedness and community. It involves stepping into the worlds of others, playing Elbow's (1973) believing game.

Linking Classroom Community and Research Community

As I drew the line which connects Herder to Dewey to Berthoff/Elbow, it was becoming clearer and clearer to me that the essential ingredient for success in *both* my classroom and my research is supportive community. Regarding my classroom, I first glimpsed its importance during my analysis of the "Boundary Conversations" data. Regarding McCarthy's and my collaboration, it was not until the second study, as I have already explained, that I saw that fifty-fifty communal sharing has nothing to do with numbers. It has to do with two people's experiencing the joys of contributing in their own unique ways to a project they share. It also involves taking from the fruits of collaboration what each person uniquely needs. Thus, I was beginning to see that McCarthy and I, in our own modest way, were enacting Dewey's (1927/1988) vision of democratic community. Dewey writes:

> From the standpoint of the individual, [community] consists in having a responsible share according to capacity in forming and directing the activities of the groups to which one belongs and in participating according to need in the values which the groups sustain. From the standpoint of the

groups, it demands liberation of the potentialities of members of a group in harmony with the interests and goods which are common. (p. 147)

Understanding McCarthy's and my collaboration in light of Dewey led me, over time, to realize that this was the sort of democratic association—however idealistic—I also wanted to build with my teaching. That is, I hoped to help my students use their unique skills to contribute to group work, and, at the same time, I hoped my classroom would provide opportunities for individuals to realize their different potentials. But at the conclusion of our second study this was not yet fully clear to me. Classroom community, however, eventually became the focus of our third piece of collaborative, integrative teacher research. But this is to get ahead of McCarthy's and my story. We pause now to reprint our second study, "Is Expressivism Dead?"

IS EXPRESSIVISM DEAD? RECONSIDERING ITS ROMANTIC ROOTS AND ITS RELATION TO SOCIAL CONSTRUCTIONISM

Steve Fishman and Lucille McCarthy

In the 1980s expressivism as a philosophy of composition came increasingly under attack, and social constructionism—the view that good writers must master the accepted practices of a discourse community—was widely adopted as an alternative. The purpose of this article is to defend expressivism against this attack, particularly against two charges. First, responding to the charge that expressivism, following the romantics, is tied to the ideal of the isolated writer, Steve Fishman argues on historical grounds that it was the social reform dimension of German romanticism that inspired expressivism. Second, Lucille McCarthy responds to the charge that expressivism disempowers students because it does not help them learn disciplinary and professional languages. She presents Fishman's class as one which is committed both to the mastery of philosophic method and to the development of student voices, committed, that is, to achieving social constructionist goals within an expressivist environment. Part I presents a theoretical perspective on expressivism; Part II shows the practical implementation of that theory in the classroom.

This article first appeared in *College English, 54* (October 1992), 647-661. Copyright 1992 by the National Council of Teachers of English. Reprinted with permission.

I: Peter Elbow and the Romantic Movement: A defense of Expressivism
Steve Fishman

In the past decade, expressivism, the view that creating text involves exploring personal experience and voice, has generated significant criticism. David Bartholomae says that to teach writing as an expression of individual thoughts and feelings is to make students "suckers" and "powerless" ("Reply" 128; "Inventing"). Patricia Bizzell, pursuing a similar line of attack, charges that by failing to teach academic language, expressivists harm students in two ways. One, encouraging students to write in everyday language puts them at a disadvantage when they must write within the academic disciplines. Two, since mastering academic discourse, for Bizzell, is also learning new ways of thinking, expressivists limit students' chances to develop academically valued ways of thinking ("Cognition"; "What Happens").

In further challenges to expressivist ideology, James Berlin and John Trimbur argue that it serves the forces of political and economic conservatism, and Burton Hatlen claims expressivist pedagogy wrongly supposes that students already have within themselves everything they need in order to write well. Even a theorist as sympathetic to the expressivist position as C. H. Knoblauch concludes that expressivist assumptions can lead to misguided teaching, to romantic classrooms emphasizing a type of self-actualization which the outside world would indict as sentimental and dangerous.

At the center of each of these criticisms is the view that, as heirs to romanticism, contemporary expressivists have a naive view of the writer as independent, as possessing innate abilities to discover truth. This charge—that expressivist pedagogy focuses upon personal growth while ignoring the social settings of specified skills and bodies of knowledge— is a familiar one in discussions of American education. In an earlier generation, Richard Hofstadter described John Dewey's child-centered curriculum as "romantic" and "primitive." Hofstadter claimed that, for Dewey and his educational reformers, "the child came into this world trailing clouds of glory, and it was the holy office of the teacher to see that he remained free" (368).

Just as Hofstadter criticized Dewey for a false view of the spontaneous tendencies of the child, so contemporary critics blame expressivists for a false view of the self-generating writer. Discussing the work of Peter

Elbow, James Berlin claims that, for Elbow, "It is, after all, only the individual acting alone and apart from others, who can determine the existent, the good, and the possible" (486). And Burton Hatlen, referring to Elbow's *Writing With Power*, concludes:

> Elbow's centering of "voice" ... clearly demonstrates the degree to which the assumptions of Romantic Idealism have pervaded the New Rhetoric. For what is the source of this "voice," if not some "deeper," more "authentic" self that is, for Elbow, as for the New Rhetoric generally, the only ultimate certainty in a world of shifting appearances? (72)

To defend the work of Peter Elbow against charges that, for expressivists, the individual is self-sufficient and ultimate, I will try to show that, although Elbow shares with eighteenth-century German romanticism a reverence for personal experience, it is not an experience leading to isolation. Rather, by reinserting personal experience into human interactions, Elbow, like Johann Gottfried Herder and other German romantics, hopes to increase our chances for identifying with one another and, as a result, our chances for restructuring community. To understand romanticism as championing the artist as a lonely, spontaneous genius is to adopt too narrow a view of romanticism. On the contrary, an important motive of the romantic movement was finding common ground among individuals, a reaction against the utilitarian and self-serving qualities of late eighteenth-century society. By labeling him "romantic," by seeing expressivism as isolating, Elbow's critics make it easy to neglect the communitarian objectives of his approach. My claim is that if we broaden our understanding of romanticism, if we recognize expressivism as rooted historically in the eighteenth-century German effort to find unity through diversity, we improve our chances of assessing Elbow's work fairly.

Conventionally, romanticism is seen as resisting the Enlightenment's objectification of nature and separation of nature from human purpose. The Enlightenment world operated smoothly but mechanistically and without destination, hence without meaning. The community rested on the notion of a "social contract," which, on the positive side, established that institutions are inventions subject to human control. On the negative side, the social contract established that men and women were self-sufficient in the state of nature and only driven to organize themselves to protect property and assure personal safety. In "Adversarialism in

America and the Professions," William May argues that, given this vision of individuals as independent and nature as mechanical, the eighteenth century could find no common purpose, no fraternity to go with liberty and equality. People entered into the social contract, not because they agreed on a goal for government, but because they could not physically protect themselves. The contract—the trade of liberty for protection—was simply the best compromise given that people could not trust one another. This distrust, according to May, is reflected in the system of checks and balances which marks the American form of government.

May finds similar patterns of self-interest and distrust in modern professionalism. Doctors and lawyers, for example, present a limited aspect of themselves in transactions with patients and clients. They maintain power by guarding their knowledge, erecting barriers around their privileged communities. Likewise, May claims that students come to the university under duress, seeking credentials without which they are unable to compete in the marketplace. Students see syllabi as contracts, ways to meet their specific objectives—to become an accountant, a biologist, or a philosopher.

This is the world we encounter today—professional, contractual, without common purpose, very much like the world eighteenth-century romantics faced. In response, they sought, not isolation for the creative artist, but reunification. I argue that Peter Elbow's work reflects similar concerns. To support my claim I want to highlight parallels between Elbow and Johann Gottfried Herder, the German philosopher who was student to Kant and mentor to Goethe.

In my reconstruction of German romanticism I see Herder as a forerunner of the writing-to-learn movement. Herder believes the artistic process is not just an expression of something already known, but also a groping toward destinations and forms that are not understood until artists arrive at them. According to Charles Taylor, expression for Herder is "not only the fulfillment of life but also the clarification of meaning. In the course of living adequately I not only fulfill my humanity but clarify what my humanity is about" (17). Just as Elbow, in his advocacy of freewriting, believes we must begin to write without knowing exactly where we are going, so Herder says human expression is both an embodiment and a clarification, an embodiment of a feeling already experienced but whose form is not clarified until the act of expression is complete.

Although this concern for embodying and clarifying one's feelings sounds self-absorbed, both Elbow and Herder see expression as more than self-discovery. They also see it as a means of social connection. As we strive to understand our own expressions, we seek insight in the work of others. Herder tells us that all thought is social. In his essay *On the Origin of Language,* which won the 1770 prize of the Academy of Berlin, Herder writes:

> I cannot think the first human thought, I cannot align the first reflective argument, without dialoguing in my soul or without striving to dialogue. The first human thought is hence in its very essence a preparation for the possibility of dialoguing with others. (128)

For Herder, to remain stuck within the mindset of our native language limits our chances of learning. This is true, says Herder, because we never learn about things in isolation but always in relation to something else. And in mastering new dialects we are not abandoning the old, because our native tongue is always the means for understanding new ones. Herder writes:

> Just as a child compares all images and new concepts with what it already knows, so our mind automatically matches all languages and dialects to our native language. By cultivating that language in active use, the mind is subsequently able to penetrate all the more deeply into the uniqueness of different languages. By keeping [our native] language constantly in view, when it discovers in foreign languages...gaps and deserts,...riches and abundance, it grows fonder of the riches of its own, and, where possible, enriches the poverty of its own with foreign treasures. The native language is the guide without which, in the labyrinth of many foreign languages, it must go astray. It is the support that, on the vast ocean of foreign tongues, preserves it from sinking. It imparts to the otherwise confusing manifold of languages unity. (*Fragments Concerning Recent German Literature,* 1767, qtd. in Morton 171)

This is Herder's solution to the problem of how we can fulfill our potential as individuals and at the same time establish unity with others. To learn more about self-expressions, we are driven to enter into unfamiliar expressions. And as we sympathetically understand foreign tongues—their ways of thinking, hearing, and feeling—we inevitably enrich our own. I find a similar sense of the socially unifying power of language in Elbow. The reason we write, says Elbow, is to connect with others.

Repeatedly, he speaks about writing and talking in order to "get inside the heads of other people" (*Writing Without Teachers* 50, 57, 149). "Writing," Elbow says, "is a string you send out to connect yourself with other consciousnesses" (73). Thus for Herder and Elbow our expressions are more than manifestations of ourselves; they are also the start of our dialogue with others.

In addition to a shared respect for the socially unifying quality of language, both Herder and Elbow stress the integration of personal life and public expression, the intimacy between the writer and his or her public work. In his essay "Herder and the Enlightenment," Isaiah Berlin writes that Herder was

> bitterly opposed to the view...that the purpose of the artist is to create an object whose merits are independent of the creator's personal qualities or of his intentions...or his social situation.... Herder is the true father of the doctrine that it is the artist's mission, above others, to testify in his works to the truth of his own inner experience.... (200)

Further, Berlin tells us that, for Herder, pandering to the audience, using one's skills without connection to one's inner life, violates the artistic covenant. Likewise, Elbow insists that our public texts must be grounded in our personal writing. In his effort to reinsert the personal into expression, Elbow goes so far as to claim that in order to do so writers must at times forget their audience ("Closing My Eyes"). This emphasis upon reconnecting artists with their work is a reaction against the anonymity of workers in industrial production, the separation of product from producer. If we were to employ the language of Marx, who learned from Herder via Hegel, we would call this a response to the alienation of labor. Unless our expressions testify to our inner lives, we are unable to see ourselves mirrored or clarified by them. And unless we are so mirrored, our opportunities for finding common cause or identifying with others are greatly reduced.

Finally, both Herder and Elbow are critical of the exclusionary quality of academic discourse. Herder resists Latin, the university and scientific language of the eighteenth century, because its dominance relegates other languages to lesser status. He believes every discourse generates its own ways of hearing and thinking, and from the interaction of these diverse languages an organic unity will emerge, a unity very different from the uniformity achieved by imposing a single discourse. Similarly, Elbow raises questions about the monovocal, "author-evacuated" quality of academic prose, its failure to reveal the writing context or the author's stake in his or her work ("Reflections"; "Forward"). In addition, Elbow argues for the provocative thinking, the "cooking," that occurs when different "modes or textures" of writing interact (*Embracing Contraries* 44-45).

Behind Herder's and Elbow's view that social unity can develop from sympathetic interplay among diverse forms of expression is a transformational view of society. Since, for Herder and Elbow, expressions are personal discoveries, when our exchanges with others are based upon self-expression, our exchanges can be transformative, can transform or make clearer who we are to ourselves and others. In addition, as members of a transformational group, discovering more about ourselves through sensitivity to the discoveries of others, we increase our chances for mutual identification and trust. By contrast, in Enlightenment communities— where human exchanges are based upon maximizing personal advantage and minimizing personal risk—we strive to limit personal exposure, to separate the professional from the more private aspects of our lives. Under such circumstances, we engage with others, not for open-ended goals like learning or growth, but to achieve clearly defined, utilitarian ends. In this sense, communities based upon transaction rather than transformation promote professional relationships, the separation of public and private. That is why our romantic heroes and heroines are those who transcend rules governing contractual arrangements and allow personal concerns—sympathetic projections into the experience of others—to influence their actions.

Given this distinction between Enlightenment and romantic communities, I believe that Elbow's writing group is a pre-vision of a transformational rather than a transactional community. Whereas Enlightenment exchanges are built primarily upon doubting, guarding ourselves against "holes" in our contracts with others, Elbow tells us that writing groups, although they doubt and criticize, are built primarily upon believing, upon inserting the self into the experience of others. According to Elbow,

> there is a kind of belief—serious, powerful, and a genuine giving of the self— that is possible to give even to hateful or absurd assertions. To do this requires great energy, attention, and even a kind of inner commitment. It helps to think of it as trying to get inside the head of someone who saw things this way.... To do this you must make, not an act of self-extrication, but an act of self-insertion, self-involvement—an act of projection. (*Writing Without Teachers* 149)

Elbow's believing game is an attempt to evaluate truth-claims, not by standing back, but by stepping closer to share someone else's experience and language. In taking this stand, Elbow is once again in the spirit of Herder, whose *Reflections on the Philosophy of the History of Mankind*, written and published between 1784 and 1791, dramatically challenged the Enlightenment view that history is a linear progression culminating in the culture of Western Europe. Herder denied that there was a single standard by which to judge civilizations from the outside. He makes a convincing case that each culture's values and artistic achievements must be assessed by adopting the standpoint of the insider, the native, by sympathetically inserting oneself into what Herder called a culture's "climate." Elbow's notion of believing, which also insists on sympathetic insertion into others' worlds, is crucial for understanding Elbow's notion of writing groups. Although respondents, especially at the later stages of writing, must doubt and criticize, it is only when respondents report their personal experience of the text, and when writers "believe" them, that writing groups are successful. This way, according to Elbow, writers discover what their words do to their readers, what happens when they send out their "strings" to others. By asking us to bring personal aspects of ourselves to writing groups and by asking us to step into the language of others, Elbow increases our chances for identifying with one another, for transformation as opposed to transaction, for blending rather than separating the personal and public. In Elbow's encouragement of multiple languages and the community that emerges from their sympathetic interaction, we hear resonances of Herder's appreciation of diverse cultures and the value of their interplay. In this way, both Herder and Elbow stand against Enlightenment relations based upon distrust and defense of individual rights.

According to this analysis of Elbow's work and its alignment with German romanticism, expressivism is far from viewing the writer as an independent, spontaneous genius. In his efforts to reinsert the self into writing and interpretation and in his awareness that social unity can emerge from exploring multiple languages, Elbow envisions a more radical sort of communion than contemporary societies easily allow. Why, then, have critics like James Berlin and Burton Hatlen characterized Elbow as romantic and, therefore, as atomistic and isolating?

In his book *Culture and Society: 1780-1950*, Raymond Williams suggests that romanticism is understood as isolating because of a particular development in its history, namely, the estrangement of nineteenth-century English poets from their readership. But Williams points out that this is hardly the full story of romanticism. He claims that Blake, Coleridge, Shelley, and Keats were "deeply interested" and "involved" in the study and criticism of the society of their day (30). However, from the beginning to the close of the nineteenth century, says Williams, changes in audience led to the professionalization of writing and the isolation of the poet. Instead of a system of patronage, writers became dependent upon reader subscriptions and, later, upon publishing houses. Some writers were successful, but others, estranged from their readership, resented their dependence on market relations.

With the treatment of writing as a commodity, writers became increasingly isolated in their resistance to the demands of mass production. Raymond Williams argues that it was these later developments among English poets which led to the characterization of the romantic writer as alienated and unique. Although English poets shared German romanticism's abhorrence of utilitarian interactions, they abandoned efforts toward communion as their isolation in industrial society became more pronounced. Whereas Herder in the late eighteenth century embraced folk art and the vernacular, English poets a century later were estranged from popular taste.

Critics who paint Elbow with the romantic brush and connect him to a naive view of the isolated, independent writer have done a disservice to him by ignoring an important aspect of romanticism. In the context of Herder and eighteenth-century German thought, Elbow's expressivism is far from supporting individualism or self-absorption. On the contrary, Elbow's work challenges the transactional and defensive character of current exchanges. His emphasis upon believing—the sympathetic hearing of diverse languages, public and private, professional and non-professional, personal and philosophical—is rooted in a romanticism that seeks not isolation but new ways to identify with one another and, thereby, new grounds for social communion.

II: THE HIGH WIRE: SOCIAL CONSTRUCTIONIST GOALS IN AN EXPRESSIVIST COMMUNITY
Lucille McCarthy

Contrary to what Bartholomae, Berlin, and Bizzell have said, the goal of the expressivists—to help students grow in their ability to understand their own experiences—is not incompatible with learning disciplinary language. I wish to describe how Steve Fishman, in his Introduction to Philosophy course, creates an expressivist context, a transformational community, in which to achieve social constructionist goals. By social constructionist goals, I mean introducing students systematically to the rules of a disciplinary language that would otherwise be inaccessible to them. "It's a high-wire act," Fishman told me,

> and I feel like I'm being pulled in two directions, my professors from gradu-
> ate school whispering in one ear, "Initiate 'em into philosophy with a capital
> P, with close critical analysis of canonic texts." In my other ear is sounding
> my own conviction based on twenty-five years of teaching: students don't
> learn very well unless they have an emotional connection. If they cannot
> relate their own lives to philosophy, their familiar languages to the new one,
> the papers they write will be no more than products of a mind game. They
> won't be their own, and they won't help them live their lives.

Philosophic method is, for Fishman, "bankrupt" when unanchored by the question, How does this affect my life? In adopting this position, he echoes Herder's and Elbow's belief that the work of artists and writers must reflect their personal experiences. As Fishman put it, philosophic method cut off from lived experience is

> irresponsible, without conscience, for sale the highest bidder. And lived
> experience apart from method remains mute, without the tools to unzip
> itself, to trace its roots and make connections with its full history.... If
> philosophy doesn't illuminate personal experience, what's the point? It may
> have aesthetic value, like a crossword puzzle, but I never wanted to do
> philosophy that way.

Fishman and I began our study in the fall of 1989, collecting, in two of his introductory classes, one that fall and one the following spring, a variety of naturalistic data, each semester focusing on five students (McCarthy and Fishman, "Boundary Conversations"). Midway through the fall term I interviewed the five students and asked them to describe the class. As they spoke, I heard the mix of personal and philosophic voices that Fishman had told me he wanted. Kerri Ritter, a twenty-two-year-old senior English major from Michigan, described students sharing their opinions and listening to each other in supportive ways. Then, she explained, they questioned each other. Although Kerri did not use these terms, students were playing Elbow's believing and doubting games. She told me,

> In this class we don't go by the book; we learn from each other. We sit in a circle, and Steve begins class with a big question like What is it to fail? or Why do we go to college? or What's the ideal marriage? or How do we come to know something? We freewrite for ten minutes, and when discussion begins, we all tell our feelings and opinions. It's like we're all contributing to a center, and everyone gets very involved. In other classes you can drift off and get the notes later; in this class you've got to listen to the other person.
>
> ... When someone states an opinion, we see if we can understand it and help the person develop it. Then we challenge it. We ask, Why do you think that? How do you know that? Where does that idea come from?

Kerri's description of the class hints at the interplay between personal and philosophic language in Fishman's classroom. As Kerri listened to other students, she was drawing closer to them, identifying with them and trying on their language in order to understand and help them articulate their points of view. As she questioned them, she was stepping away from them, employing the more analytic language of philosophy to ask questions of clarification, evidence, and argument.

In my own observation of Fishman's classroom I noted the same interplay. As the course progressed, students came to know each other so well and were listening so attentively that on several occasions they finished sentences for each other; they were able to take each other's fragmentary ideas and develop them in ways that seemed to please the originator. On two occasions I even saw students help Fishman articulate points he was trying to make. In this same environment I also heard students disagree with each other, and both they and Fishman offered counterexamples, often from their own lives, to test a principle some student had advanced. This doubting took place in an atmosphere in which poorly defined positions were seen not as errors but as tools for developing the discussion.

Although students became increasingly comfortable bringing their own experience into the classroom, at first many, including Kerri, found it difficult; they feared looking stupid or being "way off." Fishman was keenly aware of this initial difficulty. After all, he said, they hardly ever do it in college classes, and they're being judged by their peers. "So,"

Fishman explained, "for me, good teaching is building a trusting community. I've got to make my class safe so the personal can come forward to motivate the philosophic, so we can get an interaction of the two. There's nothing more deadly than a philosophic discussion when students don't care."

Unlike Kerri Ritter, who needed the trusting environment in order to *present* her views, Laurie Wilson, a twenty-six-year-old junior art major from North Carolina, needed it in order to *question* her views. Laurie began our mid-semester interview saying she was not used to a class in which there were no right answers, only endless questions. "Philosophers are always digging deeper," she said. "I had no idea there were so many ways to see things." As she began Introduction to Philosophy, Laurie was vocal in defense of her positions and unwilling to consider alternatives. She told me she was a person of strong convictions who, at times, "blasted" her views at friends and family, even "lashing out" when she knew that she was right. In Fishman's class, however, Laurie found herself in an environment tolerating a multiplicity of ideas.

The personal concern that fueled Laurie's philosophic inquiry in the second of her two papers was the way criminals are treated in correctional facilities. She believed they have too many luxuries and too many rights, a view she took from her father, a guard in a maximum security prison. In her first draft, a narrative of personal experience with which Fishman has students begin all essays, Laurie recounted a visit to this prison:

> Outside, a large area was fenced in with double fences trimmed in crushed razor-blade wire. This intimidated me very much. But then I went inside. The prison inside the fence looked like a Holiday Inn. There was a well-equipped gym, a library, a hospital, a kitchen, a school, and much more. The cell blocks were equipped with the largest t.v.'s I've ever seen. My brother even mentioned that when he grew up he wouldn't mind living there. My mom was shocked. She responded by saying he didn't want to go to prison because someone would tell him when to eat, sleep, and exercise. He answered that she told him that at home anyway.

Although society meant well in providing prisoners with these facilities, Laurie continued, it just failed to see the truth: that inmates need to be punished for their crimes. Several times her father had been attacked by inmates who had then sued him; she was very close to her father, and she worried about him. Laurie's draft set up exactly the writing situation Fishman hopes for. Her emotional stake would provide the energy and commitment to conduct philosophic research.

In his response to her first-draft narrative, Fishman told Laurie that underlying it was an important value conflict, a conflict between two views of punishment—the retributive and the rehabilitative. First, he asked her to clarify both views: her own, which resembled the Biblical eye-for-an-eye justice, and the alternative, which emphasized rehabilitation. Second, Fishman asked Laurie to state arguments for both sides. Finally, he suggested that she "try to link these two views of punishment with two different views of human nature," two different theories of why people commit crimes. Fishman was asking Laurie for philosophic thinking—first, to clarify her key concepts, the two views of punishment; then, to offer arguments in favor of each as well as explore their different assumptions and consequences.

As Laurie wrote her final draft in early December, she allowed me to record a composing-aloud protocol. She began by struggling to take on the position and language of others. She realized that her opponents, the rehabilitators, might argue that their view makes economic sense: rehabilitating a criminal saves society money in the long run. She even suggested that the rehabilitators do not go far enough in helping prisoners reintegrate into society. This was the beginning of modifying her own position, of moving away from the view that all prisoners should be punished to the view that prisoners' treatment should be a function of their attitudes and their crimes. Having moved closer to the opposing position, Laurie began to sharpen her own in relation to it. She concluded, like the rehabilitators, that some criminals *can* be reformed. But, unlike the rehabilitators, she also concluded that that some *cannot*:

> Maybe I believe it depends on the crime and the motive and if the prisoner wants to be helped. When evil emerges as the prisoner's main characteristic—when they've committed atrocious crimes and don't want anyone's help—those are people who should be imprisoned for life with no luxuries. I guess we need the compassion to help the people who are willing to be helped and the backbone to severely punish the others.

In this situation Laurie had, to use Herder's and Elbow's terms, risked identifying with the expressions of others, and in the process she had clarified her own.

The expressivist context, I believe, facilitated Laurie's growth in two ways. First, Laurie knew her position would be treated sympathetically. People would help her develop her position and bolster it as best they could before challenging it. Second, the doubting and critical analysis was carried out in a spirit of exploration. Laurie saw Fishman's questioning of her first-draft narrative as part of the development of her idea, part of the sifting to see what was weak and strong about it. Had she seen his response as an attack, I believe she would have hardened rather than examined and modified her position. For Laurie, the sympathetic listening in Fishman's expressivist community helped her achieve his goal for her: to bring philosophic reasoning and lived experience together in enriching ways.

Laurie's story shows how Fishman introduces philosophic methods of analysis in an expressivist environment. But what about the voices of his graduate school professors asking about classic texts? Five weeks into the course, as the class continued to discuss "big questions" like those Kerri mentioned, Fishman introduced philosophic texts to provide additional ways of seeing these questions. Among these works were two Platonic dialogues, Descartes's *Meditations*, chapters from Dewey's *Reconstruction in Philosophy*, Russell's *Marriage and Morals*, and essays by John Stuart Mill and Harriet Taylor. Fishman purposely delayed introducing these until the fifth week when students had, as he put it, "created some texts of their own." He had learned that students' voices can be easily drowned out by the authority of such literature and, as with philosophic method, he wasn't interested in having students learn these works in and of themselves. Instead, he wanted students to see that these texts could be used to illuminate their personal concerns and, conversely, that their personal concerns could motivate a close reading of the literature.

Beginning class discussion of *The Apology*, Plato's account of Socrates' imprisonment, Fishman posed a student-centered question. He asked them to put themselves in Socrates' predicament. "Would you attempt to escape? Would you feel loyal to Athens?" After ten minutes of freewriting, the discussion began. Laurie said she learned from this discussion that Socrates was open to others' ideas. She admired him, she told me on two occasions, because he was receptive to all arguments: "He was flexible, able to stay neutral and listen to his friends' arguments. He told them, 'If you have a better stance, I'll consider it.' He weighed all views before deciding." Putting herself in Socrates's position had helped Laurie understand Plato's dialogue. Her interpretation was, I believe, tied to her growing ability to take on the perspectives of others.

Whereas Laurie read Socrates as a symbol of openmindedness, Ginny Lewis, a twenty-one-year-old junior English major from North Carolina, saw him as a rebel standing up to authority. She told me,

> When I thought about the conflict Socrates was in, I realized how committed he was to questioning the accepted beliefs of the time and also how unwilling people are to do that. I know *I* wouldn't want to risk death or being a social outcast. I've never questioned things much. Usually, I just accept them.

Ginny, who started out the course eager to align herself with others' opinions, was, like Laurie, reading Socrates in a way which reflected her own concerns: he was for Ginny a questioner of the status quo. She told me that she was so impressed with Socrates' questioning of authority she had used him in papers for two other courses that semester, a commonality among classes she had never experienced before. Ginny's and Laurie's quite different readings of *The Apology* resulted from Fishman's insistence that there be an interplay between the assigned reading and students' own struggles.

I have told these stories about Fishman's classroom to show that, in this setting at least, the expressivist and social constructionist approaches are not mutually exclusive. Far from isolating students from one another and making them "suckers" by depriving them of the chance to learn academic discourse, Fishman's commitment to student language led to close listening and intimacy within the class and at the same time helped students master disciplinary methods and texts. Fishman believes students are empowered, not by suppressing their own voices to mimic the philosophic language that he has achieved over thirty years, but by struggling to use it for their own ends, by groping to interweave it with their familiar discourses.

CONCLUSION

What do we learn from this double study? First, we believe that the current debate between rival philosophies of composition should be redirected to consider the mixed quality of actual classroom practice. The debate between proponents of expressivism and social constructionism assumes these philosophies must be accepted in their entirety and that they are mutually exclusive. However, McCarthy's study of Fishman's classroom challenges this assumption. She finds in Fishman's introductory philosophy course a complex mix of expressivist and social construction-ist approaches. Although social construction theorists have argued that to master disciplinary language students must set aside their personal languages, in Fishman's class this conclusion is not altogether valid. He assigned reading and writing in ways that promoted the interaction of personal and disciplinary languages. And rather than interfering with the learning of academic discourse, the interweaving of the personal and philosophic seemed to encourage the development of both. Specifically, for Laurie, her philosophical exploration of the discourse she had learned from her father caused her to reposition herself in relation to it. She told McCarthy four months after the course ended that she now listened more carefully to her father's comments about his work and evaluated more critically the conversations between him and her brother, now a student of criminal justice.

In sum, we believe that recent attempts to distinguish among competing philosophies of composition, coupled with vigorous efforts to promote one theory or the other, have obscured the possibility that teachers in practice are likely to combine features of various approaches. Examining actual practice in classrooms would move us from judging philosophies of composition in the abstract to understanding when and how they interact in particular disciplines and classrooms.

Second, Fishman's reassessment of Elbow's work, highlighting the contrast between transformational and transactional communities, reminds us that classroom environments reflect larger social environ-ments. By showing that current expressivism is rooted in the eighteenth-century German romantic movement, Fishman aligns Elbow with those who, rather than emphasizing the independence of artistic genius, seek a more cooperative basis for community. This effort puts Elbow and other expressivists in conflict with the transactional and utilitarian basis of much of present-day American education. This transactional quality can be seen, for example, in the widespread portrayal by university adminis-trators of students as consumers and of syllabi as legally enforceable contracts. Whereas these dominant modes of interaction borrow from the Enlightenment, from ideas emphasizing contract and self-interest, Elbow and the expressivists are part of a tradition that emphasizes transforma-tional relations, relations based on trust and mutual support.

Fishman's linking of Elbow with the German romantic Herder shows that there is more to expressivism than personal writing and self-discovery. Fishman attempts to put into practice three key Herderian and expressivist principles and, in doing so, provides clues to how transformational classrooms might work. We conclude by pointing to these three principles. First, Herder and Elbow emphasize the integration of the personal and public when they claim that one's work must reflect one's life. Fishman takes this into his classroom by attempting to integrate ordinary student discourse and philosophic discourse, everyday concerns and philosophic ones. Second, Herder and Elbow emphasize the idiosyncratic quality of different languages. They teach that there is no fixed hierarchy of languages or cultures and that to understand them we must step inside them. In Fishman's classroom this means sympathetic listening on the part of both students and teacher. It means modeling how to try on new language, how to move closer to unfamiliar views and discourse. And third, Herder and Elbow underscore the groping and recursive quality of expression. They teach that expression is fulfillment as well as clarification, that we do not know where our expressions are going until we complete them. In Fishman's classroom this principle translates into acceptance of confusion and tentative starts, encouragement of doubt and criticism in the name of open-ended exploration.

Works Cited

Bartholomae, David. "Inventing the University." *When a Writer Can't Write: Studies in Writer's Block and Other Composing-Process Problems.* Ed. Mike Rose. New York: Guilford, 1985. 134-165.

——. "A Reply to Stephen North." *Pre/Text* 11 (1990): 121-132.

Berlin, Isaiah. *Vico and Herder: Two Studies in the History of Ideas.* New York: Viking, 1976.

Berlin, James. "Rhetoric and Ideology in the Writing Class." *College English* 50 (1988): 477-494.

Bizzell, Patricia. "Cognition, Convention, and Certainty: What We Need to Know about Writing." *Pre/Text* 3 (1982): 213-243.

——. "What Happens When Basic Writers Come to College?" *College Composition and Communication* 37 (1986): 294-301.

Elbow, Peter. "Closing My Eyes as I Speak: An Argument for Ignoring Audience." *College English* 49 (1987): 50-69.

——. *Embracing Contraries: Explorations in Learning and Teaching.* New York: Oxford UP, 1986.

——. "Forward: About Academic Personal Expressive Writing." *Pre/Text* 11 (1990): 7-22.

——. "Reflections on Academic Discourse: How It Relates to Freshmen and Colleagues." *College English* 53 (1991): 135-155.

——. *Writing With Power.* New York: Oxford UP, 1981.

——. *Writing Without Teachers.* New York: Oxford UP, 1973.

Hatlen, Burton. "Old Wine and New Bottles." *Only Connect: Uniting Reading and Writing.* Ed. Thomas Newkirk. Upper Montclair, NJ: Boynton/Cook, 1986. 59-86.

Herder, Johann Gottfried. *On the Origin of Language.* Trans. Alexander Gode. Chicago: U of Chicago P, 1966.

——. *Reflections on the Philosophy of the History of Mankind.* Trans. T. O. Churchill. Chicago: U of Chicago P, 1968.

Hofstadter, Richard. *Anti-Intellectualism in American Life.* New York: Knopf, 1966.

Knoblauch, C. H. "Rhetorical Constructions: Dialogue and Commitment." *College English* 50 (1988): 125-140.

May, William F. "Adversarialism in America and the Professions." *Soundings* 69 (1986): 77-98.

McCarthy, Lucille P., and Stephen M. Fishman. "Boundary Conversations: Conflicting Ways of Knowing in Philosophy and Interdisciplinary Research." *Research in the Teaching of English* 25 (1991): 419-468.

Morton, Michael. *Herder and the Poetics of Thought.* University Park: Penn State UP, 1989.

Taylor, Charles. *Hegel.* New York: Cambridge UP, 1975.

Trimbur, John. "Consensus and Difference in Collaborative Learning." *College English* 51 (1989): 602-616.

Williams, Raymond. *Culture and Society: 1780-1950.* New York: Columbia UP, 1958, 1983.

TURNABOUT: STENHOUSIAN RESEARCH BRINGS BAD NEWS ABOUT BERTHOFFIAN-EXPRESSIVIST PEDAGOGY

Steve Fishman with Lucille McCarthy

O ur first two collaborative projects showed that Lucille McCarthy's systematic inquiries generated information about my classroom which escaped my own observations and journal reflections. I had read David Kaiser's note at the bottom of his draft, but his anger meant little until McCarthy told me she heard similar frustration in her interviews with Ginny Lewis. Likewise, Laurie Wilson's essay about punishment and incarceration was just another well-written student paper to me until McCarthy's patient questioning and post-semester conversations revealed Laurie's struggle to reshape views bearing her father's and brother's seals of approval.

UPGRADING OUR SOCIAL SCIENCE TECHNIQUES

Both of our first two studies relied on information we had collected in my fall 1989 Intro to Philosophy course. However, our data collection procedures were limited. I made entries in a daily teaching journal and photocopied all my students' papers. Although McCarthy did extensive phone interviewing, she actually visited my class only twice that semester. For our third project—given how impressed I was with the results of McCarthy's Stenhousian techniques—I arranged for my fall 1993 class to meet in my university's television studio, outfitted with four overhead recording cameras and numerous microphones throughout the room. Students had to cram their knees behind narrow desks, and the microphones were not always sensitive enough, but I was now determined to collect every Stenhousian datum I could find.

THE FOCUS AND FORM OF OUR THIRD STUDY

The focus of McCarthy's and my third project also took advantage of what we learned from our earlier work. If my classroom emphasis on expressivist writing and Berthoffian self-discovery was not isolating pupils like David Kaiser and Laurie Wilson, what was it doing to my students' relationships? What sort of community was it fostering in my classroom? Taffy Davies, a senior political science major who was part of our first study, gave me a clue. In a late-semester conversation, she told me she completed the assigned readings because she wanted to be an active part of the group, and doing the readings was her ticket in. So Lucille and I started our exploration of my Intro classroom community expecting to show that emphasis on personal writing and experience instead of isolating students, actually helps them become self-motivated participants in a close-knit, highly purposeful group. In the end, however, it would turn out that my initial hunch was inadequate, that Taffy Davies was the exception rather than the rule, and that the social structure of my classroom was far more complicated than I had imagined.

As to the form of our third study, "Community in the Expressivist Classroom," it mirrored our second. McCarthy and I divided the article into theoretical and classroom sections, and I, once again, took primary responsibility for writing the first part and Lucille primary responsibility for the second. Our earlier work had demonstrated the value of organizing our data around well-developed theoretical categories, and we decided to continue the same strategy. However, as in our previous project, the division of our report into two parts and our utilization of two distinct voices were not designed to limit the interplay of my theoretical explorations and McCarthy's analysis. Rather, our division was intended to provide the space we needed to fully employ our different strength while still listening carefully to one another. In fact, it was the back and forth between theory and classroom events which led me to surrender my original understanding of my classroom community, prompting me in subsequent semesters to alter my teaching in radical ways.

OUR THIRD STUDY BEGINS WITH SOCIAL THEORY

My efforts to find relevant theory for our third study were hardly an initial shopping trip. Somewhere in the back of my mind, I had always sensed that important class discussions in my course were those which shook free of institutional demands, like grades and attendance, and moved from contractual to more committed and wholehearted ground. That is, what I thought were moments of discovery in my class seemed to be characterized by my students' and my becoming involved in subject matter in ways that made time pass quickly. Those were the discussions which the bell interrupted, and, surprised when I checked my watch, I wondered where the period had flown.

This sense of class involvement, this feeling that we sometimes moved to unifying ground, resonated with certain social theories I had long contemplated. Years before I found the work of 19th-century sociologist Ferdinand Tonnies (1887/1993) clarifying for me. I was especially taken with his contrast of moral, close-knit village life (*gemeinschaft*) and competitive, contract-driven urban life (*gesellschaft*). I quickly made these distinctions my own, applying them to my relations with students and letting them color my contacts with facilitating strangers: the lawyers, doctors, and real estate agents in my life. To Tonnies's theoretical framework, I later connected the liberal-communitarian debate about the function of government, siding with the communitarians, embracing the neo-Aristotelian views of Alisdair MacIntyre (1981) on the importance of internal as opposed to external rewards of practice. So when I went looking for theories with which to approach my classroom's social structure, I was revisiting concepts at the center of strong personal and professional concerns. In applying these categories to my Intro course in fall 1993, I expected simply to gain a clearer understanding of what had been my long-standing suspicion: expressivist techniques help my students bring forward and value difference, and such respect for difference promotes a Tonnies-like caring village (a *gemeinschaft*) in my classroom.

APPLYING SOCIAL THEORY TO MY CLASSROOM

Initially, McCarthy's data seemed to support my hunch. Students described my class to Lucille as a family. One pupil, Myra Brandon, said I was more like a brother than a teacher. Fishman is like everyone else, Myra told Lucille, making mistakes and learning alongside the rest of us. Further, as McCarthy and I reviewed class videotapes, we realized I was using students' stories and backgrounds to grant them individualized expertise: small-town savvy and big-city street-smarts, workplace wisdom and responsible student know-how, radical feminist sensibilities and conservative traditional ones.

A Zenith Teaching Moment

About halfway through our project, a classroom moment occurred which seemed to symbolize what I took to be the desirable (*gemeinschaft*) social consequences of my Berthoffian, narrative-as-self-discovery approach. At the start of a class discussion on women's rights, I announced I would stay on the sidelines as a notetaker to allow students to lead their own conversation. I asked them to organize it around questions I had assigned about an essay by Harriet Taylor (1851/1970), John Stuart Mill's wife and collaborator. Thirty minutes into the period, there was a lull when the spontaneous pattern of one student answering a question and then calling on another to take the next question halted. I was sitting near Tate Osborne, keeping my head down, when I heard him whisper to his neighbor, "You do it, Blue. You take the next one." But Blue Pittman did not stir. After a long half-minute silence, Tate finally said, "Okay, if no one else will do it, I guess I will," and the pattern of responding and calling on another student revived.

At the time, Tate's volunteering seemed the zenith of my teaching life. He came forward, I thought, because he wanted to serve the group. In his voice, I heard Tonnies's ideal *gemeinschaft*, a group held together by devotion to common cause, shared experience, and the joys of internal rewards. McCarthy's Stenhousian data seemed to support my interpretation of this special narrative moment. In postdiscussion interviews, students indicated they volunteered because they did not want to let me down, because they wanted to be able to conduct their own discussion, wanted to show they could learn without my help.

A Nadir Teaching Moment

But things did not stay rosy for me very long. Unlike our first two studies, where our thinking moved along pretty steadily in one direction, I was jolted just a few sessions after our women's rights discussion. Once more, it was Tate Osborne. Throughout the semester, I had been giving short quizzes on the assigned readings to encourage their timely completion. In fact, I told students not to study for these quizzes or worry about the grades they earned on them. My purpose, I explained, was simply to stimulate everyone to make a good faith effort to understand and complete the assignments. A few days after the Harriet Taylor class, as I was handing back the latest set of quizzes, someone asked Tate why he generally did well on the exams. With a big smile, Tate said, "Because I never let myself get confused by doing the readings."

Although I held my tongue, I was totally deflated. I sensed that, despite his smile, Tate was telling the truth. Fortunately or unfortunately—I am not sure which—McCarthy was at the ready with her data. What Tate had said publicly in class, she told me, many students were saying to her in private. The readings, they explained to Lucille, were too difficult, hindered rather than enriched class discussion, and were assigned, one student speculated, just to make things difficult.

During the remaining weeks of the semester, I enlisted the class in a search for ways to make the readings more accessible, but nothing worked. By the close of the term, I decided I had squandered the one chance most of my Intro students would ever have to encounter and use the philosophic canon, and I resolved that next semester things would be different. However, and sadly, all I knew to do was to invoke external threats and rewards. When I gave out my spring 1994 Intro syllabus the following January, I indicated the first, full-period, essay exam would be on the third day of class.

OUR THIRD STUDY'S EFFECTS ON MY TEACHING

Bringing the Curriculum Back into the Classroom

"Community in the Expressivist Classroom" pushed me into significant changes in my teaching. Although I did not do away with my use of personal writing, I did work hard to blend it with more traditional techniques, like exams and study questions on the readings, in an effort to force students to engage the curriculum. This solution, however, was only the first step in what would turn out to be an ongoing reconstruction of my teaching. In time, and in the wake of future classroom studies with McCarthy, I would come to see my dilemma in broader terms than the ones with which I initially framed it. Instead of employing threats of exams to force students to take the philosophic readings seriously, I eventually saw my challenge as showing students ways in which they could use philosophic subject matter to satisfy and expand their own concerns. That is, I gradually saw my task as utilizing my authority not to coerce students to engage the curriculum but to organize my class so they could better see ways they themselves could use the curriculum.

Revisioning the *Gemeinschaft*, Democratic Classroom

Reconciling the student-curriculum dilemma was just part of the pedagogical reshaping precipitated by our third collaborative project. It also led me to see the social structures in my expressivist classroom in new ways. When, in the early 1980s, I heard the National Writing Project's call to be a learner in my own classroom, I did not anticipate it would have the complex ramifications our third study made visible to me. When I first heard the teacher–as–co-learner idea at a workshop in 1983, it sounded a deep chord in me, as I explain in Chapter 2. This strategy seemed not only more democratic and fair but also a good chance to model for students at least one set of learning strategies (mine), a way to reveal my own learning enthusiasms, challenges, and fears so my students would be encouraged to reveal theirs. It also appeared to be a way to display the seriousness with which I took the classroom assignments. Since I was writing with students—doing the papers, exams, and in-class freewrites along with them—students would see we were not involved in mere busy work.

However, Tate Osborne's announcement that he was ignoring assigned texts signaled that my we-are-all-learners approach was having only limited success establishing a *gemeinschaft* community devoted to exploring the philosophic canon. Unbeknownst to me, my stress on equality was also promoting a rights-based (*gesellschaft*) structure in which one set of rules for everybody implied that there could be no leadership without consent of the governed. This *gesellschaft* consequence of my approach defeated my chances of getting students to work with the curriculum because they respected my communal leadership and wanted to be part of the group. This rights-based equality was leading students, at times, to work not for the group but for their own individual interests.

Thus, our third study left me in a stream of complicated ideological currents. I was knee-deep in the challenge of treating each student equally and encouraging his or her individual self-direction while, at the same, trying to promote the internal rewards of cooperation and conjoint philosophic thinking and reading. In other words, if I were going to reach the *gemeinschaft* side of the expressivist classroom, I had to steer my Berthoffian, self-discovery canoe around *gesellschaft* shoals. That is, while trying to use my Berthoffian stress on personal writing to develop a cooperative group of inquirers, I had to be aware that this same approach could also lead students to see themselves as autonomous individuals competing for academic awards. The challenge of working with these two consequences—*gemeinschaft* and *gesellschaft*—of expressivist teaching remains with me to this day.

Our Third Study's Effects on Our Research

Perfecting Our Stenhousian Techniques

As a reading of "Community in the Expressivist Classroom" shows, videotaping turned out to be essential. As already indicated, McCarthy's systematic review of these tapes helped us recognize *gemeinschaft* in the way I called on students across the semester. It was no longer Tate Osborne, but Tate from small-town Stanfield, North Carolina, not just Kent Davis, but Kent, the older student fireman, and Myra Brandon became Myra, the good-hearted, class den mother. Results of McCarthy's analysis interacted with my speculations on social and political theory. This data-theory integration gave us our first confirmation that equality in my classroom, as I had anticipated, was not sameness, not a formula, like one correct answer per question. To the contrary, although each student's comments were going into a single class discussion pie, students did not feel a similar response was expected from everyone. Equality seemed more about uniqueness, mutual care, need, and respect than single-standard competition or uniformity.

Of course, McCarthy's social science work was also crucial in revealing that this view of my classroom as a caring, close-knit village was only one part of the story. Her indexing of student writing and oral interviews was key to my interpretation of the second critical incident involving Tate, the moment which forced me to acknowledge that students were not doing the course readings, that a form of contracting, self-interested, *gesellschaft* society was also very much alive and well in my classroom.

Valuing Berthoffian Narrative Methodology

"Community in the Expressivist Classroom" is our first investigation which turns on sudden and surprising incidents. As I have just explained, the contexts which McCarthy and I develop around these incidents are the result of her social science inquiry. However, we see our sensitivity to these moments as Berthoffian, rather than Stenhousian, because they do not emerge from repeated categorizing or analysis of data. Quite the opposite, they jump out at us, exciting our storytelling inclinations, our sense that something has occurred which deserves attention. I take this sort of sensitivity as central to Berthoff's emphasis on narrative methodology. That is, these critical incidents set off our narrative antennae not just because they are essential to our classroom stories but because they are essential to our life-long intellectual journeys as well. Moments like those involving Tate strike me because they change not only the way I see my students' learning and my teaching but also because they alter the way I see the story of my ideational life. It is for this reason that I characterize the emotional Geiger counters we use during classroom inquiry as "Berthoffian investigatory tools."

Other practitioner inquirers who write about their methods also discuss the significance of critical incidents for classroom research (see Hubbard & Power, 1993; Newman, 1998). However, their discussions are included in the course of elaborate and helpful, but thoroughly Stenhousian, advice: ways to collect data, store them, reshuffle them, analyze them, and share them. In my view, these practitioners underplay the Berthoffian significance of these incidents, the way they are rooted in the stories of teachers' own intellectual and pedagogical histories. For example, the theory behind "Community in the Expressivist Classroom" explores the nature of equality, commitment, and shared values in cooperative inquiry. These concerns, as I have explained, have long been woven into my daily experience. Why? Because if nothing else, there is a touch of the perpetual outsider about me, the figure darkened by porch shadows forever window-staring at firelit hearths. This sense of isolation makes me edgy and watchful. No wonder, then, that I have spent much of my life dreaming communal utopias, overlooking their potential for domination and overzealousness to find the belonging I have continually sought.

So when Tate Osborne looks up from his crinkled paper to mumble, "Okay, if no one else will do it, I guess I will," it is hardly surprising that I say to myself, something important is going on here. Likewise, it is obvious why my Berthoffian Geiger counter goes off when a few days later Tate says he is not doing the readings. When Tate speaks, he unwittingly tumbles my house of cards, betrays the failure of my efforts to create Plato's academy in my classroom, to present course readings as sacred texts I am pledged to pass on safely to Tate and his classmates.

Given the strong attention teacher-research theorists give to elaborate data gathering and analysis, some practitioner inquirers may be led to overlook the significance of their own intellectual backgrounds. In my experience, no first day of notetaking is really the first day. It is, more accurately, another chapter in an ongoing exploratory life, and without articulating these broader connections, teacher-researchers may miss important sources of motivation and insight for completion and extension of their work.

It is the fact that, for Lucille and me, classroom research has helped us write central chapters in our own intellectual lives that makes Berthoff's stress on narrative methodology so helpful. It is also why, at a deep level, our work, no matter its starting point or stimulating occasion, circles back to re-examine and see anew the same underlying themes: alternative communal visions, different ideals of equality, various ways of knowing, learning, and teaching. In short, our own research suggests that the more closely we integrate our teacher stories with our own long-term intellectual journeys, the more powerful will be their potential for illumination.

OUR THIRD STUDY'S EFFECTS ON OUR COLLABORATION

As foreshadowed in Chapter 5, McCarthy and I gained insight from "Community in the Expressivist Classroom" about what shared work meant in our collaboration. Not only was it impossible for us to divide our labor and responsibilities in ways which were numerically equal, our enriched view of democratic arrangements helped explain why we could not swap tasks for very long when these rubbed against the grain of our fundamental inclinations. In the final sections of Chapter 3, Lucille explains the new appreciation of qualitative, as opposed to quantitative, equality we both developed when, early in our joint research, we switched insider-outsider roles. The discomfort of that semester-long experiment, with Lucille as insider-teacher and me as research-outsider, was more understandable after we completed our study of community in my classroom. We now saw that our switch was motivated from a sense of fairness, the sort of I'm-no-different-from-you orientation that, beginning in the 1980s, I employed in my own teaching. There is something healthy and eye-opening about this sort of authority sharing, and it can also be an effective style of leadership. But as we came to recognize other ways to understand fair and democratic participation—more *gemeinschaft* ways—we saw that we could be equals not by being the same but by employing our different skills as best we possibly could for a common cause.

Finally, our third study taught us to respect our Berthoffian instinct for important stories, for dramatic moments whose deep roots allowed us to build illuminative teacher tales, to blend data and theory in ways that produced meaningful classroom research. Although we continued, in subsequent projects, to videotape, photocopy, and keep journals, Lucille and I came away from our third piece more open to special classroom incidents. In fact, in our very next project, our new confidence in our narrative sensitivities came quickly into the foreground. But, oddly, somewhere between our third and fourth projects, we forgot the importance of theory. Lucille and I discuss that mishap in Chapter 9. At this juncture, however, we reprint our third study, "Community in the Expressivist Classroom."

COMMUNITY IN THE EXPRESSIVIST CLASSROOM: JUGGLING LIBERAL AND COMMUNITARIAN VISIONS

Steve Fishman and Lucille McCarthy

I n our article "Is Expressivism Dead?" we discussed ways in which social constructionist goals can be achieved in an expressivist classroom. We found that classroom techniques and objectives are more hybrid than is acknowledged in current theoretical debates about pedagogy in the composition field. Whereas our earlier study focused on individual students' writing, our present research looks at relationships among students and between students and teacher in an expressivist environment. As a result, our present work highlights issues of community, in particular, the diverse forms of authority, reward, and structure which develop in a classroom that emphasizes self-discovery.

Although community and power relationships between students and teachers have been a concern for composition researchers for at least a decade (J. Berlin; Bizzell; Clark; Harris; Kent; Pratt, "Utopias," *Imperial*; and Shor), many questions remain. Two of these are the focus of this article: 1. What happens to teacherly authority and grades when empha-

This article first appeared in *College English*, 57 (January 1995), 62-81. Copyright 1995 by the National Council of Teachers of English. Reprinted with permission.

sis is upon honoring students' voices as well as the teacher's disciplinary one? 2. What communal structures emerge when emphasis is on generating and positioning difference in the classroom?

In the opening part of our two-part article, Steve Fishman, drawing upon sociological and political theory, takes up the first of these questions and suggests that teacherly authority can be established along a spectrum with liberal emphasis on individual equality at one extreme and communitarian emphasis on organic wholeness at the other. Current discussion in composition studies generally favors the liberal view that, at least ideally, communities are assemblies of independent, equal members who convene to discuss differences and, where possible, work to achieve individual objectives (Bullock et al.; Ellsworth; Orner; Trimbur). By contrasting this liberal view with an opposing view of community as an organism of cooperating heterogeneous parts, Fishman offers new vantages from which to view classroom authority. In the process, he struggles with one of the problems central to community theory: how to take advantage of what we find freeing in the liberal emphasis on individual equality without ignoring what is desirable in the communitarian emphasis on coherence and shared values. From a pedagogical point of view, Fishman struggles with how to encourage student-teacher equality while, at the same time, generating faith in his own leadership as disciplinary-initiator. He finds that he draws upon both liberal and communitarian ways of establishing authority. In particular, he learns that he uses his liberal authority to construct a situation in which he can exercise communitarian leadership. He also discovers that at times he juggles these alternatives inappropriately, confusing both himself and his students.

In the closing part of our two-part article, Lucille McCarthy provides a naturalistic account that speaks to the second of our two questions, describing communal structures in Fishman's expressivist classroom and observing how different voices are generated and positioned. Her study also returns to our first question concerning teacherly authority and grades. As she focuses on the liberal aspects of Fishman's class—respect for individual rights and voices—she provides details about the ways in which his liberality limits his disciplinary authority, specifically his power to introduce classic philosophic texts to his students. As she focuses on the communitarian aspects—group commitment to common practices—she shows how this ideal confuses his attempts to assign student grades. McCarthy concludes by describing how, from this teacherly struggle, Fishman works toward clearer understanding of the liberal and communitarian visions in his expressivist Introduction to Philosophy classroom.

LIBERAL *GESELLSCHAFT* AND COMMUNITARIAN *GEMEINSCHAFT* IN THE CLASSROOM
Steve Fishman

I characterize traditional power relationships between teacher and university student as those of master-stranger. In my own undergraduate and graduate experiences at Columbia University in the 1950s and 1960s, professorial control was used in lordly and mysterious ways. Within this orientation, my teachers presented classic texts and asked students to emulate these works without explicit instruction about techniques or procedures. My professors assumed students were philistine strangers, lifting the professional gate for only those few who proved themselves worthy, who managed to develop their own strategies for replicating the disciplinary paradigms. Although I chafed under this approach, I lacked the imagination to create alternatives and spent my first fifteen years of teaching reproducing significant features of the lordly approach I so abhorred. My teaching in those early years stressed lecture, explication of classic texts, and demonstration of philosophic arguments.

However, in a 1983 Writing Across the Curriculum workshop I learned about expressivist pedagogy, and, feeling liberated, I radically altered my teaching. Impressed by the call to become another learner in my class, to share my drafts as well as my answers to my own student assignments, I began a ten-year journey toward surrendering masterly authority in my classroom. But expressivism has proven to be a pedagogy with complex social consequences. Its liberal tendency, which led me to treat myself as just another student, had the welcome consequence of promoting the communitarian ideal of organic solidarity. However, it also had the undesirable consequence of undermining my capacity to function as communitarian leader, that is, as disciplinary-initiator. Confronted with these confusions, I join the composition field's current quest for informative models of classroom structures and student-teacher relationships.

Our field currently offers a variety of metaphors for classroom community, including Pratt's "contact zones" (*Imperial*), Young's "cities of strangers," and Giroux's "border crossings." To these models, I add three more ways of looking at classroom community which I take from social and political theory: 1. the distinction between *gemeinschaft* and *gesellschaft* relations, classically elaborated by Ferdinand Tonnies in 1887; 2. the idea of rights-based as opposed to common value-based societies, central to liberal-communitarian debates in political philosophy; and 3. the contrast between internal and external rewards of practice, discussed most recently by Alasdair MacIntyre. I introduce these models and concepts because they enlighten the conflicts in my classroom between various communal visions, sources of authority, and types of reward. These polar concepts intertwine and reverberate with one another, but, in what follows, gemeinschaft and gesellschaft are my starting points.

In the late nineteenth century, Tonnies contrasted agricultural and industrial societies, arguing that relationships in pre-industrial villages, for example, revolve around common goods that reflect deeply rooted family patterns, or what Tonnies calls "Gemeinschafts of blood" (42). To be in gemeinschaft is to form a totality with others, to share common ancestors, land, or ideas. Time and again, Tonnies reminds us that gemeinschaft is organic, a whole whose various parts serve their unique functions while working toward a common good. Gemeinschaft transactions are for the benefit of the organism—family, town, guild, or church—rather than for individuals themselves. As Tonnies explains:

> Family life is the general basis of life in the Gemeinschaft. It subsists in village and town life. The village community and the town themselves can be considered as large families, the various clans and houses representing the elementary organisms of its body; guilds, corporations, and offices, the tissues and organs of the town. Here original kinship and inherited status remain an essential, or at least the most important, condition of participating fully in common property and other rights. (228)

As organic, family-based communities give way to modern, urban societies, gemeinschaft arrangements are replaced by gesellschaft ones. According to Tonnies, the constitutive relationships of village life are displaced by utilitarian exchanges among unattached, urban individuals. City people "come from all corners of the earth, being curious and hungry for money and pleasure" (228). They are uncomfortable with their class, discontent with their life-stations, and use rather than enjoy one another. Their dealings with others are instrumental, means to personal ends, rather than efforts at caring. Tonnies argues, "In Gesellschaft every person strives for that which is to his own advantage, and he affirms the actions of others only in so far and as long as they can further his interest" (77). Since relationships in gesellschaft occur between independent, contracting parties acting in their own interests, their exchanges are limited and professional, their contracts made and broken with relative ease.

Tonnies's distinction between gemeinschaft and gesellschaft associations helps me see confusions about authority in my classroom previously hidden from me. Over the past ten years, as I moved more and more into the expressivist camp, I emphasized the liberal aspect of expressivism. I tried hard to be a co-learner in my classroom, to soften the intimidating quality of canonic texts, and to emphasize student and teacher self-discovery. Although I largely achieved these particular expressivist objectives, I found that as it became easier to reach equality and self-discovery, it became harder to get students to read classic philosophic texts, students often skipping assignments or protesting that such reading was too difficult. This development led me to worry that my classes were becoming "touchy-feely," paradigms of student indulgence and teacher irresponsibility.

When I borrow Tonnies's terms, however, I can create another interpretation of my frustration. This second interpretation suggests that there are at least two ways I establish teacherly authority. There are gesellschaft ways in which I contract to deliver certain grades to individual students for certain kinds of work. In other words, for the liberal or gesellschaft dimension of expressivism, authority rests on formal properties, my evenhanded application of classroom rules and contracts. But there are also gemeinschaft ways in which I motivate students to work, not for individual gain like grades, but for communal ends that benefit all members of the group. In other words, for the communitarian or gemeinschaft dimension of expressivism, authority rests on trust, my ability to convince students I'm working in their best interests. Drawing upon Tonnies, I can see my classes as confused efforts to use both gesellschaft and gemeinschaft ways of developing authority rather than as abject failures to develop any authority at all.

When I employ Tonnies's communal models, I also discover a previously hidden social consequence of expressivist liberalism within the contractual situation, namely, that as I establish individual equality for myself and my students, I also bring about intimacy, trust, and friendship, the sorts of relationships which are unpredictable and hard to govern in accordance with contracts. So within this liberal, expressivist context, a second ideal emerges, a gemeinschaft in which contracts are left behind and authority is generated by shared devotion to common goals—in my own classroom, devotion to an environment in which certain forms of philosophic inquiry can flourish. Using Tonnies's two communal ideals, therefore, I understand better my inability to direct students to my disciplinary canon. I had succeeded so well in becoming an equal co-learner with my students that, as we moved closer to a gemeinschaft environment of trust, I was unable to establish my disciplinary-initiator authority well enough to motivate students to read difficult texts.

The gemeinschaft-gesellschaft distinction clarifies the multiple ways I relate to my students and the different ways of generating authority these relationships afford. The liberal or contractual way is appealing because of its safety. It is based upon rules, and however those rules are established, they clarify legitimate expectations and responsibilities for all who are party to them. In important ways the liberal approach limits our risks since the rules, if successful, minimize surprise and shift responsibility from personal judgment to agreed-upon contracts. By contrast, the allure of gemeinschaft is its promise of less rule-governed relations, the chances for fuller cooperation, contact, and acceptance.

This leaves me with a model of teaching in which I begin in the convener's or manager's role, handing out syllabi and establishing ground rules, but because of tendencies in my expressivist approach, I find myself moving from manager to the role of wise elder or disciplinary-initiator. Tonnies's suggestion that learning and initiation occur in familial rather than contractual situations helps explicate my disciplinary-initiator role. He writes:

> Handicraft and art are passed on [in gemeinschaft] by teaching and example, like a creed, as if they were a dogma and religious mystery. They are, therefore, more easily preserved within the family, handed down to the sons, shared by the brothers. (63)

When I play this gemeinschaft teacherly role, disciplinary canons can take on the power of sacred texts, and classroom routines can become rituals devoted to the perfection of academic practices. This Tonnian concept of gemeinschaft captures one model of the classroom which generates much of my teacherly passion, exciting the zealot in me who, I admit, wants to convert all my students into responsible, innovative, fair, and open-minded philosophers. However, despite the attractiveness of this particular classroom ideal, I recognize that intimacy and full trust have their dark sides, their potential for manipulation and victimization. Advantages and disadvantages of the gemeinschaft and gesellschaft ideals of community—ideals which are both present in my expressivist classroom—come forth clearly in the ongoing communitarian-liberal debates within political philosophy to which I now turn.

Communitarians are the contemporary proponents of gemeinschaft associations, which they characterize as based upon common values, histories, and narratives. Liberals, by contrast, defend gesellschaft associations, which they characterize as based upon individual rights, on the pursuit of one's own goods in one's own way. Articulating the communitarian position are theorists like Alasdair MacIntyre, Charles Taylor, and Robert Bellah, who argue that social disintegration in industrial countries results from emphasis upon rights to the exclusion of shared values. Focus upon individual rights, communitarians claim, leaves us without a sense of common purpose. As a result, we view ourselves as isolates, weighing alternative actions to maximize personal gain. Rights-based societies are forced to get along without common moral standards or foundations. This means, following MacIntyre, that in exclusively gesellschaft or rights-based classrooms, students would see each other as competitors and have little or no appreciation of their common intellectual heritage or their shared responsibility for protecting, modifying, and developing the practices of that heritage.

In other words, communitarians would argue that chiefly gesellschaft classrooms focus too narrowly on what MacIntyre calls the "external goods of practice" rather than the "internal" ones (187-96). Gesellschaft approaches stress external rewards like grades and status, whereas more gemeinschaft approaches stress internal rewards like the joys of cooperative inquiry and discovery. What interests me is that however necessary the contractual agreements and relationships in my classroom, I believe that if I do not develop some appreciation in my students for the internal rewards of philosophic inquiry, such inquiry will disappear for want of new and innovative practitioners. If my students are only interested in external rewards, the grades, they will see my disciplinary practices as forgettable means to separable ends. When I add this distinction between types of reward to what I learn from Tonnies, I see even more clearly that I am using my gesellschaft authority and its external rewards to lure my students into situations where I can exercise my gemeinschaft authority and promote internal rewards.

By contrast to communitarians who focus upon the importance of the common good and internal rewards of practice, liberals, like John Rawls and Isaiah Berlin, focus upon individual rights, in John Locke's terms, upon our rights to life, liberty, and possessions. It follows that, for liberals, the function of government is to protect individuals, to defend around every citizen a zone of freedom (however broad or narrow) which is inviolate against any claim, power, or class. And, since liberals also believe that the many goods in life—justice and generosity, courage and prudence, genius and public welfare—are often incompatible, individuals will necessarily face difficult choices (I. Berlin 167-68). This means that, for liberals, freedom of individual choice is the ultimate value, and governments should insure individual freedoms rather than promote any particular conclusion about the good life.

John Stuart Mill's *On Liberty* captures aspects of liberalism's essence. Mill tells us, for example, that although alcoholism is harmful, both to addicts and to those around them, we should protect the rights of those who wish to drink excessively (80-85). In other words, although we may know what is good for alcoholics better than alcoholics themselves know, Mill counsels against direct intervention since he believes it is better to risk self-inflicted harm than lose opportunities to exercise the individual choice and moral courage which enable us to be human.

It follows that liberals, like Mill (perhaps because of his revulsion at the dictatorial nature of his own education), would stare in disbelief at my proposal to employ gemeinschaft authority or position myself in the classroom as elder representative of sacred practice. They would view such an approach as encouraging faith in authority and tradition, leaving students unprotected, without rights—encouraging dependence rather than the independence required by political democracy. However superior the knowledge of teachers may be, however benevolent their intentions, most liberals believe that faith in tradition or gemeinschaft authority is just too dangerous whatever its short-term desirability.

Liberals' distrust of gemeinschaft unity in the classroom is matched by their distrust of it in the larger society. They argue that gemeinschaft solidarity and organic wholeness spawn authoritarianism. When overall structure and wholeness are uppermost, those who are unhappy with their allotted stations are marginalized, and there is little room for dissent. To liberals' objections, communitarians answer that emphasis upon equality in liberal society makes people unhappy with their differences. Communitarians say that, despite their dangers, organic structures, at the least, help people make sense of their differences, enabling them to see themselves as contributors to a whole whose prosperity they share. Communitarians try to turn the tables on liberals by arguing that, without a sense of belonging, citizens in a liberal society lack identity with their commonwealth or nation and, as a result, refuse to participate in public life. According to communitarians, it is the disintegration of public life in liberal society, not organicism and gemeinschaft solidarity, which spawns dictatorship.

Interestingly, John Dewey, who saw himself as a "radical liberal" (*Liberalism* 45), sides with communitarians when he analyzes the ills of modern American democracy. Dewey presents America's political ennui as the result, in part, of an overemphasis upon individualism. For Dewey, individuals are never isolated from or suppressed by society because they are constituted by their social memberships. Viewing freedom as independence from others is, according to Dewey, "an unnamed form of insanity" (*Democracy* 44). In *The Public and Its Problems*, he defines social democracy organically: ideally, in democracy, individuals have a share "according to capacity" in directing activities of the group and participate "according to need" in the fruits that group work sustains (147). It would follow, for Dewey, that students in our classrooms should be treated as equals, not in the quantitative sense of having equal votes or even getting equal grades for equal work, but in the qualitative sense of making their own distinctive contributions and extracting their own distinctive rewards from class associations. As much as it might grind against certain liberal inclinations, Dewey says equivalence is not mathematical or physical sameness. Rather, it is measured by our distinctive capacities to give and take from associated actions. In other words, Dewey puts welfare above mathematical equivalence. Applied to schooling, it means we must demand of our students and of ourselves as teachers the best and most distinctive contributions we can give, and this implies different standards for each of us. In this way, Dewey suggests, we can realize the difficult task of preserving both equality and difference in our classrooms.

Nevertheless, liberals would insist that the fruitfulness of communitarian oneness is overstated. Most liberals believe the best we can do is agree on ways to extend and defend individual liberties. They believe that governments which do more, which encourage a common vision of the good life, threaten political democracy. They argue that past communities displaying singular purpose have ignored or victimized significant portions of their populations. (For recent and detailed liberal critiques of communitarianism, see Galston; Kymlicka; Phillips.)

No matter the persuasiveness of communitarians like Tonnies, MacIntrye, and Taylor on one side or liberals like Mill, Isaiah Berlin, and Rawls on the other, my primary concern with the gemeinschaft-gesellschaft distinction and with the liberal-communitarian debate has to do with insights they provide about my expressivist approach. These distinctions help me recognize the dialectic in my classroom between two communal ideals, two types of teacherly authority and student reward. The metaphor I propose for my teaching is juggling, in particular, juggling the roles of gesellschaft convener and gemeinschaft initiator. I play the convener, establish liberal authority, in order to protect students' rights to the values and languages they bring to my class. I play the initiator role, establish communitarian authority, in order to honor, modify, and enhance the practices and conversations of the discipline I represent.

Of the two kinds of authority, I find it more difficult to generate the gemeinschaft sort, at least in part because of my university setting. My university is dominantly gesellschaft, students working independently, signing syllabi as contracts with four or five teachers each semester. Yet, despite this gesellschaft or liberal context, I continued to strive to build communitarian organicism, to develop moments when my classroom treats the philosophic enterprise as if it were a family tradition or religious quest. Each semester, there seem to be classes in which I am driven to replace the rows of individual, gesellschaft desks with a communitarian or gemeinschaft dining table around which I lead students in the study of holy texts. That is, I have had a blind instinct that the learning I seek for my students involves, at least at certain times, a sense of family or guild, and, during these moments, it requires mutual faith in the power of the experienced initiator-teacher.

Looking at my Introduction to Philosophy course with Tonnies and the liberal-communitarian debate in mind shows me two kinds of authority in my classroom and how they can work together, how one kind of authority (liberal) can sometimes lead to the other (communitarian). But it also reveals moments when they work at cross-purposes. As a result, I see better why some gemeinschaft or communitarian moments conflict with gesellschaft, liberal ones, and why some of the classroom events that are most important to me are impossible to reward with gesellschaft grades. I have in mind Tate Osborne as he looked up from his crumpled paper to mumble, "Well, if no one wants to answer question three, I suppose I will." I think of Aaron Wilhite reaching across his desk at the end of a class period to hand out assignments I'd forgotten to distribute. But that's another part of our study, the part my colleague, Lucille McCarthy, is in a better position to report.

TEACHING AS JUGGLING CLASSROOM IDEALS
Lucille McCarthy

In my closing section of this two-part essay, I describe Steve Fishman's and my efforts, first to articulate the social structures in his course—the way differences are positioned—and then to link these arrangements to his growing awareness of the interaction of gesellschaft and gemeinschaft ideals in his expressivist classroom. In Fall, 1993, we began our observations of Fishman's Introduction to Philosophy class, a group of twenty-three students from various majors. By mid-semester we agreed that students were gaining confidence in their voices within an open and trusting atmosphere, and many students spoke of self-discovery. For example, Aaron Wilhite, a business major from Los Angeles and 6' 5" power forward on the basketball team, told me in an interview at mid-semester about his first paper. It was a philosophic exploration of personal values which helped him remember he was not self-made. He had not become a Division I basketball player all by himself. In fact, he had been luckier than most of his friends in the support he had received along the way, and he realized it was time to pay back. Aaron also reported he had become more confident about speaking up in class: "In discussion I can say whatever's on my mind, and I know my views will be respected and used."

Aaron's testimony about self-discovery and growing confidence was echoed by others in the class. Rayvis Key, a chemistry major and cross-country runner from Pilot Mountain, N.C., remembered a discussion early in the semester on ideal views of marriage. It was the first time Rayvis had heard other people's ideas on this topic, and they helped him articulate his own. "I've never felt so valued as a class member," Rayvis commented. "Even quiet people like Aaron have a lot to contribute. Dr. Fishman makes us braver because he's open with us too. We know he won't tear us down for anything we say." These students' comments, coupled with other data, led me to believe this class was an expressivist's dream come true.

That Fishman helps his students to self-discovery by combining personal narrative with philosophic method had become clear to us in our earlier studies (see also McCarthy and Fishman, "Boundary Conversations"). However, we were now more interested in what happens *among* students and teacher when individual self-discovery is promoted. We had read James Berlin's theoretical conclusion that expressivisim leads to social isolation. According to Berlin, individuals connect with one another in an expressivist environment only insofar as their "privately determined truths" happen to correspond, any communal arrangements existing only to serve individuals (486). In our observations of Fishman's expressivist classroom, however, we were seeing something quite different.

Far from self-absorbed and isolated individuals, we saw caring students who genuinely wanted to hear from one another. In fact, as they described the class to me at mid-semester, they spoke of a kind of brotherly and sisterly affection. Aaron described class members as having a "close bond" and explained that when they ran into each other on campus or in the gym, they said "Hey" and talked about class or laughed at something Fishman had said. Aaron told me, "This isn't like my other classes where I don't know anybody. In here we're like brothers and sisters. No one's afraid to talk, and everyone is accepted. We're so close we can even disagree with each other, and no one holds a grudge." Aaron speculated that if someone were to threaten this "fun and caring atmosphere "—that is, say something personally offensive to Fishman or a fellow student—that person would "feel heat from the group." Myra Brandon, an arts and sciences major from Winston-Salem, agreed and included Fishman in the group: "He's like one of us, a brother who's learning alongside us. He makes mistakes too, and he's not afraid to make fun of himself."

The "close bond" Aaron and Myra described was evident in my mid-semester visits and class videotapes. Students chatted animatedly and laughed together before class started, and they continued discussing as they walked out. They and Fishman referred to each other by nick-names they'd created together and frequently recalled shared stories or events. In fact, the group seemed to be writing a kind of communal history. Each class began with a ritual reading of the classnotes, a summary of the previous session written by a different student each time. I felt I was watching a kind of multi-voiced invocation marking the movement across a border into this community from the world outside. The day's author tapped the first reader, who then ceded to the next person in the circle when the paragraph changed. At the close of the reading, the author named the next notetaker, passing on the responsibility as if he or she had survived an initiation and now beckoned to a younger sibling. Although the classnotes served serious community-defining functions, they were often greeted with riotous laughter because they were laced with underlife language (Brooke), jibes at fellow students as well as at Fishman and his assignments. These put-downs and ironic asides were marks of caring, according to Myra, even flattering to some people, and could never be pulled off except among close friends.

At mid-semester, then, Fishman and I were seeing a classroom in which, despite James Berlin's predictions, students were talking about *both* self-discovery *and* brother/sisterhood, individual insight as well as commitment to the group. As we analyzed this data, we struggled to find language to describe the communal patterns we were seeing. Our first breakthrough came as we watched a videotape in which students, after reading parts of Dewey's *Reconstruction in Philosophy*, were exploring definitions of modernity. Fishman asked them, "What does it mean to be modern?" and then called on one student after another. In the middle of that discussion, Fishman turned to twenty-eight-year-old Kent Davis, a fireman, and asked, "Kent, what's the view from the firehouse? What would they say down there? Hey, someone get a mike on Kent." Fishman stopped the videotape and turned to me. "I remind myself of Fred Allen on 'Allen's Alley.' I'm a radio talk-show host, interviewing experts, getting the news from various places to bake into my pie." Although Fishman worried for a minute he might actually be no more than an entertainer, his hearing himself play talk-show host alerted us to the fact that his class was indeed made up of student "experts," people speaking from somewhere, standing for something, and thereby contributing uniquely to the common project. From that moment on, we paid attention to these roles.

In addition to Kent the fireman, there were, among others, Shannon Garraghan, a business major, to whom Fishman turned for a feminist's point of view; Mac Cozier, the dredlocked soccer star and class clown who played faultless straightman to Fishman's bumbling teacher; Myra Brandon, the caretaker; Rayvis Key, the earnest student always on the right page; Blue Pittman, baseball player and future minister; Tate Osborne, the Good Ol' Southern Boy; and Aaron, basketball star and, as it turned out, former L.A. gang member. Fishman, too, revealed where he was coming from. Early in the semester he shared his freewrite about growing up in the Bronx, a thin Jewish boy frightened by World War II and subways.

That students and teacher had by mid-semester defined unique roles for themselves may not be so surprising. Expressivist pedagogy often results in students writing their histories as they develop their own voices. Fishman had consciously asked students do this in the first three weeks of class, putting off introducing philosophic texts until students had heard their own voices. Several recounted to me at mid-semester an early class freewrite about their hometown values. They had been fascinated by their differences, remembering particularly the interaction between Aaron and Tate Osborne, an earth science major and baseball player from Stanfield, N.C., population 900. On the videotape I watched as Tate explained he had grown up believing in fair play and honesty, knowing and trusting nearly everyone in town. Although small town life has its disadvantages, Tate admitted, he plans to return to Stanfield after college. As discussion progressed, Tate recounted a fight he'd been involved in one Saturday night outside a local bar. A man was hitting his girlfriend, and Tate jumped in to protect her. He didn't know the victim, but he did know that the match was unfair. And, he told the class, he would do it again.

As the video continued, I saw Aaron lean forward and shake his head. In L.A., he said, if you see a fight, you keep right on going. If it doesn't concern you directly, you stay out of it. Meddling in others' affairs, even if you see someone being victimized, is just too dangerous. Aaron was amazed Tate would take such a chance. Tate was shocked Aaron wouldn't.

Fishman and I were, then, at mid-semester observing students contributing uniquely to the group, playing roles developed within this expressivist environment. Fishman's class apparently was not, like many at the university, comprised of interchangeable students competing for the same answer. Rather, members' differences loomed large. But how, exactly, were these differences organized? What did they accomplish?

Although Fred Allen as pie baker was better than nothing, we knew we did not yet have our organizing concepts. So we turned to social and political theory and experienced our second breakthrough. We had read Tonnies the previous summer and now realized his description of organic community, gemeinschaft, might help us describe certain moments in Fishman's class. In this model, community members are like different parts of the human organism—hands, ears, blood, feet—each performing its own function toward a common goal: keeping the body alive. Might we say that at times students in Fishman's class were cooperating for benefit of the whole rather than competing for personal gain? Were we seeing gemeinschaft organicism developing within the broader class framework of gesellschaft individualism? We had evidence, in fact, that students at times put group welfare ahead of their own. Shannon and Rayvis both told me they had revealed personal information they'd rarely told anyone in order to "help out" the discussion. They had sensed the group's need at a particular moment for examples only they could supply, and they trusted the group to respect their confidences.

As we went back and forth between our data and Tonnies's theory of communal organization, John Dewey was also in our heads. Dewey's vision of social democracy resembles gemeinschaft, an organic whole whose members contribute to and take from common projects in distinctive ways, each "according to capacity" (*Public* 147). And when we contrasted Dewey's and Tonnies's organicism to the liberal ideal of community as an assembly of political equals, we got further clarification. Whereas many liberals view community members as mathematically equal, each guaranteed the right to maximize personal advantage, Dewey understands equality among members in qualitative terms and points to the family as an example. The baby is equal, not because she's the same as other members, but because she plays her appointed role, her needs taken care of without being sacrificed to the superior strength of other members (*Public* 150; Fishman 318-22).

Dewey's and Tonnies's metaphors of community as family appealed to us because they echoed what I had first heard from students. Like these theorists, students seemed to be appealing to an idealized family, several commenting that the care and respect in Fishman's class were actually greater than that they experienced at home. For example, when Aaron described Introduction to Philosophy as one big family, he assured me it was not like his own. "*My* family is crazy," he said.

So when Fishman and I returned to our data, we had Dewey's and Tonnies's images of organicism in mind. And in class discussion on November 18, gemeinschaft began to emerge for us as we watched students work together toward a shared goal. While Fishman sat quietly by, his students baked their own philosophic pie. They came to class with their answers to take-home questions on Harriet Taylor's 1851 essay, "Enfranchisement of Women," and these provided a framework for the hour-long conversation. But it was particular moves by several students that insured the group's success, and these thrilled Fishman. After class, he told me, "I looked up when Tate volunteered to take question three, and I saw his seriousness, this right-handed pitcher with a mustache and crewcut. Tate decided to risk himself, to take responsibility for the group, and at that moment I thought, 'This is what I live for.'"

Tate's action stood out because discussion on the first two questions had been initiated by pairs of students, one calling on the other in friendly tag-team operations. And the videotape shows Tate, in the twenty-second pause before he spoke, hoping to repeat that, touching his baseball teammate, Blue Pittman, and whispering, "Call on someone." When Blue would not, Tate stepped forward: "Well, if no one wants to answer question three, I suppose I will." Tate at that moment took a leadership role, not for personal gain or external rewards but for the sake of the group.

As Fishman and I analyzed the November 18 videotape, he told me, "It was everything I could want: kids listening, looking at one another, answering each other. Everything they did was for internal rewards and the common good." In fact, students conducted their exploration so patiently they achieved what for Fishman is a primary internal reward of philosophic practice: a genuine discovery. They were able to juxtapose their own and other's views in ways that gave some of them at least fresh angles on their original positions. For example, Scott Mosier, a psychology major from Delaware, described such a discovery as the class explored an example of gender inequality proposed by Shannon: the furor over the recent admission of a female to the all-male Citadel Military College of South Carolina. Scott wrote in his Class Reflection Log, "At first, I felt strongly with Tate and others that a female shouldn't be allowed into the Citadel, that such a long-standing tradition should be left alone. But then Mac remembered the time when blacks couldn't participate. This brought a new light on the issue." Rayvis Key focused less on particular discoveries when he spoke to me a few days later than he did on class cooperation. "We wanted to succeed," he told me, "to be self-sufficient. We didn't want Fishman to have to jump in, and I think that discussion shows we've come a long way. We can learn by ourselves."

The story of Fishman's class is, so far, almost unbearably rosy. There is, however, another side. If Fishman was celebrating the communal success of his class on November 18, he was, by November 23, telling me he felt "disappointed," "rejected," "downhearted," and "insulted." He lamented, "I've taken risks in that class, broadened the relationship with those students beyond the usual professional classroom contract. I've treated them with dignity, but they're not affording me the same respect. I've been trying to bridge between their lives and the texts. They're doing fine with life, but they're not reading."

What insulted Fishman was his realization that although many students had indeed contributed admirably to group practices on November 18, some had apparently not read Taylor at all, had written answers to their study questions during class. This was particularly dispiriting because students had asked for these questions to help them understand texts they claimed were too difficult. Tate, in fact, had dramatically brought underlife language to the surface two weeks earlier when he explained to Fishman and the class that he had not let reading interfere with his in-class performance. In admitting this publicly, students later told me, Tate was speaking for many of them. But now students were not taking the study questions seriously either. Fishman lamented,

> I bring them into the decision-making, hoping they'll feel greater commit-
> ment to our work together, but they're disrespectful. That's the problem with
> starting with personal experience; students are going to leave this course
> thinking they've done philosophy. And that's not fair to them. They've not
> done the reading, so they've not really tasted the challenge and rigor of
> philosophy. If they're to become sophisticated in their own discussions,
> they've got to understand something of what's already been said.

In late November, then, with students ignoring assigned texts, Fishman not only felt insulted, he also felt guilty: he believed he was not doing a good job of philosophic initiation.

In order to understand Fishman's unhappiness, we tried out our theoretical tools. Our first explanation of Fishman's inability to motivate student reading was simple: a collision between Fishman himself as gemeinschaft leader and his students as gesellschaft contractors. So at first, when Fishman was most down, he blamed his students: "They are probably just like most other people in the culture. They're after the best contract they can get, the highest grade for the least work."

On second thought, however, Fishman blamed himself. He had demoted external rewards in favor of internal ones, putting only "satisfactory" or "unsatisfactory" on student responses to study questions. And then when internal rewards didn't work—when students didn't enjoy the reading or see how reading might enhance class discovery— Fishman felt powerless. He had no incentives with which to direct students to the philosophic texts he thought were essential, although not sufficient, for their initiation.

So our collision theory, we realized after the semester ended, was not the whole story. Fishman's unhappiness also came because the gemeinschaft moments in his expressivist classroom represented an incomplete version of gemeinschaft. Although we had glimpsed an element of organicism—students contributing uniquely to common ends—some crucial components were missing. An organism has a head, but Fishman was, as students repeatedly testified, an equal, not an experienced guide. He was their "brother." So Fishman's classroom was a gathering of novices without an elder. And as such it was cut off from its history. Despite all his students' grateful talk about self-discovery, Fishman felt he'd shortchanged them.

Fishman had hoped students' commitment to the group and taste of internal rewards in class discussion would provide motivation when it came time for the demanding texts. If students did not care about Harriet Taylor or Dewey or Plato, they would read in order to be part of the group. However, it was their very success in establishing their own voices and roles within the group which led students to resist the reading. Many of them were people who had seldom, if ever, been "experts" in any classroom, and they were so excited by their own voices and discoveries that they saw the texts as unwelcome intruders. Blue Pittman, for example, told me class was just not as exciting when Fishman directed them to the texts, and, in a spirit of genuine helpfulness, he explained this to Fishman in his Class Reflection Log. Blue pointed out that whereas many hands were raised during discussions of personal issues, only a few people talked about the texts. Myra Brandon was also dismayed by the reading, and when I asked her why she thought Dr. Fishman assigned it, she smiled and raised her eyebrow. "To punish us, I think."

Students' views of the texts obviously bore little resemblance to Fishman's. Far from sacred scripts, the charter documents of a rich, 2500-year heritage of inquiry, students saw the reading as unexciting, irrelevant, and just too hard. Fishman, now with neither gemeinschaft nor gesellschaft authority, was beside himself by late November with a class he said felt out of control. Instead of the situation ten years earlier where teacher and texts were masters, and students were strangers, he now had the reverse. The canon had become the outsider. Although he spoke to the class about his disappointment, and several students apologized for writing answers during discussion, few ever actually wrestled with the reading assignments. The class just got better and better at philosophic discussions—that is, as long as they were talking about issues directly related to their lives.

Because Fishman tried to play both the role of liberal brother and that of gemeinschaft elder, grades, as I have suggested, were a problem. In a well functioning organic community, there are no grades. Successes and failures are based on how well one carries out one's unique function. As Dewey suggests, in an organic community there are different standards for everyone, and, ideally, there are no external rewards. Rewards come instead from the satisfaction of contributing to the common good—in Fishman's class, to the maintenance of shared philosophic inquiry. However, when it came time to give external rewards, to grade students' writing, and students disagreed with Fishman, he was upset, not because they argued with him, but because of the arguments they used. Rather than focusing on what they wrote, some students questioned Fishman's expertise, suggesting he knew no more about philosophic practice than they. This bothered him because he realized if he was ever to have moments of ideal organic functioning, members would have to exhibit a faith in their leader not evident in his class.

Fishman was particularly bothered by Blue Pittman's mid-November reflections on his essay grade because they highlighted Fishman's and Blue's very different assumptions about Fishman's status in the gemeinschaft moments in this classroom community. Blue maintained, in a conversation with me, that his B+ would have been an A in any English class, and when Fishman offered the class Blue's and Fishman's papers as models, Blue saw as many flaws in Fishman's as in his own. Fishman was shocked. He had left that modeling class in late October, celebrating; he had shown students what he valued in both papers, and they had indeed challenged him and offered as many suggestions for his as for Blue's. This pleased Fishman because he interpreted it in gemeinschaft terms: he was the experienced practitioner whose initiates were preparing to become full-fledged members of the guild. But Blue viewed it differently.

He saw the reading of the papers, with its implicit reference to grades, not as a gemeinschaft moment of group cooperation, but as a gesellschaft competition between himself and Fishman.

Although Fishman was temporarily upset with Blue, he once again realized he himself was responsible for the confusion. On reflection after the semester ended, Fishman saw the foolhardiness of attempting to discuss external rewards, rooted in the contractual gesellschaft classroom of equals, within what he had confusedly hoped would be a gemeinschaft, idealized family classroom. He saw how these two ideals, both stimulated by his expressivist commitment, were, at that class moment, in conflict. He was again dismayed—this time, not by Blue, but by the problems he himself had created for students.

Despite the clashes between the communal ideals of gemeinshaft and gesellschaft, the Fall semester of 1993 ended with students more closely bonded than ever, many claiming they learned a great deal about themselves and others, some even saying they'd changed core values and positions. Aaron, for example, wrote in his Class Reflection Log that he would not only take with him a fresh version of his own history, he also respected women and Southerners in new ways. And Fishman admitted, ultimately, that something very special had happened in that class. People felt part of a group, important, respected, cared for.

CONCLUSION
Steve Fishman and Lucille McCarthy

What do we learn from this double study? We return to the two questions with which we began. One, our initial question: what happens to teacherly authority and grades when emphasis is upon honoring student voices as well as disciplinary texts and traditions? We found that Fishman's expressivist techniques provided him with a rich opportunity for meeting these twin goals. However, Fishman's dual attempts were not equally successful. He had more difficulty developing classroom space for his discipline's texts than he did generating a safe place for student expression.

How do we account for Fishman's difficulties? These were, we believe, caused by the presence in Fishman's class of two competing forms of authority—liberal and communitarian—and their very different visions of community and reward. Fishman's expressivist techniques led him, in their liberal tendencies, to become just another classmate: his students' "brother," as several phrased it. However, these same expressivist techniques, especially those that led to the development of distinctive student roles, also promoted gemeinschaft, moments when class members cooperated as an idealized family. This happened because class achievement of the equality portion of the liberal vision generated intimacy, trust, and shared secrets, and, thereby, set the stage for the communitarian commitment to shared goals.

Paradoxically, however, Fishman's near success in reaching the liberal ideal of equality with his students made it difficult for him to realize the communitarian ideal of experienced elder, the knowledgeable practitioner introducing newcomers to the wisdom of his tradition. And, because of these competing visions, he also confused his students and himself at grade time with mixed messages about liberal external rewards and communitarian internal ones. So it was the clash of liberal and communitarian classroom ideals, both rooted in expressivism, which created Fishman's trouble.

Two, our second question: what communal structures emerge when emphasis is on generating and positioning differences in the classroom? The expressivist techniques Fishman employed, his efforts to be just another student in his class, his willingness to make students "experts," to ask them for information he honestly did not have, worked well to generate differences. As students developed their classroom roles, their differences were positioned and valued as if they were vital parts of an organism working toward a common goal, in this instance the maintenance and enrichment of philosophic inquiry. Frequently students reported that they contributed to class discussion in an effort to add fresh perspectives and complicate the treatment of issues.

Although we recognize that organicism has been vigorously challenged by liberal theorists, we still find it helpful to view at least certain moments in Fishman's classroom as organic wholes or systems, a metaphor first suggested to us by Fishman's own students. And although we acknowledge that such systems can at times be too hierarchical and the roles they prescribe for their members too limiting, we found that most students in Fishman's class flourished as they established clear parts for themselves in the unfolding classroom drama. In addition, the organic metaphor, as developed by Tonnies and Dewey, suggested ways in which both student difference and equality could be encouraged. For while it is true that not all parts of an organism are equal in the sense they are all the same, they can be equal in the sense they contribute their best to a common objective.

In Fishman's classroom, the image of organicism as ideal family was, thus, a fruitful way of thinking about positioning difference, a way of preserving difference without its becoming a source of jealousy or win-loss debate. Students within this organic atmosphere accomplished what we believe many teachers hope for: they listened carefully to one another, explored their differences, experimented with novel points of view, and were pleased to report modifications of their initial positions.

We end this study with the same call with which we concluded our earlier *College English* piece. Fishman's struggle with alternating visions of the ideal classroom, with alternating views of reward and authority, shows the complexity of the expressivist classroom. Whereas most discussions of classroom community in our field revolve around theoretical debate between either-or alternatives, our study suggests that in actual classrooms the communal alternatives are richer and more mixed than our field's theoretical discussions would have us believe. Again, we ask other researchers to bridge the theory-practice gap by grounding their discussions of communal theory in classroom data.

WORKS CITED

Bellah, Robert N., Richard Madsen, William M. Sullivan, Ann Swidler, and Steven M. Tipton. *Habits of the Heart: Individualism and Commitment in American Life*. New York: Harper & Row, 1985.

Berlin, Isaiah. *Four Essays on Liberty*. New York: Oxford UP, 1970.

Berlin, James. "Rhetoric and Ideology in the Writing Class." *College English* 50 (1988): 477-94.

Bizzell, Patricia. *Academic Discourse and Critical Consciousness*. Pittsburgh: U of Pittsburgh P, 1992.

Brooke, Robert. "Underlife and Writing Instruction." *College Composition and Communication* 38 (1987): 141-53.

Bullock, Richard, John Trimbur, and Charles Schuster. *The Politics of Writing Instruction: Postsecondary*. Portsmouth, NH: Heinemann, Boynton/Cook, 1991.

Clark, Gregory. "Rescuing the Discourse of Community." *College Composition and Communication* 43 (1994): 61-74.

Dewey, John. *Democracy and Education*. 1916. New York: Free P, 1967.

———. *Liberalism and Social Action*. Vol.11 of *The Later Works (1935-1937)*. Ed. Jo Ann Boydston. Carbondale: Southern Illinois UP, 1991. 3-65.

———. *The Public and Its Problems*. 1927. Athens, OH: Swallow P, 1988.

———. *Reconstruction in Philosophy*. 1920. Boston: Beacon P, 1962.

Ellsworth, Elizabeth. "Why Doesn't This Feel Empowering? Working through the Repressive Myths of Critical Pedagogy." *Feminisms and Critical Pedagogy.* Ed. Carmen Luke and Jennifer Gore. New York: Routledge, 1992.

Fishman, Stephen. "Explicating Our Tacit Tradition: John Dewey and Composition Studies." *College Composition and Communication* 44 (1993): 315-30.

Fishman, Stephen M., and Lucille Parkinson McCarthy. "Is Expressivism Dead? Reconsidering Its Romantic Roots and Its Relation to Social Constructionism." *College English* 54 (1992): 647-61.

Galston, William A. *Liberal Purposes: Goods, Virtues, and Diversity in the Liberal State.* Cambridge: Cambridge UP, 1991.

Giroux, Henry A. *Border Crossings: Cultural Workers and the Politics of Education.* New York: Routledge, 1992.

Harris, Joseph. "The Idea of Community in the Study of Writing." *College Composition and Communication* 40 (1989): 11-22.

Locke, John. "Of Political or Civil Society." In *Of Civil Government.* 1690. Chicago: Gateway, 1955. 62-77.

Kent, Thomas. "On the Very Idea of a Discourse Community." *College Composition and Communication* 42 (1991): 425-45.

Kymlicka, Will. *Liberalism, Community and Culture.* Oxford: Clarendon P, 1989.

MacIntyre, Alasdair. *After Virtue.* Notre Dame: U of Notre Dame P, 1981.

McCarthy, Lucille P., and Stephen M. Fishman. "Boundary Conversations: Conflicting Ways of Knowing in Philosophy and Interdisciplinary Research." *Research in the Teaching of English* 25 (1991): 419-68.

Mill, John Stuart. *On Liberty.* 1859. Arlington Heights: Harlan Davidson, Inc., 1947.

Orner, Mimi. "Interrupting the Calls for Student Voice in 'Liberatory' Education: A Feminist Poststructuralist Perspective." *Feminisms and Critical Pedagogy.* Ed. Carmen Luke and Jennifer Gore. New York: Routledge, 1992.

Phillips, Derek. *Looking Backward: A Critical Appraisal of Communitarian Thought.* Princeton: Princeton UP, 1993.

Pratt, Mary Louise. "Linguistic Utopias." *The Linguistics of Writing: Arguments between Language and Literature.* Ed. Nigel Fabb, Derek Attridge, Alan Durant, and Colin McCabe. Manchester: Manchester UP, 1987. 48-66.

———. *Imperial Eyes: Travel Writing and Transculturation.* New York: Routledge, 1992.

Rawls, John. *A Theory of Justice.* Cambridge: Harvard UP, 1971.

Shor, Ira. *Empowering Education: Critical Teaching for Social Change.* Chicago: U of Chicago P, 1992.

Taylor, Charles. *The Ethics of Authenticity.* Cambridge: Harvard UP, 1991.

Taylor, Harriet. "Enfranchisement of Women." *Essays on Sexual Equality.* Ed. Alice S. Rossi. Chicago: U of Chicago P, 1970. 93-121.

Tonnies, Ferdinand. *Community and Society.* 1887. Trans. Charles P. Loomis. New Brunswick: Transaction Publishers, 1993.

Trimbur, John. "Consensus and Difference in Collaborative Learning." *College English* 51 (1989): 602-16.

Young, Iris Marion. *Justice and the Politics of Difference.* Princeton: Princeton UP, 1990.

Don't Swap Pedagogical Recipes without Swapping Theoretical Ones

Steve Fishman with Lucille McCarthy

The fourth and final classroom study we include in this volume—
"Teaching for Student Change: A Deweyan Alternative to Radical
Pedagogy"—led us unexpectedly back to John Dewey's philosophy and to a wider context for our integration of Stenhousian social
science and Berthoffian narrative inquiry. But that was the ending point
of our fourth collaborative project, not the start.

Study number four began with a shared discomfort Lucille McCarthy
and I felt as we read claims that classrooms should encourage student
confrontation. These claims came from a variety of sources. For example,
critical pedagogists argue that without some form of instructor intervention or "backloading," by which teachers challenge prejudices embedded
in student language, pupils will remain blind to their own ideologies
(Shor, 1996, p. 41; see also Fitts & France, 1995; Shor, 1992). Along
similar lines, radical feminists hold that misogynist and homophobic
talk in classrooms and student texts needs to be directly confronted if
schools are to reform mainstream attitudes (Jarratt, 1996). And, likewise,
writers focused on minority issues suggest that traditional schoolroom
practices—what counts as normal school talk and decorum, the collective

"we" of classroom conversation—if left unquestioned, perpetuate our culture's, as well as our schools', injustices (hooks, 1994).

TELLING A TEACHER STORY BUT NEGLECTING THEORY

McCarthy's and my questions about confrontational classrooms were brought into focus by Mary Louise Pratt's "Arts of the Contact Zone" (1991). In her article, Pratt applies to classroom practice a sociolinguistic theory about ways colonized people adopt for their own purposes the literary forms of the ruling class. Just as powerful literature occurs at the borders of dominant and subordinate cultures, Pratt argues, so, too, significant learning occurs in classrooms in which students understand their differences as clashes between dominant and oppressed peoples. She advises that students engage in a form of intellectual disrobing to recognize the prejudices of their own views, the legacies of privilege and subordination, the stories of colonization and resistance they have inherited. But in her article, Pratt does more than lay out a theory. She also invokes her success with Stanford students to support her claim that agonistic or "contact zone" classrooms bring about—via pupil-to-pupil confrontation—acknowledgment of cultural imperialism, embarrassment at institutionalized oppression, and, as a result, dramatic student transformation.

My skepticism about Pratt's claims of dramatic student change, as well as my uneasiness about the wisdom of such confrontational strategy, was, of course, colored by my Berthoffian inclinations, my romantic desire for a community which is safe for personal voice and common cause. My negative response was also the result of the teacher research I had been doing with McCarthy. As I have explained, our discovery that students who share their personal experiences do not isolate themselves or antagonize others but, rather, generate sympathetic listening led us in subsequent projects to study my classroom's social space. And what we discovered suggested that fruitful discussion, at least in my Intro to Philosophy course, was the result of student respect for classmates and their unique contributions to common inquiry. That is, despite other shortcomings we identified in my trusting classroom environment, we found that students like Tate Osborne could hear classmates with quite different views and then feel secure enough, in a subsequent class session, to openly discuss the results of reexamining his own beliefs (Chapter 8, this volume; see also Fishman & McCarthy, 1998, p. 93).

Pratt's claims for confrontational pedagogy, then, appeared to challenge both McCarthy's and my findings as well as the overall wisdom of my Berthoffian approach, and my first reaction was, ironically, overly oppositional. Learning in my own class, I said to myself, never occurs via confrontation. In fact, so sure was I that learning is always the result of sympathetic consideration of dissonant points of view that whenever my own students' exchanges became heated, I interceded to stop them. Unlike Pratt, I wanted to reduce the chances of student embarrassment rather than promote them. In sum, at the start of my fourth project with McCarthy, I would have sworn there were no productive student confrontations in my classroom at all.

So, if we doubted the presence of fruitful, no-holds-barred debate in my Intro course, what was McCarthy's and my focus as we set out to explore Pratt's contact-zone pedagogy? We decided to look closely at those heated exchanges which arose spontaneously in my classroom, the very ones I moved to abort. And what McCarthy found when she looked behind these clashes surprised us. Her student interviews revealed a rich classroom underlife, mumbled conversations, secretly passed notes, and out-of-class relationships of which I was totally unaware.

For example, it turned out that a series of increasingly acrimonious questions and responses between Kyle Newman and Andrew Fitzpatrick about freedom of the will in my fall 1994 class—a series I interrupted when I thought they had gone back and forth in disagreement too many times—was better understood in the context of their family lives than their philosophic beliefs. After extensive interviewing, McCarthy learned that Kyle's older brother was often dismissive of Kyle in ways that resembled Andrew's style in our class. In surprisingly parallel ways, her interviews also showed that Andrew found Kyle highly offensive because Kyle's manner of questioning recalled Andrew's own father's approach, and Andrew and his father did not get along. This connection between negative family patterns and classroom exchanges was a revelation not only to McCarthy and me but to these two young men as well. Neither realized the source of his anger, each claimed, until speaking about it in the interview setting. McCarthy's data suggested, then, that if instead of quieting Kyle and Andrew, I had pushed them to reveal more about their differences, I might have engendered even worse feelings between the two with little promise of philosophic gain for either.

To make matters worse, McCarthy uncovered additional evidence of my ignorance of underlife forces influencing my students' exchanges. When she asked for classmates' reactions to the Kyle-Andrew disagreement, she found that the majority sided with Kyle, not because of the way he defended his views, but because they thought Kyle more attractive. Some of the women in class even confessed to trading notes which ridiculed Andrew's language and demeanor as too academic and pretentious. My hesitancy to adopt a confrontational pedagogy, then, appeared vindicated by McCarthy's data. To promote an extended debate between these two antagonists would have been to imagine I understood what the conflict was really about and how their classmates really viewed it. McCarthy's interviews and my talk with Kyle showed I was in the dark about both.

In addition to my ignorance, McCarthy also found that student connections outside of class—their participation in on-campus social organizations and athletic teams—made many of them reluctant to publicly voice their differences and explore unpopular, or controversial, opinions in class. As the published account of our fourth study shows, a number of students worried about how they would be perceived by others. Eric Shelton relates that he held his tongue in my course—refused to reveal his personal history and views—for fear he might be perceived as racist. Likewise, Sarah Marcotte explains that she denied her desire to openly speak in favor of blacks because of her concern that black classmates might think it presumptuous for a white person to do so. The more we looked beneath my students' conversations, the more I became convinced that much of the thinking behind what they said in class—and refused to say—was hidden from my view.

As a consequence of McCarthy's systematic inquiries, I became more uneasy than ever about encouraging all-out student confrontations. Since I was unwilling to try it in my classroom, we initially centered our fourth study around urging teachers to use caution when enacting contact-zone pedagogy. As we prepared to send our manuscript to *College English*, I was pleased with our work. It seemed plain to me that we were offering our readers more than just a teacher story or reminiscence. Thanks to McCarthy's systematic and triangulated investigations, I believed we had interesting data illustrating the dangers of pushing students into self-disclosures they might not in less confrontational classrooms make. To her credit, McCarthy was less sanguine about our work than I. Whereas the storyteller in me was insisting our dramatic account of Kyle's and Andrew's encounter would carry the day, the social scientist in McCarthy was doubting that my classroom as counterexample to Pratt's pedagogy would carry much weight with our readers.

STENHOUSIAN PEER REVIEW IN TEACHER RESEARCH

Two anonymous *College English* reviewers gave our manuscript a resounding thumbs-down. One respondent was particularly disgusted, asking "With all due respect, who cares about Fishman's classroom?" Louise Smith, *CE* editor, was kind enough, however, to allow us another try. Deciding we had been too negative and one-sided in our approach to contact-zone teaching, we tried to balance our cautions about it by showing sympathy for the frustration that radical pedagogists have with the conservatism of American public schools. We also attempted to acknowledge the insight which teachers—especially of minority and ESL pupils—derive from applying contact-zone theory to their students' efforts to learn mainstream ways without betraying their own.

A second round of reviews by *College English* yielded the same thumbs-down result. But in the long run, this second round turned out to be fortunate. Louise Smith, going out of her way once again to be fair, had added a new reviewer for the evaluation of our revised manuscript, and this third respondent gave us valuable criticism. In essence, he or she said, Pratt provides a theory to explain and contextualize her classroom practice, but Fishman offers none to support his. This reviewer went even further, suggesting that my pedagogy seemed to be Deweyan and that, although we briefly referred to Dewey at the close of our submission, we had in no way sufficiently developed or explored his theory's role in my classroom.

With this outside reviewer's help, it did not take us long to refocus our study. He or she helped us use theory to gain enough distance from our work to see our data differently, to realize that, in our attention to the potential risks of contact-zone teaching, we had blocked out Berthoff's advice about the importance of integrating theory with any exchange of pedagogy. As I foreshadow at the close of Chapter 5, our efforts to artic- ulate Deweyan concepts eventually helped us see both our collaboration and my classroom in more complex ways.

Recognizing Fruitful Conflict in My Classroom

With regard to my Intro course, Deweyan theory helped us complexify our view of pupil conflict. Writ large in Dewey's (1933/1960) work is the idea that thinking arises as an accompaniment of doubt, a hazard or obstacle forcing us to reexamine our strategies and goals. But Dewey also recognizes that, despite the importance of challenge and dissonance for learning, inquiry depends upon cooperation: shared values, common objects of allegiance, and what he calls "social intelligence" (1916/1967; 1938/1963).

Mindful of Dewey's view of the value of both conflict and coopera-tion for learning, we were able to reinterpret our data. For the first time, I could recognize and acknowledge the moments of productive conflict in my Intro course. Eventually we reshaped "Teaching for Student Change" so that, instead of denying the importance of pupil confrontation, we distinguish among types and contexts for pupil confrontation. We suggest that cooperative classroom situations can do more than simply seduce pupils into mainline consensus. They can also help students feel comfortable about sharing and living with their differences. We also suggest that teachers focus on the quality or process of classroom debate, attending more to its effect on student habits—their open-mindedness, courage, and sincerity—than on the specific beliefs or ideas which students take from such debate. We conclude that, whereas we see no evidence of the sudden and dramatic student changes which Pratt (1991) claims for contact-zone classrooms, we can show that student conflict in my more cooperative setting does produce pupil change. The student change we uncover, however, in contrast to Pratt's, is slow, piecemeal, and grudging. In the end, the reshaping of our article—adding Dewey's theory of learning and communal inquiry to our pedagogical recipe—led us to jettison the Kyle-Andrew exchange since it appeared unproductive for both students. Instead, we focus our revised study on the student change precipitated by a memorable—and conflict-filled—classroom exchange which also took place during fall 1994, a session in which my Intro students applied the free-will issue to the plight of Native Americans.

Before outlining the form our final report took and its implications for teaching and classroom research, I note that one immediate result of adding a strong theoretical ingredient to what had been an exclusively pedagogical discussion was that our revised manuscript was quickly accepted by Joseph Harris at *College Composition and Communication* and appeared in the October 1996 issue.

THE FORM AND METHOD OF OUR FOURTH CLASSROOM REPORT

The final version of "Teaching for Student Change" is divided into three sections. We begin by placing Pratt's pedagogy in the context of radical and feminist theory. We then contrast Pratt's orientation to Dewey's, paying special attention to the ways in which my own ideology borrows from Dewey's view of the cooperative aspects of learning. Finally, in the main section of our article, we examine the nature of student change in my "cooperative" classroom.

An Integrated Voice

Overall, "Teaching for Student Change" is more fully integrated than our earlier studies in two ways. First, McCarthy and I adopt a "we" voice throughout. That is, there are no separately authored sections, no changes of voice to spotlight either theory or classroom application. The principal reason is that theory only took shape during the course of our project. As already indicated, we did not start our research hoping to examine or evaluate Deweyan theory in my classroom. It just worked out that, after much of our data had been collected, we could finally recognize, with the help of peer review criticism, that we were watching a class whose under-pinnings were Deweyan. That is, my theory was so embedded in my practice that I did not understand it very well until someone else pointed it out.

An Integrated Method

Stenhousian Techniques on the Trail of Student Change
In addition to its "we" voice, the second way in which this study is more integrated is that our methods combined Stenhouse and Berthoff more seamlessly than in previous projects. Obviously, as our interviews about the Kyle-Andrew exchange show, our version of Stenhousian systematic,

self-critical inquiry was at work. McCarthy and I collected endless data, including videotapes, students' written texts, and numerous interviews. Her careful theme and pattern analysis as she sifted the data was crucial. Her coding of pupil texts and interviews helped us identify and follow the zigzag quality of student change in my Intro course: the ways students tried on novel views, retreated back to familiar ones, and then practiced, once again, their new ideas as they slowly—and, often, as if fearing disloyalty to sacred vows—challenged their deep-seated beliefs. In addition, our desire to be in conversation with other researchers, as Stenhouse urges, and our willingness to submit our work for peer review, as he also urges, were both important for our research. In these respects, then, the spirit of our inquiry was Stenhousian.

However, having enumerated all these analytic tools, what stands out for me about the methodology of "Teaching for Student Change" is McCarthy's and my use of our Berthoffian narrative sensitivities, our commitment to tell the story of one particularly dramatic class discussion. When we finally set aside the Kyle-Andrew encounter, we immediately turned to the one session of my Intro course that semester which both Lucille and I knew, from the start, was critical, one of those moments that bore upon the deepest parts of our teaching and intellectual lives.

A Berthoffian Nose for Story as an Instrument of Research

What was the nature of this critical incident? It was, once again, a glimpse into classroom cooperation or *gemeinschaft*, a moment when students and I forgot our marketplace or *gesellschaft* roles—degree candidate, wage earner, career seeker—and became more fully engaged and identified with the flow of classroom questioning and reflecting.

There was a focal point during that particular fall 1994 class discussion, a question I posed—Are Native Americans responsible for their high degree of suicide and alcoholism?—which caught my class's attention. At some implicit level, nearly everyone quickly knew we were talking about broader issues of racism and colonialism in America. Yet, despite the fact that there were 3 African American students sitting among 16 white students, no one was willing, at first, to face the issue directly. Then Shanderic Downs, who is black, pushed us closer. He said, "I don't blame the Indians for drinking. Everything they had was taken away; they had no hope," and he says it haltingly, quietly, half hiding his mouth behind his large hands. Of the first six students I call on, only Shanderic defends Native Americans, and, of the six, only Shanderic is black. So something dramatic and tense has entered the class. I mean I feel it in my chest and spine.

Then Karla Hembrick, also African American, sitting next to Shanderic, and even shyer than he, pushes us over the edge. "I know why Shanderic is sympathetic with the Indians," she says. "He's black, and blacks have suffered in this country just as bad." Almost everyone gets into it then, some white students supporting Shanderic's view, others denying it, talking about their own poverty and how no one gives white people any special breaks, and others just mumbling with their heads down toward their books. But we are taking turns and listening and showing respect until Martin Cibulskis, from New Zealand, says "Indians should just get off their butts; they're lazy, that's why they're so poor," and Sarah Marcotte and Kelly Snowden become enraged and start shouting at Martin, which sets off outcries from the far end of the room so that I intercede with my left arm raised and my right hand tapping my pencil eraser furiously on my desk. When I had gotten a few students' attention, I succeed in restoring calm by asking Ben Weart, who once traveled to Arizona, to describe the Indian reservation he visited there.

As indicated earlier, when McCarthy and I began our study we were on the lookout for drawbacks of student confrontation. But when we left my class's discussion of Native American oppression, we sensed that—whatever our preconceptions—we had witnessed something worth studying and that we needed to use all of McCarthy's social science skills to clarify its impact upon the participants, on Shanderic and Karla, on Martin and Sarah, and even on Eric Shelton, who mumbled but did not speak. In sum, as we worked on "Teaching for Student Change," McCarthy's Stenhousian positivism was integrated with Berthoffian narrative methodology, our own bodily and emotional register of what was important in my classroom. On the positivist side, we wanted to be systematic in our data collection, using multiple informants and various methods to triangulate the account we produced. We also wanted to reduce our biases, the chances of presuming we knew what my students experienced or could trust our initial interpretation of what had occurred. On the narrative side, we allowed our felt sense of student interest and energy—our Berthoffian noses for the dramatic—to redirect McCarthy's data collection efforts and, ultimately, the focus of our paper.

OUR FOURTH STUDY'S EFFECTS ON MY TEACHING

Recognizing and Shaping Productive Confrontation

McCarthy's and my fourth collaboration influenced my teaching in several ways. First, it opened me to productive confrontation in my classroom. In the process, it also clarified my aims for such confrontation, namely, increased student sensitivity to difference and self-criticism as opposed to alteration of student beliefs in order to bring them into line with my own.

Recognizing the Complexities behind Student Comments

The second significant classroom insight I took from this project was my high degree of ignorance about what lies behind students' in-class comments. Although in earlier studies I was surprised by what McCarthy's Stenhousian techniques revealed about my students, I was particularly impressed this time. Her inquiries helped me realize that encouraging students to recount personal experience in order to situate their views is not always desirable or feasible. As readers will see in "Teaching for Student Change," it turned out in Eric Shelton's case that there was a lot behind his silence following Shanderic's comments, and my respect for Eric's unwillingness to respond was, ultimately, productive. The Kyle-Andrew exchange also reveals that sometimes students themselves are not fully aware of the attitudes fueling their own disagreements. So, despite my continued belief in the value of connected knowing, our fourth classroom project made clear that I have to use my best on-the-spot judgment about when to push students to talk more about their backgrounds and when not to.

My ignorance about the complexities behind my students' comments particularly strikes me because my natural inclination is to assume their experiences are like my own. In other words, I generally imagine their lives are as ordinary, middle class, and mainstream as mine. "Teaching for Student Change" alerts me that this is rarely the case and that I need to use care in encouraging my pupils to situate their beliefs, something I do, as I have said, so we can better discuss the forces—the language, communities, and practices—supporting these beliefs. Not only am I continually surprised by the personal tragedies my students have endured, I am also frequently taken aback by their sensitivity.

Kyle Newman, for example, came to my office in an agitated mood the day after his disagreement with Andrew Fitzpatrick. Kyle was a senior from New Orleans who, at the time, intended to go to law school. He was in his mid-twenties, well-spoken, and appeared supremely confident in class. Yet my impression of him proved off-target. As soon he sat down that afternoon, he quickly began, "Did you see what Andrew did to me yesterday? When he said, 'With you, Kyle, it's always determinism this and determinism that. I'm tired of hearing about it!' he destroyed everything I've been building all semester. I've lost my credibility with the class, and there's no way I can go back."

In my efforts to calm Kyle, I told him that, from what I had observed, Andrew was a sensitive person who did not mean to offend him. I reminded him that Andrew's belief in free will was probably connected to his belief in God, and I suggested that when people feel strongly about an issue their words sometimes sound harsher than they intend. After we talked for a while, Kyle finally accepted my interpretation, and he did attend all subsequent classes. Sadly, however, Andrew's attendance became sporadic. I took him to be a very capable student, but I sensed he felt underappreciated in my class. His brief debate with Kyle seemed to be a turning point, and thereafter he took only a marginal role in class discussion despite my efforts to bring him back to the center.

Of course, I cannot and do not want to know everything about my students, nor would I want them to know everything about me. And I cannot protect them from every possible slight and affront. But I hold to the idea that my classroom, if it is to be effective, need not mirror the often harsh structure or competitive nature of out-of-school life. "Teaching for Student Change" not only alerts me to the possibility of fruitful classroom confrontation and the complexities of students' backgrounds, it also helps me see how much I want my courses to be as safe as I can make them for discussion and reconsideration of student belief. As a result, although I do, on occasion, push students to say more than they initially reveal about their views, I try to let them take the lead. Although I frequently offer the personal stories behind my own beliefs as an invitation for students to do the same, I generally leave it to them to decide how much of their out-of-school life they reveal to me and their classmates.

OUR FOURTH STUDY'S IMPLICATIONS FOR TEACHER RESEARCH

Integrating Stenhouse, Berthoff, and Theory

Our fourth study brings home to us, once again, the importance for teacher research of making theory explicit. Given McCarthy's and my intended audience—the peers and journals for which we write—a classroom story, no matter how dramatic, is not enough. Our experience writing "Teaching for Student Change" suggests that no matter how much data is collected, no matter how much theory is implicit in our classroom account, that theory needs to be explicitly related to competing points of view and applied to the local setting in ways which illuminate it and make the research more transferable.

More generally, we have learned the value of integrating Stenhousian systematic data collection, Berthoffian narrative, and explicit theory. Such a hybrid methodology yields teacher stories of more general interest, accounts which illuminate different philosophies of education as well as multiple informant perspectives. By themselves, teacher stories can, of course, offer compelling practical lessons and memorable student and teacher triumphs and failures. But as our final study shows, teacher stories, without theory, can be limiting. I needed Dewey's theories of learning and communal inquiry before I could become an outsider to my teaching, see myself anew, and experience practice-changing discovery. And because such goals are, in my view, what teacher research is all about, McCarthy's and my weaving together different research approaches with provocative theory is, I believe, worth the effort.

Experimenting with Methods and Report Forms

Our fourth project's integrated report form, the significant role that peer criticism played, and the readjustment of our focus from Kyle and Andrew to the Shanderic class, all suggest the advisability of methodological experimentation. Although McCarthy and I began our collaboration with strong commitments to the Stenhouse and Berthoff approaches, respectively, in the course of our work we have learned to be flexible, using these methods and report forms in various ways. At times, McCarthy has written sections which are thoroughly social science in tone and APA style in format, and I have written personally, trying to satisfy my Berthoffian inclinations and narrative instincts. At other times, as in this fourth study, "Teaching for Student Change," we integrate these approaches more thoroughly than we have in the past. This is not to say, however, that a blended or "we" voice is always appropriate. In fact, in studies subsequent to this one, we have returned to individually authored parts and have separated the theoretical from the applied sections (see Fishman & McCarthy, 1998).

OUR FOURTH STUDY'S EFFECTS ON OUR COLLABORATION

As McCarthy and I were concluding our fourth study, we were simultaneously planning a more ambitious project. We were sketching chapters for a book-length manuscript that would examine feminist, liberal, and communitarian influences on my pedagogy. It seemed a splendid undertaking at the time—and it still does—but its scope was large, and I was unsure how we might get started. Almost three months after we completed "Teaching for Student Change," McCarthy and I were talking about our future work when I told her I was not sure I had the courage for the encompassing project we had planned. "But a book on Dewey makes sense to me," I said. "It seems something the two of us could do." This was at the end of November 1995, and our chat made apparent to us that "Teaching for Student Change" was a critical incident in our research lives. It took a while, but this study eventually moved us into a clearing where our future research, which had appeared so difficult, now seemed to fit more comfortably into our histories, to carry forward the narratives of both our lives.

This shift in our research focus made sense because our fourth classroom study had pushed us to face Dewey's work head-on, and a larger project would enable us to continue this work, to look at Dewey more fully and carefully. A book-length investigation also made sense because it would allow us to expand the methods and report forms we developed in our second and third classroom projects. I could do the first half of the book, examining Dewey's pedagogical theory, and in the second half, Lucille could investigate the failures and successes of trying to operationalize Deweyan theory in my classroom.

So the most profound impact of "Teaching for Student Change" on our collaboration was that it opened the door on a 2-year effort to bridge the gap between Dewey's theory and actual classroom practice. This opening of a new research project turned out to be especially satisfying since, as I have already hinted, while our work moved forward onto fresh ground, it also seemed to move backward, helping us trace and deepen our earlier paths. We give way now for the public form of our fourth study, "Teaching for Student Change."

TEACHING FOR STUDENT CHANGE: A DEWEYAN ALTERNATIVE TO RADICAL PEDAGOGY

Steve Fishman and Lucille McCarthy

For at least a decade, composition researchers have argued that instruction should aim for social reform. These calls come from a variety of sectors: social constructionist, critical pedagogist, and feminist (James Berlin; Bizzell; Brodkey; Giroux; Luke and Gore; Shor; Trimbur). Prominent among the pedagogical tools of such reform is the idea of critique, the view that instruction should help students see their individual and social realities as alterable constructs, not as transcendent or immutable structures. In other words, we should help students recognize the values, discourses, and institutional practices which have shaped and help maintain their realities (Frazer and Lacey 20-25; Weiler 113-15). But the ultimate goal of such instruction is not simply critique, but critique leading to reform. As Henry Giroux puts it, we want instruction to help students develop "the language of possibility" or reconstruction as well as deconstruction (52). This focus on challenging student beliefs as a means of cultural reform has a rich history in American thought. As early as 1916, John Dewey envisioned the classroom as a vehicle for social change, emphasizing ways in which classrooms could foster the cooper-

This article first appeared in *College Composition and Communication*, 47 (October 1996), 342-366. Copyright 1996 by the National Council of Teachers of English. Reprinted with permission.

ative and community-building skills he believed necessary for inclusive and participatory democracy (*Democracy*, chapters 6-8).

However, more recently, some social reformers in composition studies have challenged the view, long associated with progressive education, that classrooms should be relatively safe and cooperative places. Whereas Dewey saw community as built upon common values and goals, these theorists and teachers, interested in confronting injustice more directly, have increasingly focused on "dispute and diversity" rather than "politeness and common ground" (Hayes 300). This reflects a growing impatience with the slow pace of social reform in America. The assumption is that "teaching for radical change" will speed reform and that this requires that students' subjectivities—especially their sexist, classist, racist, and homophobic discourses—be vigorously challenged (Sciachitano 300; Weiler 136, 144-45). This approach echoes that of bell hooks, who argues that safe classrooms protect the status quo and that politeness is disrespectful of students because it dismisses classroom diversity. Instead, hooks urges us to accept painful confrontation, to encourage tension and conflict, even if this leads students to dislike their classes and teachers (42). Susan Jarratt continues hooks' approach, opening her article, "Feminism and Composition: The Case for Conflict," with examples of sexist and racist student language which, she says, go unchallenged in classes which establish supportive and accepting climates (105-06).

The spirit of this sort of teaching for radical change seems to be broadened by Mary Louise Pratt, who more fully develops the hooks-Jarratt distinction between safe, polite classrooms and dangerous ones. Pratt also describes her students' transformations, how pain and rage lead to new revelation and respect in her course on culture, ideas, and values. She tells us her classrooms are places of powerful emotion where no one can hide, where everyone's identity is on the line. She writes,

> All the students in the class had the experience...of having their cultures discussed and objectified in ways that horrified them, all the students experienced face-to-face the ignorance and incomprehension, and occasionally the hostility of others.... Along with rage, incomprehension, and pain, there were exhilarating moments of wonder and revelation, mutual understanding, and new wisdom—the joys of the contact zone. (39)

And in his "Fault Lines in the Contact Zone," Richard E. Miller extends this argument for confronting diversity, claiming the conservative nature of current teacher preparation prevents us from allowing powerful words in our classrooms, from opening ourselves to unsolicited, oppositional, and transgressive student language.

For an example of radical pedagogy in action, we refer to the October 1992 *CCC* "Symposium on Feminist Composition," in which Karen Hayes describes her confrontation with one of her students, Al. She calls this confrontation invaluable, telling us that Al's sexist, classist, and racist slurs stirred minority students to face issues they might otherwise have avoided. Her debates with Al, she says, raised student consciousness in ways she never could have accomplished alone. In fact, she herself was so stirred by Al's outrageousness that she was able, in front of the entire class, to "flatly state that I disagreed with and was actually offended by his remarks" (303). Hayes believes that her students, especially females, were empowered by her willingness to confront Al and that this resulted in significant student change.

In sum, whereas relatively safe, cooperative classrooms—the sort Dewey pioneered, and Elbow, Murray, and Noddings have more recently forwarded—once seemed progressive, now some feminists and critical teachers argue that these so-called polite classes are actually *non*-progressive. They camouflage refusals to recognize the diversity, hierarchy, and injustice which exist both in our own classrooms and throughout society.

Our intention in this article is to defend a Deweyan approach as an effective alternative to radical or confrontational pedagogy. In saying that it is an alternative, we do not mean that Dewey thought that learning is risk-free or non-conflictual (*Experience and Nature* 201; *Reconstruction* 26). To the contrary, he makes clear that advance in science and art involves sharing and exploring sharply divergent ideas ("Authority" 142; *How We Think* 264). However, we believe the Deweyan approach is sufficiently different from radical pedagogy to represent an alternative for teachers who find certain kinds of conflict unattractive but who seek student critique and change. For although Dewey recognizes the importance of dissonance, he stresses that conflict must always occur within the context of appreciation for cooperative inquiry and the virtues which sustain it (*How We Think* 270-71). Although we do not deny that confrontation may result in student change for practitioners of radical pedagogy, and while Deweyan teachers may also use conflict to achieve student change, we believe that, given the different principles guiding Deweyan and radical classrooms, the nature of dissonance in each will be quite different.

After briefly outlining Dewey's educational theory, we will present a study of one of our classrooms—Steve Fishman's—in which he tries to follow Deweyan pedagogy, privilege diversity, and effect student transformation. In particular, we focus on the way students and teacher in this one classroom experienced various kinds of dissonance, which types they pursued, which types they aborted. In offering this classroom account, we not only present an alternative to radical pedagogy, we intend to achieve two other purposes as well, namely, to further explore a major figure in what Emig has called composition studies' "tacit tradition" (see also Fishman; Russell; Jones; Newkirk; Phelps), and to answer calls for studies of student experience in classrooms of change (Harris 36; Pratt 38).

DEWEYAN EDUCATIONAL THEORY BEHIND FISHMAN'S TEACHING

Two Educational Principles

From Dewey's extensive writings we extract two principles of learning. First, school learning should parallel learning which occurs in more natural settings ("Authority" 322-23; *Experience and Education* 52). That is, since maturation outside school is prompted by problems and difficulties, predicaments requiring reflection and readjustment, classrooms, according to Dewey, should simulate situations which allow students to experience genuine perplexity. As Dewey puts it,

> Thinking begins in what may fairly enough be called a *forked-road* situation, a situation that is ambiguous, that presents a dilemma, that proposes alternatives.... One can think reflectively only when one is willing to endure suspense and to undergo the trouble of searching.... To be genuinely thoughtful, we must be willing to sustain and protract that state of doubt which is the stimulus to thorough inquiry. (*How We Think* 14-16)

In emphasizing the importance of perplexity in education, Dewey distinguishes learning from assimilation and training. The latter he characterizes as leading to stability, conformity, and closed-mindedness, whereas the former results in experimentation, questioning, and open-ness. He warns that students who are not challenged by difference and who are left to feel comfortable in a "finished" world, will not develop "intelligence"—that is, the ability to respond to the inevitable uncertain-ties and fluctuations in real life. He writes, "The individual, the self, centered in a settled world which owns and sponsors it, and which in turn it owns and enjoys, is finished, closed. Surrender of what is possessed, disowning of what supports one in secure ease, is involved in all inquiry and discovery" (*Experience and Nature* 201).

Second, since learning in natural settings is not only a risky activity but also a social one—a process in which people develop shared language to achieve common goals—school learning, according to Dewey, should focus on the skills and virtues of cooperative inquiry (*Experience and Education* 58). These include respect for the intelligence, personality, and creativity of others; recognition that everyone has something to contribute to conjoint activity; and trust that evaluation of difference is a collective process ("Authority" 142; *Ethics* 329; "Need" 11-13). Dewey believes students have a natural disposition toward these virtues, a natural inclination to contribute what they can to common projects. He argues that the child wants to "work out something specifically his own, which he may contribute to the common stock, while he, in turn, participates in the productions of others.... The child is born with a natural desire to give out, to do, and that means to serve" ("Ethical Principles" 118-20).

Three Pedagogical Corollaries

Given these two Deweyan principles, what are the implications for teachers? One, lecture is replaced by student activity. Since perplexity is necessary for learning, lecture is called into question because it is an effort to deliver solutions to problems owned by others. That is, unless students themselves own the problems and actively explore them, solutions lack significance. As Dewey puts it, solutions cannot be passed from teacher to student "like bricks" (*Democracy* 4). Rather, only when students expe-rience perplexity and shape the problem in their own way can they supply the energy necessary for learning. In Dewey's words: "Since learning is something that the pupil has to do himself and for himself, the initiative lies with the learner. The teacher is a guide and director; he steers the boat, but the energy that propels it must come from those who are learning" (*How We Think* 36).

Two, the teacher sets the conditions for learning. Since knowledge cannot be passed directly, it follows for Dewey that the teacher must educate indirectly by shaping the classroom environment ("Child" 209; *Democracy* 19). This means establishing situations in which students face dilemmas they find interesting and relevant to their own lives. "Unless the activity lays hold on the emotions and desires, unless it offers an outlet for energy that means something to the individual himself, his *mind* will turn in aversion from it, even though externally he keeps at it" (*How We Think* 218).

Three, teachers and students must alternate roles to develop common understanding. Since instruction must be indirect, since students must own the problems and find their way to their own solutions, the instructor's leadership should be unobtrusive, the teacher being careful "not to forestall the contributions of pupils" (*How We Think* 270). As Dewey tells us, in shared classroom activity "the teacher is a learner, and the learner is, without knowing it, a teacher—and upon the whole, the less consciousness there is, on either side, of either giving or receiving instruction, the better" (*Democracy* 160). In other words, instructor and students should engage in cooperative inquiry so that they alternate roles, becoming sufficiently sensitive to one another's contributions that they develop common understanding (*Democracy* 30; "Need" 10).

Dewey's Educational Goals and Ideology

Dewey's educational goals focus on the development of certain habits and dispositions rather than on the acquisition of a fixed body of knowledge or belief. He maintains the world is changing. He calls it "unstable, uncannily unstable" (*Experience and Nature* 38). As a result, he wants students to think for themselves, to be able to engage in the ongoing critical and constructive tasks demanded by the human condition ("Construction"). That is, Dewey wants students to develop flexibility or "intelligence"—the ability to respond to novel situations, access their culture's resources, reshape their plans, and take positive residue from these experiences. Of course this critical and constructive process must be done, if it is to be moral, in cooperation with others.

It follows that Dewey would oppose teachers who have static pedagogical ends, for example, particular political positions they want students to adopt before leaving their classrooms. For Dewey, such educational objectives put too much emphasis on a relatively minor product of the educative experience. It is not particular political or ethical stances which he wants for students. This would be too much like indoctrination. Rather, he tells us:

> [Education] is a process of development, of growth. And it is the *process* and not merely the result that is important. A truly healthy person is not something fixed and completed. He is a person whose processes and activities go on in such a way that he will continue to be healthy. Similarly an educated person is the person who has the power to go on and get more education. ("Need" 4)

In our own time, Dewey's educational objectives, "growth" and "enriched experience," are so familiar, they may seem devoid of ideological bias. However, it is hardly necessary to say they are not. They reflect Dewey's deep conviction that there are no absolute, transcendent truths ("From Absolutism"). Rather, all claims—religious, political, scientific, and ethical—are social constructions, fallible and always subject to revision (see Kymlicka 64). Dewey's goals also reflect his liberal respect for the individual, the value of eccentricity and personal uniqueness, because without individual challenges to cultural constructions, he believes, there can be no social reform or adjustment (*Reconstruction* 188).

Fishman's Educational Goals and Ideology

Like Dewey, Fishman's ideology is liberal. In other words, at the core of Fishman's teaching is a respect for the integrity of each student and a commitment to defend that student's right to think for himself or herself. In the classroom this means he wants to grant each student as much liberty as is commensurate with granting similar liberties to every one of that student's classmates. He aims to be tolerant about pupils' deeply held beliefs and to profess a neutrality which encourages the critical and constructive skills which he and Dewey hold dear. As a consequence, Fishman tries to intercede in student debate only when he believes someone's liberties and opportunities to make up his or her own mind are being transgressed.

However, Fishman's liberalism, like Dewey's, is not simply focused on what political theorists call "negative liberty," the don't-tread-on-me sorts of individual protections just described (see Barber; Isaiah Berlin; Shklar). Fishman is also concerned with so-called "positive liberty," with creating a classroom which encourages students to step out of their private realms, find common projects, and, in conjunction with class-mates, make their unique contributions to such projects. He does not want students to remain isolates, advocates of positions which a compet-itive environment forces them to defend at all costs. Rather, Fishman, with Dewey, believes that learning at its best is a cooperative affair, and thus he strives to help his students develop the virtues needed to main-tain conjoint inquiry. (For more on Fishman's pedagogy and ideology, see Fishman and McCarthy "Expressivism," "Community"; McCarthy and Fishman "Boundary".)

In what follows, we describe Steve Fishman's Introduction to Philosophy class to illustrate Dewey's educational theory. We intend to show that Deweyan pedagogy can, like radical alternatives, effect student change, but without surrendering the cooperative classrooms which Dewey sought.

THE CLASSROOM STUDY

Fishman's fall 1994 Intro class was a group of 19 students from a variety of majors who took the class to satisfy a graduation requirement. Of these students, all were Americans except for one New Zealander; eight were women, and three were African-Americans. Students came from a variety of rural and urban settings, a number were first generation college students, and all were within the ages of 20-23.

Fishman, at this point in his career, was a full professor who had been teaching 27 years at a large state university in the South. For the past 10 years, he had experimented with his pedagogy, becoming increasingly aware of his commitment to Deweyan theory and practice. McCarthy came to this collaborative project well acquainted with Fishman, having for 5 years worked with him on studies of his classroom. She was thus far from a neutral observer, often conversing with Fishman about his class-room assignments and structures. And just as McCarthy and Fishman continually discussed Fishman's teaching, so too they worked together to develop and carry out their research design.

As we began the study in fall 1994, McCarthy collected a variety of types of data in Fishman's class: student interviews, classroom observa-tions, videotapes, and student texts. Our central questions were (1) What kinds of student change occurred in Fishman's classroom? and (2) What were students' attitudes to Fishman's indirect approach to racist, sexist, classist, and homophobic views, his respect for individual differences, and his commitment to group cooperation?

We found that pupils in Fishman's Intro to Philosophy class, although they generally denied they had altered their perspectives, actually did change their views toward key issues. In addition, we discovered that, unlike the apparently dramatic transformations in Pratt's class, change for Fishman's students was slow and piecemeal, involving reversals and inconsistencies, and taking place in fits and starts. In this sense, they reflected Dewey's view of change. As he says, when we are in a condition of doubt, we grope toward the solution in an obscure light.

> In the thinking by which a conclusion is actually reached, observations are made that turn out to be aside from the point; false clues are followed; fruitless suggestions are entertained; superfluous moves are made.... There are temporary stopping places, landings of past thought that are also stations of departure for subsequent thought. We do not reach *the* conclusion at a single jump. (*How We Think* 74-75)

We also found that Fishman's students were, generally, wary of win-or-lose confrontation and eager to maintain group cooperation. They thus confirmed Dewey's view that students are highly socially motivated and want to contribute to and preserve conjoint activity. Because Fishman's students wanted to maintain their relations with classmates, with whom many shared extracurricular activities, when sensitive issues like racism were the focus of discussion, they became unusually respectful and careful of one another. Granted that Jarratt, hooks, and Miller are correct, that many *teachers* prefer politeness to confrontation, we found that in this particular class *students* were equally disinclined to push their differences too far.

Setting Conditions for Student Perplexity and Ownership

As evidence for our findings, we focus on two sessions of Fishman's Intro to Philosophy class, November 15 and 29, 1994, the first and final days of his free will–determinism unit. By this point in the semester, Fishman and his students knew each other quite well. For ten weeks they had sat in a circle discussing topics both philosophic and deeply personal, for example, the existence of God, survival of the soul, sexual morality, and the politics of marriage. "The purpose of the class," Sarah Marcotte, a sophomore biology major from Connecticut, told McCarthy in mid-November, "is to get people to recognize other points of view and think about them and question their own views. People then either change, or they solidify. And Dr. Fishman genuinely wants to hear from everyone. He won't forget even the students who want to be forgotten." Misty Goforth, Sarah's softball teammate from North Carolina, added, "The class climate is tolerant. I'm friends outside with people in the class, and even though we take opposing views, no one gets angry. That really surprises me. We respect each other."

Fishman planned the November 15th class with the goal of generating student doubt and involvement. "I want to get students to reflect," he explained, "and I try to do this by putting them in a position where their beliefs will conflict." Fishman knew student beliefs would not come forward if he lectured, if students remained passive, distanced from the material and one another as he doled out information. He commented, "This unit deals with a pretty abstract issue in determinism and free will, and it's difficult for kids to find its relevance to their own lives. So I try to edge them closer with something they care about, something they'll feel some energy about. And if I'm to get students to question one another, I'll need some strong differences." So Fishman began the unit with a freewrite he hoped would bring the free will–determinism issue closer to home and, at the same time, generate perplexity.

At the beginning of the period, Fishman and his students (and McCarthy, who was observing), freewrote for 15 minutes. In the hour-long discussion which followed, a number of differences and perplexities emerged. Fishman's two-part, focused freewrite asked students: (1) Are you free? Are you responsible for yourself, making your own decisions, such as the one to come to this university? (2) What would you say to those who argue that adolescent Native Americans are *not* free, *not* responsible for their high rates of alcoholism and suicide, who say their behavior is caused by 350 years of oppression by white Europeans?

Fishman asked students to write about Native Americans because he thought the racial issue it might raise was important and might stimulate interest in the philosophic problem of free will and determinism. He chose Native Americans because he did not want to go at black-white race discrimination straight on. Given his allegiance to Dewey's principle that the teacher sets the conditions for generating ideas rather than transmitting them directly, Fishman wanted students to take responsibility for deciding whether or not to explore an issue which, in a mixed class in the South, would be highly charged. In other words, he was inviting students to discuss a fundamental social dilemma, but only when they felt ready and only in their own way.

With the 15-minute freewrite complete, Fishman "interviewed" six students, asking them to read from their freewrites, hoping to get some differences on the table. Five of these six students, all white, said they were free. They made their own decisions, completely uninfluenced by forces outside themselves. And, they said, so do adolescent Native Americans. Standing by himself in opposition to these five proponents of free will was Shanderic Downs, one of the three African Americans in the class. Fishman later recounted, "As they spoke, I thought to myself, what a great conflict! Everybody but Shanderic is saying they're free. He was isolated, and that made his voice even more powerful. And his willingness to go against other students showed he was owning his position. I also sensed that others in the class were feeling as I did, that attention and interest were building."

Shanderic, a sophomore criminal justice major from Louisiana, and starter on the basketball team, was third of the six students Fishman called on. Although Shanderic did, like the others, say he was responsible for himself, freely making his own decisions, he took a determinist position regarding adolescent Native Americans. They are *not* responsible for their alcoholism and suicides, he argued, but rather other social forces are at work. Shanderic spoke quietly, his hands partially covering his mouth: "The Indians were betrayed, moved from place to place. There was no trust. They have no belonging in the world. They can't always cope, so they drink."

As Shanderic spoke, Fishman leaned forward and nodded with interest, betraying neither his excitement about the unfolding classroom drama nor his position on this issue: "Okay, okay, Shanderic. So you disagree with Martin and Eric. You're saying Native Americans were pushed out of the mainstream." He then announced to the class, "Now we have three people saying they themselves are independent, but only two of the three agree about Native Americans." Fishman was getting what he wanted. Student writing and thinking were becoming the classroom texts, and his apparent neutrality as a questioner was working. Students were responding in a way that suggested they saw Fishman as a learner and that they had information which he and their classmates needed.

Shanderic's determinist language did indeed stand out from the free will discourse of Martin and Eric, who preceded him, and April, Tara, and Kelly, who followed. Martin Cibulskis, a senior finance major from Aukland, New Zealand, had begun the discussion saying, "The Indians don't want to face their problems, so they take the cheap way out. In our country we have pretty much the same thing. Our native people have just as much opportunity as anybody, but they'd rather take welfare than work." Eric Shelton, a junior business major from Maryland, echoed Martin: "No one's making you kill yourself. It's your choice. And if you want to drink, you'll drink. No one's holding a gun to your head." April Drake and Tara Coble, both from North Carolina, and, finally, Kelly Snowden, from Ohio, all agreed that Native Americans were responsible for their own problems. Kelly wondered, "How long can you use ancestry for an excuse? When is your life your own? I know it was whites who introduced alcohol to the Indians, but that was many years ago." Although Kelly apparently was committed to her free will position, she concluded with a conciliatory locution we heard frequently during the semester: "Still, I can see the other standpoint."

During the 20 minutes it took to establish these two opposing positions, Fishman played neutral interviewer, modeling the virtues of cooperative inquiry. He respectfully questioned students, restated their positions to make sure he got them right, thanked them, and reported results to the class. He then noted them on a pad in front of him. "Shanderic's all by himself," Fishman said, like a student who had made an important discovery.

Just as Fishman was ending his final interview with Kelly, Karla Hembrick raised her hand: "I have a comment." In what followed, this quiet African-American student, who seldom volunteered, made explicit the analogy which Shanderic had only implied. Speaking quickly, she said, "I know why Shanderic is alone. It's because the struggles of Native Americans are similar to African Americans. Just because one's ancestors did something, you cannot say it was just a single event and it's over with. The effects of oppression are lasting. That's why Shanderic is sympathetic."

When Karla finished, the room was silent, as if students were, for the first time, owning up to the problem they faced: the sharply divergent nature of their experiences and perspectives. Karla had accepted Fishman's invitation to take the issue of freedom and determinism personally and to engage with the problems in her own way. And now, because of what she had said, the class was no longer speaking about a relatively distant concern, but about the very real differences between blacks and whites right there in that room. After a brief pause, Fishman responded to Karla in the appreciative tone of someone taking in a piece of important information. "So, Karla, you think that's why Shanderic is more sympathetic."

The conflicting narratives about Native Americans which were generated by Fishman's freewrite presented the opportunity for conjoint exploration and evaluation of alternative points of view. Students now owned the free will and determinism issue because they had tied it to their own deeply held and opposing perspectives on race, equality, and achievement. Five white students had argued, Horatio Alger-like, that everyone is free to make it on his or her own; no excuses are acceptable. Shanderic and Karla disagreed. Circumstances, they said, determine what people do. This first part of class discussion suggests that Fishman had succeeded in setting the conditions for student ownership and per-plexity, a context in which minority and divergent voices could emerge. The ensuing class conversation suggests that his style of questioning and listening also offered students a model for cooperative inquiry, a shared exploration of difference which resulted in student change.

Students Cooperatively Exploring and Evaluating Difference

John White, a senior business major from Chicago and the third African American in the class, began the exploration by probing the free will position. He criticized a major assumption underlying the view that the Indians' plight is their own fault. Without directly saying so, John was offering an interpretation of Native Americans' behavior as an act of political resistance rather than a deficiency. "Everyone is assuming that Indians *want* to bring themselves up, that they *want* to succeed in our culture." From his seat next to Karla and Shanderic, John continued, "I was under the impression the Indians were tied strongly to the land, and that when their culture was destroyed, they lost their identity. And who's to say they want to take on ours?" Although John's story seemed to be leading him to a thoroughgoing determinist position, he constructed the kind of hybrid and logically inconsistent position we often heard from students as they considered new ideas. In this case, John, a business major, was aware of economic barriers erected against minority groups in America, but as a fundamentalist Christian, he was committed to holding people responsible for their moral decisions. Therefore, he concluded, Native Americans should not be blamed for their poverty—the result of prejudice in the business world—but they should be held responsible for their personal conduct, their decisions to drink or commit suicide. Whatever John's thinking, as he reasoned out his position, teacher and students appeared to listen attentively, Fishman nodding to John and taking notes.

If John raised questions about Native Americans' responsibility by criticizing one of the majority's unexpressed assumptions, Shanderic extended John's point by connecting it to African Americans. Shanderic suggested that not only was it a mistake to assume Indians wanted to join the mainstream but were not capable; it was also wrong to assume this about African Americans. He began by admitting that when he had originally spoken about the Indians, he had not made the connection between their situation and the plight of African Americans. Karla had helped him in that regard. In effect, Shanderic was bearing witness to what Dewey sees as the value of cooperative inquiry: the chance for students to construct meaning together, to be teacher and student to one another. Karla, by displaying sympathetic listening, had given value to Shanderic's position, and now Shanderic, although it took him a while, was acknowledging he had learned from Karla and that her comments had helped him reconstruct his views.

But Shanderic didn't leave it at that. Because he had been a learner to Karla, he could now, after listening to John, become a teacher to the class once again. As Shanderic thought about it, he said, he remembered slaves who committed suicide by throwing themselves off transport ships. He explained, "Like the Indians, they committed suicide rather than be chained. They knew what was ahead of them, and they'd rather be dead. They had no future in the white world, and they shouldn't be blamed." He then appealed to personal experience to make a further political point, to illustrate the sometimes irreconcilable gaps between subordinate and dominant cultures. "You know what we were saying about robbing the Indians' land? Well, back home, my grandmother told me, my grandfather passed away, and some people came who showed her a piece of paper with an X on it. My grandfather couldn't read, and so they put an X on a deed and said the land was theirs. My grandmother and eight of my uncles had to leave their seven acres." In other words, Shanderic tried to explain that African Americans, like native Indians, brought very different views of justice and ownership to the land dealings they had with the majority whites.

Fishman was once again appreciative but non-committal, a position many students in later interviews indicated made it possible for them to speak out, and he restated Shanderic's point: "Oh, so a similar thing happened to Native Americans and your grandfather."

"Yes," Shanderic replied.

Discussion went on in this way, exploring the position that Shanderic, Karla, and John had presented until about 10 minutes were left in the period. At that point, several students attempted to resurrect the free will position which had, since its initial popularity, been seriously challenged. Misty began her defense of free will by developing an analogy. In effect, her argument was that she and Native Americans were alike in essential respects. Like them, her life is filled with hardships; however, since *she* is free, they must be free as well. "I think everyone has problems," Misty said, "their own reasons for drinking or suicide. White people and women do it too. But who can white people blame? I'm not a Native American, so I can't blame my stresses on the past. But I've got problems too, and if I'm alcoholic or commit suicide, I've got to face the fact it's my fault." What seemed exciting to Fishman about Misty's comments was that they appeared to reflect close listening to Shanderic. She seemed to imitate his argument, using the similarities between herself and the Indians to argue for her point of view.

Eric and Martin, early advocates of free will sitting next to Misty and quiet since the beginning of class, nodded their approval. However, from Misty's other side, came a challenge from her softball teammate, Sarah. Turning to look directly at Misty, Sarah questioned her analogy: "You're not like the Indians. Your family has risen above. You have problems, but they're different. Native Americans can't escape 350 years of oppression."

Martin, speaking for the first time since the start of class, articulated the conclusion that he thought Misty had only implied, that Native Americans are lazy. Interrupting Sarah, Martin asked, "Why can't the Indians escape? They're not held back by their culture. They have opportunities. It's that they won't get off their butts."

The videotape shows Kelly, who was seated between Misty and Sarah, and who was one of the five original free will spokespersons, grimace and lean forward. Adopting determinist language, Kelly snapped at Martin: "They can't escape because society won't let them." Sarah, a determinist who had earlier opposed Kelly, now joined her in the attack against Martin: "That's our life, not theirs!" John chimed in from the other side of the classroom: "Maybe they don't *want* opportunity. Maybe they just want to be on the land!"

At this point, Fishman reentered the conversation because, as he recounted later, students seemed to be shouting their disagreements rather than carefully considering Martin's position or questioning him further. Fishman was uncomfortable with this sort of confrontation, a departure from the sympathetic listening which had marked the discussion until then. That is, Kelly and Sarah, as if frustrated by what they took to be Martin's inattention, gave up any attempt to understand Martin or more fully explain themselves. Instead, they simply repeated their position in loud voices as if shouting might persuade him. And John, also showing frustration, seemed to adopt a similar strategy. As a result, Fishman moved to abort this confrontation and redirect discussion to potentially more productive ground. With just seconds left in the period, he asked a question intended to elicit more reliable information about Native Americans: "Can you tell me this? Has anyone ever been on a reservation?" The period ended with Ben Weart describing his visit to a Native American site in Arizona.

Whereas some advocates of social reform, as we explained above, urge teachers to directly confront prejudiced discourse whenever it occurs, Fishman ignored this advice in his response to Martin at the end of class. Rather than pursuing Martin, challenging him about what seemed to be a racist remark—Indians should "get off their butts"— Fishman showed sympathy for Martin by letting him off the hot seat. In doing so, Fishman was following a Deweyan principle, that people cannot be handed ideas like bricks—not by shouting students any more than by heavy-handed lecturers.

Fishman's objection to what happened at the end of class was not so much that it was a confrontation, but that it was what he considered an unproductive confrontation. After all, Fishman had been very accepting of Shanderic, the third speaker at the beginning of class, who had confronted the first two, Martin and Eric, differing with them directly. And he was equally grateful for the contributions to collective inquiry by John and Misty, both of whom challenged the positions of various classmates. These sorts of confrontation, in which students were hearing each other and building upon one another's remarks, were the very exchanges Fishman thought central to joint evaluation. His decision to abort the one-line challenges to Martin was because they seemed to preclude the careful listening and respectful speaking Fishman believes are required or productive reflection. As Dewey reminds us, if communication is to yield understanding, we must take care about the way we present our ideas. "Seeds are sown," he writes, "not by virtue of being thrown out at random, but by being so distributed to take root and have a chance for growth" (*Public* 177).

What happened to the seeds that were sown in Fishman's November 15th class? What were their effects upon Fishman's students? In the weeks which followed the introduction to the free will-determinism unit, McCarthy interviewed students and examined their work to see what kinds of change occurred.

Students' Slow, Piecemeal Change

One of the appealing features of radical pedagogy is its suggestion that confrontation will bring about student transformation and, ultimately, social reform. For example, as we noted above, Pratt tells us that along with her students' experiences of rage, incomprehension, and pain came "exhilarating moments of wonder and revelation" (39). By contrast, among Fishman's students, we saw little evidence of this sort of learning or dramatic insight. However, despite his avoidance of direct confrontation, Fishman's students did show signs of slow, piecemeal change. Although we found that students, with very few exceptions, steadfastly denied that their experiences in Intro to Philosophy had changed their fundamental beliefs, many did admit that they had learned to be more sensitive or appreciative of beliefs they had previously overlooked or ignored. Students' denials of change were particularly interesting to us because we found that nearly all of them actually *did* modify their beliefs over the course of the semester.

Eric Shelton did not speak again on November 15th after his initial contribution, although we did find him nodding agreement with Misty Goforth near the end of the period. However, Eric took on special interest for us because of information revealed during one of McCarthy's interviews with Misty. About halfway through Misty's reconstruction of that class, she matter-of-factly recounted, "Eric was sitting near me, and I could hear his mumbles. He was getting angry about Shanderic's and Karla's saying it was their background. Eric was like, 'That's all you hear. They're violent because of what we did.' He feels whites are taking blame for something we didn't do, and blacks are using it as an excuse. Eric's angry because they get money from the government. He comes from a broken home, and his mom struggled to avoid that. He kept saying he was going to bite his tongue and not say anything."

When McCarthy asked Fishman if he had heard the mumblings from Eric which Misty reported, he said he had. He indicated that at one point, while listening to Shanderic, he had sensed agitation in the class from the opposite direction. He remembered that when Shanderic finished, he had turned to his right to face Eric. But when asked, "Is there anything you would like to add?" Eric shook his head no. Although Fishman was not convinced, he took him at his word. With Eric, as with Martin, Fishman followed his Deweyan instincts to offer students the opportunity to join the conjoint exploration but also to protect students, including honoring their refusals to speak.

In this regard, Fishman's ideology and approach is at variance with some radical teachers. Although the question of how to respond to student silence is a matter of controversy (see Lewis; Orner), at least some claim success with confrontation (Faris). By contrast, Fishman's Deweyan assumption that students must take responsibility for their own learning underlay his belief that it would be ineffective teaching to force Eric to address an issue which, for whatever reasons, he did not want to speak about at that moment and in that context.

What was Eric's experience during this class? What lay behind his refusal to accept Fishman's invitation to contribute to group exploration? When McCarthy asked him, it turned out that for Eric, at that moment the topic of race was just too hot to handle. He had spent his freshman year, he told her, as a minority student at a historically black college in Maryland, and he was still stinging. Supported by a baseball scholarship he found himself the only white in an English class discussing *The Autobiography of Malcolm X* and, although offended, he felt he could not speak. During class on November 15th, Eric said, he relived that experience. "I didn't want it to come down to black and white, but it did, and left class upset because I didn't speak. But I didn't want to be branded a bigot and have to defend myself. I'm actually not racist at all. I just don't believe you can blame other races. As a society we believe everyone is on their own; that's the way my mother raised me." Eric concluded, "I listened to others' opinions, but I protected myself."

Given Eric's strong commitment to the view that everyone is responsible for his or her own fate, and the complexity of his personal history with racism, how did change for him occur? It was gradual and incremental, produced by small encounters over many class periods, ye always accompanied by Eric's denials. In fact, he maintained until the end of the semester that he had *not* altered his views. And, in one of his final pieces, he reiterated his position: "I feel it is bull to blame another race for your problems. It is time for the Indians to take responsibility for their own actions and stop blaming others. Everyone is given the chance in the U.S., and it comes down to whether or not they go after it." But, he added a sentence which, for Eric, represented significant rethinking, a rethinking which resulted from his own mulling of alternative voices and texts rather than from aggressive teacher confrontation. Eric concluded, "I can understand also, however, how the white race may have been involved in many different race problems."

Although Eric clung tightly to his Horatio Alger version of free will—that if one wants to succeed, one only has to work—we watched him try out the determinist position on a number of occasions. For example, the first time McCarthy interviewed Eric, on November 18th, he assured her he would not change. "I'm pretty stubborn in the way I see things." But, he added, "This class gets me thinking. I've never been in a situation like this—where you can voice your opinion. And I've learned there are more views out there than I realized." Near the end of the 30-minute interview, Eric again declared, "I am firm; there is no way I'll change." But, once more, he had an afterthought. He *had* been affected, he said, by the assigned reading the day before. It was an article by Paul Ree, a 19th century German philosopher, who "doesn't believe in free will," and Eric had found Ree's argument convincing.[1] "We are somewhat shaped by our society, I guess," he said. But, having once conceded this glimpse into opposing territory, Eric pulled back. "Still, the decisions I make are my own."

Eric was caught. On the one hand, he was working hard to keep his free will narrative intact, his "firm belief" that people control their fates and get what they deserve. Yet, at the same time, he was opening to voices saying that things are more complex than he had imagined. In class, on November 29th, the last session on free will and determinism, Eric's inconsistency, as well as his ambivalence about his own change, were clearly displayed.

On the videotape we watch Eric struggle, not sure what to do with the differences which were, as Fishman hoped, causing Eric to reflect. After an initial freewrite and discussion about whether students had altered their original position about Native Americans, Fishman challenged Eric with a hypothetical situation: if two people, one wealthy, one poor, stole the same quantity of food, the wealthy person doing it as a prank, the poor person doing it to feed hungry siblings, would he hold them both equally responsible? Fishman later explained to McCarthy, "I knew Eric had come to trust me and that he was trying hard in class, so I thought I'd push a bit." He began questioning Eric with a characteristic non-adversarial and respectful locution.

Fishman:	Eric, I don't want to pick on you, but let me ask you this. If you were the judge, would you feel differently about these two thieves?
Eric:	Most likely.
Fishman:	Why?
Eric:	Because the poor guy did it out of necessity, to feed his brothers and sisters, whereas the rich guy could have bought it. The poor guy did it to survive.
Fishman:	Okay, okay. So both did it freely, but their circumstances are different, and this is relevant to your attitude.
Eric:	Yes.
Fishman:	Would you sentence them differently?
Eric:	Most likely. I'd be more lenient with the poor guy.
Fishman:	Eric, let me go back. Maybe I don't understand. You've been saying all along that Native Americans are responsible, but now you're suggesting we shouldn't blame the poor thief because of his environment. It seems like you're softening. (The videotape shows Eric frowning and running his hand through his hair. He mumbles something.)
Fishman:	I don't mean to give you a hard time.
Eric:	I know. (5 second pause) Well, I suppose it does depend on the pressures you've got on you. If your surroundings are bad, you'll be influenced by that. (4 second pause) I don't know. It's hard for me to explain.

Eric provides us with a portrait of a student in the midst of reconstruction. His position fluctuates, changing from one example to the next, and he clings to old views while acknowledging contradictory new ones. Despite Eric's stubbornness, he had accepted Fishman's invitation warily, to face his perplexities and to risk the pain of change. On the final day of the semester, Eric wrote in response to Fishman's question about what students would take with them from the class: "I've become a more questioning person, not just accepting everything at face value. I now look at someone's opinion from both sides, not just believing my opinion is the only right answer. I never thought about things like free will before. So this class has opened my mind to new opinions and beliefs." But Eric still wasn't quite sure what to do with these, and, in his concluding sentence, he beat a familiar retreat. "I am not saying I will take these new beliefs as my own, but I will think about them."

In Fishman's class, then, Eric was typical in adopting contradictory and hybrid positions, his process of rethinking gradual and halting, not dramatic or decisive. Eric's refusal to acknowledge change suggests that his whole life story was so built around the Horatio Alger narrative that he was probably having difficulty adjusting to views he found somewhat attractive but threatening to this narrative. For Eric to give up the free will position involved the very complicated task of composing a new life story. Nevertheless, seeds for change had been planted, and Eric had worked, if only modestly, with some potentially useful tools of self-reflection.

It was, in fact, Eric's developing ability to use these tools which most pleased Fishman. It was the sort of student change he vigorously sought. Insofar as Eric was becoming more open to differing points of view, he was increasing his chances for enriched future experience. That is, by becoming more sensitive to the complexities of race relations, he was increasing his chances for more fruitful encounters with minorities in the future. And insofar as Eric's thinking about freedom and determinism had become more sophisticated, he was taking small steps toward richer, less narrowly grooved habits of thought. In short, Fishman's Deweyan commitments made him less concerned with the particular political views with which Eric might leave the class and more concerned with what Eric would take in the way of desire for further reflection, criticism, and reconstruction (see *Reconstruction*, chapter VII).

Kelly, like Eric and the overwhelming majority of the class, also refused to acknowledge change. Yet she seemed restrained by a different belief structure than Eric. Whereas Eric was bound to a particular vision of hard work, free will, and success, Kelly seemed committed to the religious view that alteration is a sign of imperfection. Kelly, who came to college on an athletic scholarship, was from a fundamentalist family in North Jefferson, Ohio, where, she said, no one ever changes. "I've never been able in my whole life to change anyone's mind about anything." Although Kelly believed alteration was both impossible as well as undesirable, she reported opening to opposing views on a number of occasions, and, on November 15th, we watched her go from one extreme to the other, starting the period with the free will view that the Indians are responsible for their own difficulties and ending the period with a full-fledged determinist response to Martin. Kelly's final class freewrite reflects the sort of slow workings of readjustment, and its attendant inconsistencies, which also characterized Eric's in-class exchange with Fishman. She wrote, "No, my opinion hasn't changed." But then, contradicting herself, she acknowledged the complexities to which she was awakening on November 15th. "I know there is free will," she concluded, "but now I'm not so sure what type of bounds it has."

And what happened to Martin, the senior finance major from New Zealand, who was the object of shouting from three of his classmates at the end of the November 15th class? Fishman had aborted that confrontation and had refused to say what was obvious to many, that Martin's remark smacked of racism and reflected his home culture's history of minority oppression. What effect did this aborted confrontation have on Martin? Did Fishman's strategy hide an implicit acceptance of Martin's prejudiced discourse, and, thereby, deny him an opportunity for reflection and change? Or, on the other hand, did Fishman's Deweyan assumptions—his belief that learning requires careful listening, respect for individual difference, and the need for students to own their own change—work to Martin's advantage?

Our data suggest the latter. In conversations with McCarthy soon after the November 15th class, we heard Martin beginning to raise questions about his original position. We also heard an openness to his classmates and a willingness to see things from their points of view. Martin's comments indicated that this sort of give and take was a relatively new experience for him. He explained to McCarthy he had been "taken by surprise" at the vehement response he got. He thought he was merely restating the free will point of view. "I didn't see that what was saying was different from their position, but maybe I was too straightforward." In his home, by contrast, Martin said, he had seldom spoken out, his parents setting his goals for him and making sure he achieved them. He described his chemist father, a Lithuanian immigrant to New Zealand, talking at him in "no-win" situations, usually when Martin "was slacking off.... My dad was always right, and I was wrong, so I'd sit there and say nothing. Maybe that's why, until now, I've kept my opinions to myself. But philosophy class has helped me not be nervous people are accepting. That's why I wasn't scared to say my view. But I can see Shanderic's position, definitely. About slavery. Blacks didn't have any more chance to fight back than Indians."

We have no idea what would have happened had Fishman adopted a confrontational pedagogy and pushed Martin to acknowledge prejudices in his language and his culture's practices. Nor can we be sure that Martin is not saying the sorts of things he believes Fishman would want to hear. Nevertheless, Martin's conversations with McCarthy provide some evidence that Fishman's respectful and protective approach, his unwillingness to push ideas on Martin, helped Martin feel safe enough to listen. His remarks seem to corroborate our claims about the power of Fishman's accepting and cooperative approach to effect change. When recalling the November 15th class, it is the quiet, respectful voice of Shanderic, and Shanderic's reference to personal experience, that Martin reflects on, not the one-line shouts from Sarah, Kelly, or John. It thus appears that Fishman's protective move really didn't let Martin off the hook. Instead, he seems, at his own rate and without apparent defensiveness, to be reconstructing his views, allowing Shanderic's remarks to help him reconsider his beliefs about American blacks and, also perhaps, about native New Zealanders.

Students' Wariness about Confrontation and Desire to Maintain Cooperation

Dewey's belief that students want to contribute to and preserve conjoint activity was confirmed by our study. We are not claiming that students' attitudes were unaffected by Fishman's decision to avoid win-loss confrontation, nor are we claiming that these same students, under different instruction, might not welcome and learn from such confrontation. However, we found that in Fishman's class students generally wanted to sidestep this kind of conflict, be respectful of classmates, and do whatever they could to enhance and protect the class conversation.

In a mid-November interview with McCarthy, Sarah Marcotte, despite her sharp in-class response to Martin, twice illustrated this desire to appear respectful of others' views and not too forceful or presumptuous about her own. First, Sarah explained, she had, on November 15th, initially remained silent because she did not want to presume to speak about the experiences of others. Although she agreed with Shanderic's determinist view and immediately connected the plights of Native and

African Americans, she did not feel it was her place to articulate that analogy. With three African Americans in the room, Sarah feared she might misrepresent their perspective, and they would say she was "just wrong." So she waited until Karla and Shanderic, who could draw upon personal experiences, made the analogy, and then Sarah entered in a supportive role.

Second, Sarah was also careful not to speak too presumptuously about her own experience. Early in the semester, she found herself in the minority when discussing God and immortality, an atheist in the midst of believers. In fact, some of the fundamentalists in the class, including Misty and Kelly, Sarah's teammates and good friends, said Sarah was the first nonbeliever they'd ever met, the sort of person their parents had told them to stay away from. Faced with this opposition, Sarah was careful not to polarize, not to alienate those who disagreed with her. She explained to McCarthy, "If I stood up and said, 'Dammit, I'm an atheist, and I don't believe in God, and I think all you people who do are just ridiculous, and can't you see you're living a big lie?' no one would bother to reply. They'd say, she's a blithering idiot. Why try to change her mind? To heck with her." So when Sarah spoke about religion, she said, she softened her views to indicate openness to other positions "so we could have a discussion about it."

That Sarah's strategy was successful was evidenced by Kelly's comments. Although Kelly at first dreaded debate in philosophy class, recalling high school discussions about similar issues which involved shouting and name-calling, she reported that she and Sarah, despite their opposite views about God, had been able to continue exploring their differences calmly and productively outside class.

Sarah's concern about appearing too certain of one's views was echoed by Shanderic. He told McCarthy, "It would deter you away if someone spoke like they just absolutely knew it, like they're so confident in what they're saying that you should agree with them no matter what." However, he continued, this seldom happened in class because "everybody respects everybody's opinions. And they know they'll get their chance to be heard, so there's no reason to get loud. Fishman never intimidates us. He never tells us what's right, so it's easy to speak out."

Students were particularly eager to avoid offending classmates with whom they shared other campus activities. This applied to many of Fishman's students, some of whom shared social life and other classes, as well as sports teams. For example, Shanderic and Misty were not only both varsity athletes and criminal justice majors, but after philosophy, they walked together to their next class which they also shared. When Shanderic reflected for McCarthy on the sharp contrast between his and Misty's positions regarding the Native Americans, he was obviously concerned about preserving their out-of-class friendship. He said that if he were ever to bring this topic up with Misty, "I'd do it in a joking manner. I'd ask her where she gets her idea and why she won't look at the Indians' history."

When McCarthy put the same questions to Misty, her response betrayed a similar care for the relationship and a concern for Shanderic's feelings as an African American in a dominantly white college class. "I think Shanderic and I could talk about it, but he's very quiet, and you have to get to know him before he says much. If he didn't know me, it might offend him, but being he knows I'm not a racist person because I have so many African American friends, it wouldn't be bad for me to mention it. It would just be conversation." Misty and Shanderic illustrate how guarded students are once they realize they're speaking about issues that might threaten group cooperation or damage ongoing relationships. In sum, Fishman's students showed little desire to engage in heated confrontation with him or their classmates, despite the fact that sharp exchanges sometimes did occur.

CONCLUSION

Our purpose in this article has been to offer Deweyan educational practice as an alternative for teachers who, because of political ideology or educational theory, find it difficult to adopt confrontational pedagogy but embrace the goal of student change. This Deweyan alternative seeks to effect student transformation by having the teacher set the conditions for doubt, ownership, and cooperative inquiry. In doing so, the teacher is neither a lecturer nor conspicuously at the center of the class. In fact, Dewey says it is crucial that teachers become learners and allow students to become teachers. The study we present is a local one. Therefore, we do not claim that other teachers in other settings, with different perspectives and ideologies, would not be effective with a confrontational approach. What we do claim is that, in this one setting at least, politeness, coopera- tion, and conflict in the Deweyan spirit also promoted student change.

What kind of change did Fishman's Deweyan style effect? Unlike the dramatic transformations described by some advocates of radical pedagogy, the changes we report in Fishman's Intro to Philosophy class are piecemeal and episodic, with students often contradicting themselves and denying any modification of their original views. Interestingly, the patterns of change we observed in students like Eric, Kelly, and Martin, reflect the halting rhythms of learning in real life situations which Dewey himself describes.

Our study of Fishman's class also provides support for Dewey's claim that students are socially motivated, that they want to contribute to and preserve conjoint activities. Students such as Sarah, Shanderic, Misty, and Eric, wanted to keep the classroom conversation going. They worked to appear respectful of different positions and persuadable, that is, open-minded enough to be worthy of serious consideration by classmates with whom they disagreed.

We end our study with a caution about the dichotomy between Deweyan and radical or confrontational approaches. Because of the paucity of information about student experience in reform-minded class-rooms, the distinction we have been working with may be overly simple. In *Experience and Education*, Dewey seems to warn that false pedagogical dichotomies can result from discussions which are too theoretical. Our study of an actual classroom shows that the issue, finally, is not between confrontation and cooperation but, rather, between various types and mixes of both. In other words, our study reveals that confrontations do occur in Deweyan settings. Likewise, we believe, a closer look at radical classrooms would surely disclose important moments of cooperation. Therefore, we argue that, in the end, the question is not, Which is better, confrontation or cooperation? Instead, the important questions are, What is the *quality* of classroom confronta-tion? What is the *quality* of classroom cooperation? And what, ultimately, is their impact upon students' lives?

Thus we close with a call for further inquiry into the nature and quality of experiences in classrooms which privilege diversity and work for student change. We encourage studies in a variety of reform-minded settings, including those, like the one we examined, where the teacher follows Deweyan principles of cooperative inquiry, as well as ones where instructors are more directly confrontational and explicit about their ideological stance.

Note

1. Paul Ree's article was one of seven which students read from the free will–determinism section of an anthology edited by Edwards and Pap, *A Modern Introduction to Philosophy: Readings from Classical and Contemporary Sources*.

WORKS CITED

Barber, Benjamin R. "Liberal Democracy and the Costs of Consent." *Liberalism and the Moral Life*. Ed. Nancy L. Rosenblum. Boston: Harvard UP, 1989. 54-68.

Berlin, Isaiah. *Four Essays on Liberty*. Oxford: Oxford UP, 1982.

Berlin, James. "Rhetoric and Ideology in the Writing Class." *College English* 50 (1988): 477-94.

Bizzell, Patricia. *Academic Discourse and Critical Consciousness*. Pittsburgh: U of Pittsburgh P, 1992.

Brodkey, Linda. "Making a Federal Case Out of Difference: The Politics of Pedagogy, Publicity, and Postponement." *Writing Theory and Critical Theory*. Ed. John Clifford and John Schilb. New York: MLA, 1994. 236-61.

Dewey, John. "Authority and Social Change." *The Later Works, 1925-1953*. Vol. 11, 1935-1937. Ed. Jo Ann Boydston. Carbondale: Southern Illinois UP, 1991. 130-45.

——. "The Child and the Curriculum." 1902. *The School and Society; The Child and the Curriculum*. Chicago: U of Chicago P, 1990. 181-209.

——. "Construction and Criticism." *The Later Works, 1925-1953*. Vol. 5, 1929-1930. Ed. Jo Ann Boydston. Carbondale: Southern Illinois UP, 1988. 127-43.

——. *Democracy and Education*. 1916. New York: Free Press, 1967.

——. "Ethical Principles Underlying Education." 1897. *John Dewey on Education, Selected Writings*. Ed. Reginald D. Archambault. Chicago: U of Chicago P, 1964. 108-38.

——. *Ethics. The Later Works, 1925-1953*. Vol. 7, 1932. Ed. Jo Ann Boydston. Carbondale: Southern Illinois UP, 1988.

——. *Experience and Education*. 1938. New York: Macmillan, 1975.

——. *Experience and Nature*. 1st ed. 1925, 2nd ed. 1929. LaSalle: Open Court, 1989.

——. "From Absolutism to Experimentalism." *The Later Works, 1925-1953*. Vol. 5, 1929-1930. Ed. Jo Ann Boydston. Carbondale: Southern Illinois UP, 1988. 147-60.

——. *How We Think: A Restatement of the Relation of Reflective Thinking to the Educative Process*. Lexington, MA: Heath, 1933/1960.

——. "The Need for a Philosophy of Education." 1934. *John Dewey on Education, Selected Writings*. Ed. Reginald D. Archambault. Chicago: U of Chicago P, 1964. 1-14.

——. *The Public and Its Problems*. 1927. Athens: Swallow, 1988.

——. *Reconstruction in Philosophy*. 1920. Boston: Beacon, 1962.

Edwards, Paul, and Arthur Pap, eds. *A Modern Introduction to Philosophy: Readings from Classical and Contemporary Sources.* 3rd ed. New York: Free P, 1973.

Elbow, Peter. *Writing Without Teachers.* Oxford UP, 1973.

Emig, Janet. "The Tacit Tradition: The Inevitability of a Multi-Disciplinary Approach to Writing Research." *The Web of Meaning: Essays on Writing, Teaching, Learning and Thinking.* Upper Montclair: Boynton, 1983. 145-56.

Faris, Sara. "'What's in It for Me?' Two Students' Responses to a Feminist Pedagogy." *College Composition and Communication* 43 (1992): 304-07.

Fishman, Stephen M. "Explicating Our Tacit Tradition: John Dewey and Composition Studies." *College Composition and Communication* 44 (1993): 315-30.

Fishman, Stephen M., and Lucille P. McCarthy. "Is Expressivism Dead? Reconsidering Its Romantic Roots and Its Relation to Social Constructionism." *College English* 54 (1992): 647-61.

——. "Community in the Expressivist Classroom: Juggling Liberal and Communitarian Visions." *College English* 57 (1995): 62-81.

Frazer, Nancy, and Nicola Lacey. *The Politics of Community: A Feminist Critique of the Liberal-Communitarian Debate.* Toronto: U of Toronto P, 1993.

Giroux, Henry A. *Postmodernism, Feminism, and Cultural Politics: Redrawing Educational Boundaries.* Albany: State U of New York, 1991.

Harris, Joseph. "Negotiating the Contact Zone." *Journal of Basic Writing* 14 (1995): 27-42.

Hayes, Karen. "Creating Space for Difference in the Composition Class." *College Composition and Communication* 43 (1992): 300-304.

hooks, bell. *Teaching to Transgress: Education as the Practice of Freedom.* New York: Routledge, 1994.

Jarratt, Susan. "Feminism and Composition: The Case for Conflict." *Contending with Words: Composition in a Postmodern Era.* Ed. Patricia Harkin and John Schilb. New York: MLA, 1991. 105-25.

Jones, Donald. "Beyond the Postmodern Impasse of Agency: The Resounding Relevance of John Dewey's Tacit Tradition." *Journal of Advanced Composition* 16 (1996): 81-102.

Kymlicka, Will. *Liberalism, Community, and Culture.* Oxford: Clarendon, 1989.

Lewis, Magda. *Without a Word: Teaching Beyond Women's Silence.* New York: Teachers College P, 1993.

Luke, Carmen, and Jennifer Gore, eds. *Feminisms and Critical Pedagogy.* New York: Routledge, 1992.

McCarthy, Lucille P., and Stephen M. Fishman. "Boundary Conversations: Conflicting Ways of Knowing in Philosophy and Interdisciplinary Research." *Research in the Teaching of English* 25 (1991): 419-68.

Miller, Richard E. "Fault Lines in the Contact Zone." *College English* 56 (1994): 389-408.

Murray, Donald. *Learning by Teaching: Selected Articles on Writing and Teaching.* Montclair, NJ: Boynton/Cook, 1982.

Newkirk, Thomas. *More than Stories.* Portsmouth: Heinemann, 1989.

Noddings, Nel. *Caring: A Feminine Approach to Ethics and Moral Education.* Berkeley: U of California P, 1984.

Orner, Mimi. "Interrupting the Calls for Student Voice in 'Liberatory' Education: A Feminist Poststructuralist Perspective." *Feminisms and Critical Pedagogy.* Ed. Carmen Luke and Jennifer Gore. New York: Routledge, 1992. 74-89.

Phelps, Louise W. *Composition as a Human Science.* New York: Oxford UP, 1988.

Pratt, Mary Louise. "Arts of the Contact Zone." *Profession 91.* New York: MLA.
(1991): 33-40.

Russell, David R. "Vygotsky, Dewey, and Externalism: Beyond the Student/
Discipline Dichotomy." *Journal of Advanced Composition* 13 (1993): 173-97.

Shklar, Judith N. "The Liberalism of Fear." *Liberalism and the Moral Life.* Ed.
Nancy L. Rosenblum. Cambridge: Harvard UP, 1989. 21-38.

Sciachitano, Marian. "Introduction: Feminist Sophistics Pedagogy Group."
College Composition and Communication 43 (1992): 297-300.

Shor, Ira. *Empowering Education: Critical Teaching for Social Change.* Chicago:
U of Chicago P, 1992.

Trimbur, John. "Consensus and Difference in Collaborative Learning."
College English 51 (1989): 602-16.

Weiler, Kathleen. *Women Teaching for Change: Gender, Class and Power.* South
Hadley: Bergen, 1988.

Conclusion

Steve Fishman and Lucille McCarthy

I n our conclusion, we offer suggestions about ways teacher-
researchers might integrate theory and practice, insider and outsider
perspectives, and diverse methodologies. Steve Fishman begins by
focusing on the first of these integrations, presenting tips about how to
make theory a more central part of practitioner inquiry. Lucille McCarthy
follows with advice about ways to manage productive insider-outsider
collaborations as well as ways practitioner inquirers might combine
social science and narrative techniques. We also look at the consequences
of our own teacher research, examining for a final time its effects upon
our teaching and professional status.

Part 1: The Insider-Teacher's Conclusions
Steve Fishman

Integrating Theory and Practice

In my view, three conceptual areas are especially relevant to teacher
research: (1) theories of learning and knowing, (2) theories about aims of
education, and (3) theories of classroom research. In my classroom studies with McCarthy, the first and second concerns have been central issues,

and the third is the focus of this book. Let me now add details and weight to this three-part taxonomy by describing some theoretical highlights from McCarthy's and my work.

Theories about Learning and Knowing

Questions about the best ways to teach led McCarthy and me straightaway to questions about theories of learning and knowing. As our first study shows, she favored explicit instruction and modeling, and by contrast, I favored indirect instruction and "student muddling." As we explain in Chapter 3, these differences became clearer and more significant when we finally viewed them through the theoretical lenses of Belenky et al. (1986). We then saw that McCarthy's preferred teaching strategy reflected her own learning style. Because she was primarily a "received knower," she found that modeling—showing students the paradigmatic ways of writing, arguing, and speaking in particular academic disciplines—was her obvious instructional choice.

Not unexpectedly, I differed. Favoring another Belenky et al. (1986) category, I saw myself as a "constructed knower," someone needing to relate or connect academic concerns to personal ones. Thus, Belenky and her colleagues enabled us to reenvision my students (and ourselves) in the context of epistemological theory. This larger context, in turn, drove us back to the classroom to reexamine my students' performances (and our teaching) in more probing and critical ways.

Questions about teaching strategy not only led us to questions about theories of knowing and learning, they also provoked questions about the nature of knowledge. From the start, McCarthy understood knowledge as socially constructed. Different academic communities, she argued, hold different views of the world, and an accomplished learner shifts gears as he or she moves from one community—and its base of knowledge—to another. Although I could not talk about it very well, I was less concerned about stepping into or receiving others' worlds than relating these worlds to my own. Knowledge, I believed, was a bridge I perpetually built from within to without, whereas McCarthy saw knowledge as something already out there to be mastered and taken in.

As we have shown in our studies, each of these theories of knowledge had important teaching implications for us. If learning, as McCarthy initially viewed it, is primarily a matter of received knowing or taking in, then teachers can be less concerned about the interests and language which students bring to the classroom. This orientation makes it somewhat easier to stress skills acquisition. Conversely, if knowledge is, as I saw it, a construction involving both students' out-of-school and in-school lives, then ignoring pupils' personal concerns and family communities is riskier. Although McCarthy and I do not pursue these issues at great length in our four studies, we do focus in our third project on a related issue, namely, the status of internal and external classroom rewards.

My assumption that knowledge involves pupils finding connections between academic and nonacademic life means that when they are successful learners, they extend their interests to school projects. It is no longer just a matter of pleasing the teacher or parents or achieving superior grades. No, the hope is that external rewards like these yield to more internal ones. Why do I focus on internal rewards? Because they not only promote learning, as I understand it, they also generate habits of thought and personality I find desirable. However, at this point, we are already at the edge of discussions about goals of education, which only shows that the three theoretical areas of classroom concern I name at the start of my part of this conclusion are not easily kept apart. So let me now shift my focus to theories of educational aims.

Theories about Aims of Education

Classrooms whose goal is social reform and moral development, that is, classrooms whose aim is encouraging the citizenly virtues of democracy, have long been at the center of theoretical debates in education (Allen, 1999; Edelsky, 1994; Beyer, 1996; Shor, 1996). The controversy has been over which virtues are preferable and which sorts of democracy teachers ought to promote. Should it be a democracy that strives, above all, to preserve our colonial heritage and frontier self-reliance? Or should it be a democracy that educates youth to be critical, to conserve what is good from the past and reform what is dysfunctional? Is democracy a guarantee of open and free competition among self-regarding individuals? Or is it a guarantee that everyone, regardless of wealth, social class, gender, or race, will have equal chances to take from and contribute to our culture's fruits and resources?

These issues are part of the rich and complex theory implicit in teacher research. As is clear from preceding chapters in this book, I favor a *gemeinschaft* or cooperative democracy, one which strives for material as well as formal equality, one whose roots lie deep in the romantic tradition (see Rosenblum, 1987). These educational aims, as we have also seen, have significant implications for my teaching. They lead me to struggle for ways to feature student difference while promoting group work and identification of common cause.

To illustrate, when Tate Osborne volunteers during our class discussion of women's rights (Chapter 7) and when numerous students respond to Shanderic Downs during our consideration of the plight of Native Americans (Chapter 9), I see moments of what I have called *gemeinschaft* association, occasions when students are caught up in the subject matter or curriculum. These are, in my view, incidents, albeit short-lived, of pupil integrity, when students merge their genuine interests and school concerns, when they do not have to fake school attention or enthusiasm in order to please their teacher or anyone else. My desire to promote such student experiences says as much about my views of learning as my aims for education, as much about my views of implicit instruction as about the types of people I want my students to become and the types of democracy I hope they foster. Not surprisingly—and this is what makes theoretical discussions so instructive—my point of view has its serious and persuasive detractors, critics whose theoretical commitments differ markedly from mine.

To some, my indirect approach is weak on the promotion of social justice (see Fitts & France, 1995; France, 1993). In the Shanderic Downs class, for example, I refrain from "backloading" my own ideas (Shor, 1996, p. 41). Never once do I suggest to Martin Cibulskis that his telling Native Americans "to get off their butts" smacks of racism, nor do I ever chide Eric Shelton for his naive—almost callous—view that hard work is the essence of success in American society. My indirect approach runs the risk, say my critics, of preserving the status quo rather than challenging and reforming it.

This failure to intervene, my detractors continue, is only one of my pedagogy's risks. Some would also argue that my whole *gemeinschaft* approach is built entirely on sand, that alleged paradigms of historical *gemeinschaft* or social cooperation, like the polis, the small village, or colonial America, are flawed and misleading (see Phillips, 1993). In addition, my emphasis on collaborative work has frequently troubled those who believe such an approach can easily become intolerant overzealousness, a chance to smother the nonconformist, the creative and, thereby, valuable eccentric. Noted historian Richard Hofstadter (1963), for instance, worries that pedagogies like mine endanger the loner's right to conduct inquiry independently or in any way he or she sees fit. More recently, discoveries of ostracism and narrow-mindedness in writing groups at the elementary and junior high levels have led to similar worries (see Flinders, 1997; Lensmire, 1994). In a parallel vein, John Trimbur (1989) highlights the dangers of building consensus, the ways in which such agreement masks suppression of minority points of view. Following Iris Marion Young (1986), Trimbur sees democracy not as a process of cooperatively reconciling difference but as a means of encouraging, voicing, and accepting difference.

Theories about Classroom Research

In addition to reflecting on and clarifying our commitments to theories about learning, knowing, and educational aims, another conceptual area of significance for teacher-researchers has to do with the nature of research itself. Indeed, this has been the organizing framework of this book and, at present, is a central theoretical focus of the practitioner-inquiry movement.

Whereas McCarthy and I have tried for a decade to employ various combinations of Stenhousian social science and Berthoffian narrative, educational researchers in general during this period seem to have hardened the lines around the methodological theories separating them. For example, recent criticisms of Stenhouse's sort of systematic, self-critical inquiry have been especially virulent and have come from two significant sources: postmodern and neo-romantic. I offer a brief outline of both these criticisms, beginning with the postmodern.

Postmodern Criticisms of Social Science

In general, postmodernists question the epistemology (conception of knowing) and metaphysics (conception of reality) undergirding contemporary science (Kinchloe, 1993; Lather, 1991). They argue that its search for universal truth, control, and predictability, its attempts at objective reporting and neutral interpretation, rest on an inadequate world view. For postmodernists, social science relies on too static and coherent a notion of the world, a notion which downplays uncertainties and artificially separates object and agent, language and value, researcher and personal experience. Thomas Kuhn's (1962) famous account of paradigm shifts suggests that social science, like all forms of inquiry, is communally constructed, loaded with the same biases accompanying other, and in contemporary life, less privileged, forms of inquiry such as art, history, and religion. That is, according to postmodernists, no matter our investigatory methods, our findings are always indeterminate and local, and our starting points are always conventional, if not arbitrary. Worse yet, any procedure we adopt and any language we employ overlook important perspectives and silence important voices. The cost of every vantage point is violence to others.

Neo-romantic Criticisms of Social Science

Critics of social science classroom inquiry who draw on romantic sources differ from postmodernists in being bothered not so much by the foundations of social science as by its scorn for other approaches to knowledge. In opposition to social science's emphasis on technical reason, neo-romantics celebrate imagination, creativity, and will. In place of science's faith in controlled experiment, they substitute story, fable, and biography. As we mention in the introduction to this book, the 1998 Annual Convention of the Conference on College Composition and Communication (CCCC) featured numerous plenary sessions by contributors to Joseph Trimmer's (1997) anthology, *Narration as Knowledge*. By shaping its conference around narrative, CCCC leaders seemed to declare they had had enough of technical, abstract scholarship in composition and English language studies.

In view of these continuing controversies about how to do classroom research, practitioner inquirers might want to add methodological theory to their list of relevant conceptual concerns. In other words, in addition to theories about learning, knowledge, and educational goals, teacher-researchers might find it important to discuss the pros and cons of alternative research designs. Does the Berthoff approach—or something kin to it—seem most fruitful, and if so, why? Alternatively, does a more social science stance seem justifiable? And what about an amalgam of the two, a methodology similar to the one McCarthy and I have attempted to forge? This is not to say practitioner inquirers should spend as much time reflecting on their research methods as they spend using them. But, in my view, assessing and clarifying our theoretical commitments in this way is at least one means of making classroom studies more significant, more relevant and meaningful to a larger than usual readership.

A TOOLBOX OF IDEAS FOR COLLECTING THEORY

Having outlined areas of debate among classroom and teacher-research theorists, I now attend to a few practical, how-to questions. For instance, where do you find and how do you develop a taste for theories about learning and knowing, educational aims, and research? How do practitioner inquirers learn about different views of democracy, for example, or distinguish democracy's enlightenment roots from its romantic ones?

Empirical Data and Classroom Theory as Equally Important

My first suggestion is that classroom practitioners accept the notion that collecting and analyzing theory is as important as collecting and analyzing empirical data. This is a major lesson of the four studies we present in this volume, namely, that undertheorized and undercontextualized teacher stories have limited appeal. They run the risk of eliciting the response we received to an early draft of our fourth piece: "With all due respect, who cares about Fishman's class?" In other words, starting teacher research with our own stories and questions is crucial, but we also need to explore these stories and questions in ways which help articulate the intellectual history and theoretical frameworks—especially social and political—implicit in them.

My suggestion that we collect our reflections on theory may sound a bit odd. However, I deliberately take my heading for this section from the "Toolbox" feature section of the *Teacher Research* journal in order to make a point. Emphasis on developing questions and observing classroom events to answer them is so dominant in the teacher-research literature that I want to draw attention to a neglected aspect of observing. After all, what we see is a result of what we look for, a consequence of the categories with which we organize our impressions. This means good watching and interpreting of our classrooms depends upon good fashioning of our conceptual lenses.

To support my point, I note that the comment made by my Intro student Blue Pittman—in our third study—that his writing had no more mistakes than my own (and therefore his work, being equal to mine, deserved a high grade) surprised me and made me defensive. However, his comment took on added significance when I finally saw it as a reflection of *gesellschaft* or rights-based democracy. This broader context made his comments more understandable and interesting, less a challenge to my authority and more an indication of underlying social forces in my class. Similarly, Michael Howard's observation—in our first study—that J. S. Mill's *On Liberty* (1859/1947) was relevant to our discussion of responsibility to family as opposed to society also took on added meaning when I saw it through the theoretical spectacles of Belenky et al. (1986). With their epistemological framework in mind, I understood Michael's remarks as helping my class step away from the personal context in which we were conversing (doing what Belenky et al. call "connected knowing") to a broader context which relied on "critical or separate knowing."

Collecting Information about Our Theoretical Commitments

Once we are convinced of theory's importance for teacher research, the next step is to join theorists in conversation. Putting my Berthoffian spin on McCarthy's social construction view of knowledge, I suggest we have to collect data about our responses as we set sail for theoretical land, as we struggle to learn the native's ways of doing, speaking, and writing theory. Reading journals like the *Educational Researcher* and *Educational Theory* would be one way to begin such travel. Of course, a central problem for would-be theory tourists is that those faraway territories are teeming with academics. This means the native speakers use highly technical and obscure language, tongues which foreigners often find inaccessible and arid.

To counteract such travel dangers, I advise you as a theory tourist to wear a heavy sunscreen of patience wherever you go. I also recommend that you be selective about the conversations you choose to follow and the bed-and-breakfasts where you put down your bags. However, if you remember to be patient—to pay close attention to your own reactions and record them in your travel journal (to continue the Berthoffian twist I put on McCarthy's social construction view of knowledge)—then sooner or later you will find theorists who speak to you, ones to whom you can relate, ones who lead you to write a postcard home saying, "I finally met a theorist I understand! He (or she) really makes sense to me!" When that happens, take him or her as your guide. Buy everything you can of his or her writing, paying special attention to the works cited sections. These will be your maps and introductory letters to all sorts of new theoretical data about the field and yourself.

As my readers can see by now, the main implements in my theoretical toolbox are designed to help you collect what I designate as your theoretical commitments, conceptual conversations you care about, theoretical territory that makes you stop, notice, and take a picture. So do not be just a "received knower" as you travel. Get yourself in the pictures you take! Find out what is happening to you! Granted that it is important to attend carefully to the conversations you encounter on educational and social theory, it is even more important to listen closely to your own responses. That is, do not force things. Do not pretend enthusiasm and interest when it is not there. As I encourage my students (and myself), so I urge you, please practice intellectual integrity. I know this is not easy. You may get discouraged and write letters longing for home, but you will eventually get to know the new territory if you wait for honest sparks of connection (pieces of theory you easily integrate into your life). These are crucial since they help you bridge between your classroom world and the new theoretical one in ways that make you a more perceptive, determined, and probing tourist, perhaps, ultimately, the sort who decides to go native.

Analyzing Our Theoretical Commitments

My last practical tip about theory is that when you hear or find these honest sparks of connection, a conversational exchange, perhaps, or an author whose writing strikes a deeply responsive chord—incidents we might characterize as theoretically critical ones—do not be satisfied with that one postcard home. Please work to get clearer about your newly shaped theoretical positions by contextualizing them, making efforts to sympathetically understand the alternatives you reject, the implications of the ones you accept or modify. To this end, I encourage you to cradle your theoretically critical incidents, embracing them through writing, relentlessly asking yourself why you so easily make them (these parts of the new territory) your own. As these incidents accumulate, you will become clearer about the connections among your theoretical obsessions, your compelling concerns and outlooks, and at some point, you may decide you must do what it takes to become part of the conversation. You may determine that you need to join the theoretical community about which you have grown to care, that you want to influence and perfect it while, at the same time, learning more about yourself.

THEORY-DATA INTERPLAY

In stressing theory collection and analysis, as I have been doing—raising it to the same level of importance as empirical data collection and analysis—I write against a prevailing trend in teacher research. The favored idea is that theory is "grounded" and, therefore, does not require special attention: if we just do a thorough job of collecting, indexing, and coding empirical data, theory will emerge. In accepting this standpoint, teacher-researchers are responding to the Glaser and Strauss (1967) fear that we might impose an interpretive structure upon our research situation rather than allowing one to develop from responsible sensitivity to it. As a result, practitioner-inquiry strategy currently leaves theorizing until a late stage of the teacher-research process, until we know more clearly what our questions really are (see Hubbard & Power, 1993; Newman, 1990).

As is already plain, Lucille McCarthy and I take a different, more integrative, stance. We recommend that data and theory collections go hand in hand. Of course, we acknowledge there are all sorts of ways to conduct teacher research, and again, we are not suggesting our strategies are best. However, they have worked for us. For example, after watching the Michael Howard class (in our first study), I sensed something positive had occurred, but I was unsure what it was. He had suddenly changed the class outlook on the question of whether to turn in parents who had broken the law. I could hear the click of alteration in his classmates' conceptual gears, and I wanted to understand better what had happened. But I am not sure that going to ERIC and checking categories like "good class discussion" or "sudden changes in student attention," as Hubbard and Power (1993) suggest, would have helped much. Of course, it was important to know and mull the data, but what really made the difference was Lucille's and my sharing of theoretical material, specifically Belenky et al. (1986), as part of our never-ending reading group of two.

Our ongoing reading also helped me satisfy my nagging desire to figure out why Tate Osborne's revelation about avoiding class assignments was so disturbing. I knew the obvious reason—that I was doing a poor job of motivating students to deal with the curriculum—but what had really gone wrong? *Gemeinschaft* and *gesellschaft* categories were in our heads, but they did not, as Glaser and Strauss's idea of grounded theory suggests, arise from the data in a spontaneous sort of fashion. They were not ideas which came from simply cooking and coding the data. To the contrary, these concepts were part and parcel of our study from the start. That is, as theories they were highly important tools of our empirical data collection. They were the shovels and picks which McCarthy and I used to dig deeper into the tell of my classroom, to reach new layers of artifact and meaning. In the Tate class, from the very beginning, social theory determined the direction of the questions we asked my students, the sorts of interactions among them to which we closely attended.

TEACHER RESEARCH'S EFFECTS ON MY TEACHING AND PROFESSIONAL EMPOWERMENT

As I mention in the introduction to this book, almost all commentators on teacher research suggest that it improves instructional effectiveness and teacher status. Has this been true for me?

Instructional Effectiveness

I have no evidence that I am a better or more effective teacher now than I was 30 years ago when I started. Nevertheless, teacher research has generated renewed enthusiasm for me in the classroom, a kind of antidote to teacher burnout. Why? First off, when I am not engaged in systematic study of my class and things go badly, I think dark thoughts, like maybe I should have been an accordion player or furniture salesman. But when I am engaged in classroom research, a bad class becomes a valuable opportunity. I say to myself, "Wait until I tell Lucille! How can she and I use this difficulty to develop new questions and explorations?" Second, classroom study makes students more interesting to me. Not that they are always wonderful informants, but I never know when students are going to say something significant for the research. When this happens, they become the special object of my love, effort, and attention because I want to tell their stories. And, finally, conducting collaborative inquiry means I really have a co-teacher, someone who cares as much as I do about the details of my students, my pedagogy, and my curriculum.

In addition to renewed enthusiasm and interest, teacher research also allows me to "intelligize" my instructional practice, to borrow a term from my philosopher-colleague Michael Eldridge (1998, pp. 13-42). Although I cannot understand all the relevant factors in my teaching situation, nor can I control the consequences of my pedagogy, my teaching is now more intentional than it was prior to my teacher research. That is, I have a better idea of what I am trying to bring about in the classroom, the reasons behind my assignments, my in-class comments, and my decisions to build on certain student remarks while letting others slide.

Professional Empowerment

What about the second justification frequently offered in defense of teacher research? Have I been empowered by 10 years of classroom studies? Not in the sense of starting a wave of teacher research at the university where I work, and not in the sense of administrators or school trustees seeking out my views on instruction. However, my answer is more positive with regard to my ability to join conversations about education and the power of such participation. If nothing else, McCarthy and I have helped, in modest ways, to make space for teacher research in journals like *College English* and *College Composition and Communication*, periodicals which have not always honored classroom accounts and which have large circulations. We have also regularly reported on teacher research at NCTE and CCCC conventions during the decade of our work together. In short, teacher research has allowed me to exercise new power insofar as McCarthy and I have added to the momentum of the current teacher-research movement, both reflecting on practitioner inquiry as well as doing it.

Teacher Research and Personal Integration

Although I am not sure either Stenhouse or Berthoff had it in mind, the primary importance of teacher research for me is really its power to help me unify my life. As McCarthy explains at the close of Chapter 3, I have continued to play the insider role in our collaboration because of its integrative potential. Not only does it help me talk about classroom theory and practice, data and story, it also allows me to join together my writing, teaching, and research. Now some may believe this is an easy trick. Certainly, many deans think so. I cannot count the times I have heard an administrator say that good research goes hand in hand with good teaching. Really?! Just try returning to an article-in-progress after a weekend of responding to 40 or 50 student papers. And try discussing your latest conference presentation with introductory, or even advanced, students, and see how easy it is to help them understand and appreciate your own excitement. From my perspective, practitioner inquiry is one of the few ways for research to positively influence teaching, for the energy of one to add to and reinforce the energy of the other. That is, when I investigate my classroom, my interests are focused rather than divided, my activities integrated rather than dispersed. In short, teacher research helps me act with integrity.

Of course, many researchers may not share my need for coherence. In fact, I can understand why some readers might find my approach highly dangerous, a risky placing of all my eggs in one basket. If one part of my project goes wrong, my whole life is set on edge. True, but I am willing to take the chance because when I do achieve coherence or centeredness I am more alive (and empowered). There is a ricochet among my important life activities, and this increases the significance of each. Writing becomes a means of research, and research becomes a blessed opportunity to write, and both together add zest and drama to my classroom preparation and practice.

In closing, I refer to the work of the Czech-German poet Rainer Maria Rilke. Whereas Hubbard and Power (1993) quote Rilke to emphasize the importance of starting classroom inquiry with our own questions, I invoke him to champion the importance of beginning with our deepest commitments. In the first of his 10 published letters to the young poet Franz Kappus, Rilke (1903/1962) tells his correspondent that an answer to the question of whether or not Kappus should continue to write poetry has little to do with Kappus's skills and everything to do with Kappus's need to do it. Rilke advises him, wake in the "stillest hour of your night" and ask yourself, if I do not write poetry, will I die? If the answer is anything but yes, Rilke counsels Kappus, you should give up poetry and move on to something else (pp. 18-19).

While Rilke offers what is arguably an overly romantic view of how to choose a career, his answer reflects my own attitude toward teacher research. When we shape our research questions, they must be important ones. In other words, to do the difficult work of learning the language of theoretical communities, as well as the complicated work of exploring our classroom tells, I believe we need to be passionate and single-minded about what we do. With Rilke, I engage in teacher research, not just because I want to be a more effective and socially responsible teacher, but because I have to.

It goes without saying that I cannot claim such wholeheartedness is necessary for all who do teacher research. It is just that my own efforts are fueled by my sense that practitioner inquiry is worthy both as means and as ends: the doing of it being as important as the completing of it, the internal rewards—the challenge and pleasure of building from initial to concluding steps, the putting of my shoulder to a collective enterprise— as important as the published article. Otherwise put, teacher research, for me, is arduous, but its integrative qualities generate the energy I need to do it. As Rilke knew, these integrative qualities change a career into a calling. It is why, as a good Berthoffian, I find the ultimate power of teacher research is its demand that I continually rewrite my life.

Part 2: The Outside-Researcher's Conclusions
Lucille McCarthy

Steve Fishman has just offered advice about how to theorize classroom research, providing tools for integrating classroom data with broader pedagogic and political issues. Reflecting on our 10-year research history, he has buttressed his recommendations with stories about ways he and I have used theory in our own collaborative teacher research. Throughout his comments, Fishman remains, as he says, the good Berthoffian, never for long abandoning his "nose for narrative." In what follows, I also speak in my native tongue, offering Stenhousian advice to complement Steve's Berthoffian wisdom. First, I discuss insider-outsider collaboration, and second, I describe two social science techniques we have found particularly generative, one which we have already discussed, the critical incident, and the other, the think-aloud protocol, which I discuss for the first time. Because our book's aim is to influence the future of practitioner inquiry, I, like Fishman, structure my concluding remarks as advice for teacher-researchers.

LESSONS CONCERNING INSIDER-OUTSIDER COLLABORATION

Despite problems which sometimes occur when outside researchers enter classrooms, if I had to pick a single piece of wisdom for practitioner inquirers, it would be to team up with one or more outsiders. They might be peer teachers or university-based researchers, and the collaboration arrangement can, of course, take many forms. My own experience suggests a co-learning arrangement is best, a reciprocal agreement in which you and your partner(s) exchange classroom visits, share data collection and analysis, and co-author research reports. But if you cannot manage cross visitation, and if co-authoring is impossible, I suggest you meet regularly with your collaborator(s) to discuss research questions and procedures, emerging interpretations of data, and report drafts. It is my strong belief, after working with Fishman (and, across my career, with several other collaborators as well), that my research has been more fun, more imaginative, and, ultimately, more fruitful than it ever would have been had I worked alone. In sum, the clear lesson from my own research history is that several heads and hearts are better than one (see McCarthy & Fishman, 1996; McCarthy & Walvoord, 1988).

Choosing a Partner

The richness of any collaboration depends, however, on the participants' relationship. And the quality of this relationship is, in my view, less dependent on collaborators' relative positions in the educational hierarchy than on their shared commitment to the project, their mutual respect and need for one another, and their common assumption that everyone must profit equally from the work. But how do you identify such a collaborator? How do you know a collaboration will work before you have tried it out? Well, I suppose you don't, as Fishman's and my unplayed tapes reveal. All Steve and I knew about each other when we met was that the other one had skills we needed and that both of us wanted to publish. But Fishman's and my complementary abilities and our common publication goal would not have taken us far had we been unable to negotiate our roles and responsibilities, ameliorate power imbalances, and, ultimately, construct a common language—the mix of Stenhousian and Berthoffian dialects we have described. This was not easy, as we have shown, and it took us a while. But in retrospect, I believe we persisted—and continue to persist—because we have both always felt we were learning from one another, that we were, as individuals, growing within the collaboration.

My recommendation, then, is that in choosing a research partner you try to pick someone with whom you can grow. But let me be honest and admit it also helps if you and your partner share certain personality traits and values. For example, Fishman and I are, to put it bluntly, equally compulsive. Neither of us can tolerate a missed deadline, an article half read, an interview not bothered with, a stone unturned. A collaboration for either of us with someone less uptight, more laid back and relaxed, would, I believe, have been impossible. In addition, Fishman and I are equally serious about our shared project, the pursuit of good teaching.

Developing a Cooperative, "Critical" Community

So when a collaboration clicks, as it has for Fishman and me, it provides you with inquiry partners, co-learners dedicated to a mutually valued quest. It also creates a "critical" community (Phillips, 1992, p. 30). That is, throughout our work, Fishman and I question one another, challenge each other's interpretations, push for clarification, asking, What's your point? What's your evidence? And how is this relevant to our work anyway? Although these exchanges sound agonistic, they always feel safe to me. This is because I know that no matter how demanding Fishman and I are of one another or how discordant our positions, we are not playing a win-loss game. In fact, our strong differences are, as we have shown, the means to our shared end: a research report honoring both our perspectives, one we can both be proud of.

My collaborator's critical eye on my work is especially useful, I have found, during data analysis. At this stage I sit at my kitchen table reading and rereading stacks of student interview and think-aloud transcripts, piles of pupil writing, and notebooks full of my own and Fishman's observations and reflections. Over several weeks, I construct an elaborate category system on legal pads, using various colors of ink, my handwriting getting tinier and tinier as I squeeze in more data cites. At this point I want to be lost in my data forest, wandering through thickets of student and teacher language, noticing fresh connections and repeated refrains. But I often need help finding my way out. Fishman's questions as I describe my emerging constructions—or his suggestions of alternative interpretations or images or his reminders about theory—often are crucial in helping me decide which paths to follow, which to abandon. And, likewise, his responses to my early data-reduction drafts promote similar focusing and sharpening. Although in these drafts I succeed in reducing the data field and sketching preliminary narrative lines, they are, generally, still too loose and poorly theorized. But I write them knowing Fishman will come to my rescue, his theoretic and narrative instincts helping me make sense of my Stenhousian social science abundance.

Effects of Insider-Outsider Collaboration on My Research and My Classroom

It has also been my experience, as I have indicated, that successful collaborations promote practice-changing discovery. I started with Steve Fishman in 1989, a Stenhousian social scientist trained to retain my outsider expertise in data-extraction agreements with teacher-insiders. In fact, as we show in Chapter 3, my stance threatened to dominate and silence Fishman, assuming as I did the outsider advantage which Lincoln terms the "priesthood of [the] social science expert" (Maxwell & Lincoln, 1990, p. 502). I had not yet experienced the benefits—or the challenges—of sharing authority with the teacher I was studying, the potential rewards of integrating the insider's voice with my own. Neither did I foresee the role reversal we describe in Chapter 3, the moment when Fishman dared me to put the shoe on the other foot, to become the observed rather than observer, thereby illuminating for me both my teaching and my research.

This collaboration, then, while it has been difficult at times—calling for large doses of tact, flexibility, and courage on both our parts—has been extremely rewarding. Our different personalities and research orientations, our contrasting outsider and insider perspectives, have required me to step into Fishman's perspective and to articulate my own. I have been required, in effect, to become an outsider to my own practices, and this has resulted, for me, in fresh ways of seeing and going at the world.

LESSONS ABOUT INTEGRATING RESEARCH METHODS

Making the Most of Critical Incidents

In Chapters 7 and 9, Fishman describes the critical incidents which, in our third and fourth studies, arrested our attention and set our "emotional Geiger counters" beeping. Such incidents, he claims, are more the product of Berthoffian narrative methodology than Stenhousian social science, more connected to our life-long intellectual and pedagogic stories than to a particular semester's data collection. And I agree with Steve. It is true that I sense intuitively that I have just witnessed something "special"; I know it in my gut before I have time to think. However, it is also true, as

Steve himself admits, that our critical incidents have often been set up by our ongoing Stenhousian techniques and, more important, brought to fruition by them. In the case of the events around which we build our third and fourth studies—the Tate Osborne and Shanderic Downs incidents—it was the data collection we added immediately after these moments which clarified their richness for us. Steve and I both observed these incidents, and we both resonated to them, were moved, fascinated, puzzled. But it was only as I grabbed key players for follow-up interviews, eliciting their perspectives and interpretations, only as I questioned them across time, triangulating among student, teacher, and my own outsider-researcher accounts, that we began to understand why Tate and Shanderic affected us so.

My second piece of wisdom for teacher-researchers is, then, to respect your intuitions, take seriously the moments in your teaching that touch you, make you want to cry or sing or shout. Pay close attention to events you feel you need to understand or which you want to memorialize in your writing. If the moment "refuses to go away," keeping you up late or awakening you early, I urge you to study it. Gather new perspectives. Ask participants to reflect, speak, and write about it. Review videotapes and audiotapes if you have them. Converse with research partners. Try to figure out why you were so affected, which of your assumptions, your closely held beliefs, were challenged by the incident (as Fishman's were in our third and fourth studies.)

Looking back, I see that in my early Stenhousian studies I pay little attention to dramatic moments, and this is understandable. Throughout my social science training no one ever spoke about the researcher's felt sense, and it never occurred to me I was missing anything. Instead, I applied my analytic techniques to systematically collected data, confident these methods would serve up well-warranted conclusions. Across time, however, Fishman's Berthoffian zeal has chipped away more than one chink in my Stenhousian armor, and as critical moments have become more important in our work, I have learned to trust my feelings. My sense that a particular moment is full of meaning, full of narrative import, now often precedes and shapes the way I apply my social science techniques.

Adding Think-Aloud Audiotapes to Your Toolbox

A data collection method we have not discussed, but one I have found valuable throughout my career, is the think-aloud protocol. I mention it here, hoping teacher-researchers will experiment with it in their own settings, adding it to their inquiry repertoire if they find it useful. In these think-alouds, I ask students to speak into a tape recorder while they are reading or writing their class assignments. The purpose is to help me learn about their processes as well as their attitudes toward their course work. Sometimes I observe students as they record; most times I do not. In the latter case, students work at home or in their dorms, turning on the tape player to let Fishman and me eavesdrop on their learning, their struggles and resolutions as they complete class assignments.

In essence, students who agree to record these protocols consent to lift the veil on their frustrations and satisfactions, the processes that lie behind their observable behaviors and texts, and as I transcribe these tapes, I am often rewarded with rich information about pupil experience in Fishman's class. These data add to the student pictures I am creating, cross-checking and augmenting pupil interview comments, corroborating or contradicting my classroom observations or text analysis. And not only do I learn about students' thinking and feeling but also about the social situations in which they complete their out-of-class work. Although this methodology has been criticized as too intrusive, I appreciate its elasticity and the insights it provides about student work habits and learning experiences. (For more on the think-aloud tool, its strengths and limitations, see Cooper & Holzman 1983, 1985; Ericsson & Simon, 1980; Flower & Hayes, 1985; Hayes & Flower, 1983; Walvoord & McCarthy, 1990; Swarts, Flower, & Hayes, 1984).

In Fishman's and my first two projects, I draw upon composing-aloud protocols that were recorded by my five focus students as they revised their final papers for Intro to Philosophy. In these initial studies, I wanted to understand the nature of philosophic discourse and students' efforts to learn it, so I focused on (and counted) students' "conscious concerns" as they revised. What did they pay attention to while composing? What, in these students' minds, constituted "good" thinking and writing in philosophy? The think-alouds allowed me to study pupils' writing processes as they happened, to gain insight into their conceptions of this new academic language and their struggles to speak it. In these early think-alouds, I directed the 30-minute session as I had learned to do at Penn, sitting by students as they composed, noting their body language and prodding them to speak aloud when they fell silent.

In the years since those initial studies, however, I have varied my use of the think-aloud tool, frequently asking students to record when I am not present. I invite certain of my focus students—ones in whom I am

particularly interested—to think aloud when they are doing out-of-class
assignments for Fishman's course. I permit more freedom in the proce
dure than I used to, hoping students will feel comfortable, their processe
as little disrupted as possible. Because my adjustments mean that th
think-alouds are now less under my control, the data I get vary widel
When I collect students' tapes at the end of the semester, some are har
to decipher and frustratingly sparse, virtually useless in other words. Bu
when the tapes are good, when students have gotten used to—even com
to enjoy—thinking and reflecting aloud, the data enlighten me abou
their experiences in rich and exciting ways. In sum, the think-aloud too
is for me a flexible and useful one, complementing others in my kit b
providing a window into student activities usually beyond th
researcher's view. (For an example of a recent invitation to students t
record think-alouds, see the appendix.)

Final Words
Lucille McCarthy and Steve Fishman

When it came time to write this final chapter, we turned to one anothe
and said, How should we do this? What constitutes an appropriate con
clusion for a book of reflections on teacher research? It can hardly be th
same sort of ending we usually write, our customary restatement o
research findings and speculations about their implications. So we agree
Fishman would offer the lessons he has learned across our 10-yea
collaboration, and McCarthy would provide hers. We would write ou
sections separately, sharing only a general outline, and then we woul
swap. At that point, we agreed, we would figure out how to fit these part
together. You have just read the result.

What strikes us about our double byline conclusion is that, after
decade of working together, we still retain our initial propensities
Fishman's Berthoffian romanticism is as strong as ever, and McCarth
continues to center her attention on perfecting her Stenhousian socia
science methodology. Yet we are hardly unchanged. Fishman has s
mastered McCarthy's social constructionist dialect that he tells a tale o
teacher-researchers' setting sail for "theoretical land"—a new discours
community—to collect data about themselves. And McCarthy is so influ
enced by Fishman's narrative instincts that she admits she now focuse
her best social science techniques on classroom events chosen emotionally

ones that have moved her for reasons she may little understand. So we read each other's contributions to this conclusion with interest and find evidence of borrowing and modifying in both our pieces. But we have not merged our voices. We have held on to, and sharpened, the perspectives with which we began our association many years ago.

So our conclusion-writing experiment teaches us once again that our jobs as collaborators cannot be divided exactly fifty-fifty. We cannot be—nor do we want to be—just the same. Rather, we continue our efforts to achieve equity in Dewey's qualitative sense, a cooperative community in which our individual differences become our common strength, and our unique contributions forward our common enterprise.

APPENDIX
MEMO TO FOCUS STUDENTS
ABOUT THINK-ALOUDS

To: Fellow Student Researchers
From: Dr. McCarthy
Re: Tape Recording Your Writing and Reflections in Philosophy

Thank you for agreeing to join me in studying your experiences in philosophy this semester. I'll summarize here what I mentioned to you on the phone, but please feel free to call me collect if you have questions.

When to Turn on the Tape Recorder and What to Say

1. When you are writing anything for this class (study questions, questions for group, class reflection logs, drafts of papers, notes on reading, class notes, etc.) Please try to record during writing, tracking your decision making, describing where you get stuck, how you get out of trouble, how you decide to structure the piece, etc. In addition to your thinking, I am also interested in your feelings (frustration, boredom, mind wandering, excitement, understanding, etc.). Please talk also about your social situation when relevant (where you write, TV on, interruptions by phone, kids, roommates, getting up to get a snack, etc.). In other words, I am interested in a movie of your mind and body during writing. Please be detailed and honest.

2. During and after reading. Please tell me about your reading of various texts during or soon after you finish. As with your composing, describe your thinking, feelings, and social situation and interactions. Again, I'm interested in your problems and challenges as well as your successes. Please be detailed and honest.

3. Please also turn on the tape to reflect for a few minutes on what you particularly remember from the previous class. What struck you? What did you learn and why (or fail to learn)? What helped you (or failed to help): other students, the teacher, some reading or writing you or someone else did, etc.? What frustrated, angered, pleased, excited, embarrassed you? Again, there are no right answers here; my goal is to experience the class from your point of view. Please be detailed and honest.

Each time you speak into the tape, please begin by telling me the date and assignment you are working on. If you are reflecting on a class, please tell me the date of that class. In other words, be sure I know what you are composing, reading, or commenting on.

Taping Log
Please keep a log where you note the date and subject of each taping so I also have a visual record of what is on your tapes.

My Meetings with You
I will meet with you on each of my visits to UNCC this fall in order to talk further with you about your experiences in Intro to Philosophy. I will collect your tapes and logs at the end of the semester. Please keep receipts of anything you spend for this work, and I will reimburse you. Again, thanks a million.

WORKS CITED

Allen, J. (Ed.). (1999). *Class actions: Teaching for social justice in elementary and middle school.* New York: Teachers College Press.

Allen, J., Buchanan, C., Edelsky, C., & Norton, G. (1992). Teachers as "they" at NRC: The ethics of collaborative and non-collaborative classroom research. In C. Kinzer & D. Leu (Eds.), *Literacy research, theory, and practice: Views from many perspectives* (pp. 357-365). Chicago: National Reading Conference.

Altrichter, H., Posch, P., & Somekh, B. (1993). *Teachers investigate their work: An introduction to the methods of action research.* New York: Routledge.

Anderson, G. L., & Herr, K. (1999). The new paradigm wars: Is there room for rigorous practitioner knowledge in schools and universities? *Educational Researcher, 28*(5), 12-21.

Applebee, A. (1987). Musings: Teachers and the process of research. *Research in the Teaching of English, 2,* 5-7.

Atwell, N. (1984). Writing and reading literature from the inside out. *Language Arts, 61,* 240-252.

Avery, C. S. (1987). Traci: A learning-disabled child in a writing-process classroom. In G. L. Bissex & R. H. Bullock (Eds.), *Seeing for ourselves: Case-study research by teachers of writing* (pp. 59-76). Portsmouth, NH: Heinemann.

Bakhtin, M. (1981). *The dialogic imagination.* Austin: U of Texas P.

Banford, H., Berkman, M., Chin, C., Cziko, C., Fecho, B., Jumpp, D., Miller, C., & Resnick, M. (1996). *Cityscapes: Eight views from the urban classroom.* Berkeley: National Writing Project.

Banks, J. A. (1998). The lives and values of researchers: Implications for educating citizens in a multicultural society. *Educational Researcher, 27*(7), 4-17.

Bartholomae, D. (1985). Inventing the university. In M. Rose (Ed.), *When a writer can't write: Studies in writer's block and other composing-process problems* (pp. 134-165). New York: Guilford Press.

Bazerman, C. (1988). *Shaping written knowledge: The genre and activity of the experimental article in science.* Madison: U of Wisconsin P.

Becher, T. (1987). Disciplinary discourse. *Studies in Higher Education, 12,* 261-274.

Belenky, M. F., Clinchy, B. M., Goldberger, N. R., & Tarule, J. M. (1986). *Women's ways of knowing: The development of self, voice, and mind.* New York: Basic Books.

Berkenkotter, C., Huckin, T. N., & Ackerman, J. (1988). Conventions, conversations, and the writer: Case study of a student in a rhetoric Ph.D. program. *Research in the Teaching of English, 22,* 9-44.

Berlin, J. (1988). Rhetoric and ideology in the writing class. *College English, 50,* 477-494.

Berthoff, A. E. (1981). Towards a pedagogy of knowing. In A. Berthoff, *The making of meaning: Metaphors, models, and maxims for writing teachers* (pp. 48-60). Upper Montclair, NJ: Boynton/Cook. (Original work published 1978)

Berthoff, A. E. (1987a). The teacher as REsearcher. In D. Goswami & P. Stillman (Eds.), *Reclaiming the classroom: Teacher research as an agency for change* (pp. 28-39). Portsmouth, NH: Boynton/Cook-Heinemann. (Original paper presented 1979)

Berthoff, A. E. (1987b). From dialogue to dialectic to dialogue. In D. Goswami & P. Stillman (Eds.), *Reclaiming the classroom: Teacher research as an agency for change* (pp. 75-94). Portsmouth, NH: Boynton/Cook-Heinemann.

Beyer, L. (Ed.). (1996). *Creating democratic classrooms: The struggle to integrate theory and practice.* New York: Teachers College Press.

Bisplinghoff, B. S., & Allen, J. (Eds.). (1998). *Engaging teachers: Creating teaching and researching relationships.* Portsmouth, NH: Heinemann.

Bissex, G. L. (1987). What is a teacher-researcher? In G. L. Bissex & R. H. Bullock (Eds.), *Seeing for ourselves: Case-study research by teachers of writing* (pp. 3-5). Portsmouth, NH: Heinemann.

Bissex, G. L., & Bullock, R. H. (Eds.). (1987). *Seeing for ourselves: Case-study research by teachers of writing.* Portsmouth, NH: Heinemann.

Bizzell, P. (1982). Cognition, convention, and certainty: What we need to know about writing. *PRE/TEXT, 3,* 213-243.

Bizzell, P. (1992). *Academic discourse and critical consciousness.* Pittsburgh: U of Pittsburgh P.

Bleich, D. (1990). Sexism in academic styles of learning. *Journal of Advanced Composition, 10,* 231-248.

Brause, R. S., & Mayher, J. S. (Eds.) (1991). *Search and re-search: What the inquiring teacher needs to know.* London: Falmer.

Britton, J., Burgess, T., Martin, N., McLeod, A., & Rosen, H. (1975). *The development of writing abilities 11-18.* London: Macmillan.

Brodkey, L. (1987). *Academic writing as social practice.* Philadelphia: Temple UP.

Brodkey, L. (1996). *Writing permitted in designated areas only.* Minneapolis: U of Minnesota P.

Brooke, R. (1987). Underlife and writing instruction. *College Composition and Communication, 31,* 141-153.

Brookfield, S. D. (1995). *Becoming a critically reflective teacher.* San Francisco: Jossey-Bass.

Burnett, R. E., & Ewald, H. R. (1994). Rabbit trails, ephemera, and other stories: Feminist methodology and collaborative research. *Journal of Advanced Composition, 14,* 21-51.

Campbell, K. (1998). If only I had time on my side! *Teacher Research: The Journal of Classroom Inquiry, 5,* 169-171.

Carini, P. F. (1979). *The art of seeing and the visibility of the person.* Grand Forks: University of North Dakota.

Chandler, K. (1998). Saying "Y'all come" to teacher researchers: An interview with JoBeth Allen. *Teacher Researcher: The Journal of Classroom Inquiry, 5,* 47-67.

Clifford, J. (1983). On ethnographic authority. *Representations, 1,* 118-146.

Clifford, J., & Marcus, G. E. (1986). *Writing culture: The poetics and politics of ethnography.* Berkeley: U of California P.

Cochran-Smith, M., Garfield, E., & Greenberger, R. (1992). Student teachers and their teacher: Talking our way into new understandings. In N. A. Branscombe, D. Goswami, & J. Schwartz (Eds.), *Students teaching, teachers learning* (pp. 274-292). Portsmouth, NH: Boynton/Cook-Heinemann.

Cochran-Smith, M., & Lytle, S. (1993). *Inside/outside: Teacher research and knowledge.* New York: Teachers College Press.

Cochran-Smith, M., & Lytle, S. (1998). Teacher research: The question that persists. *International Journal of Leadership in Education, 1*(1), 19-36.

Cochran-Smith, M., & Lytle, S. (1999). The teacher research movement: A decade later. *Educational Researcher, 28*(7), 15-25.

Cole, A., & Knowles, J. G. (1993). Teacher development partnership research: A focus on methods and issues. *American Educational Research Journal, 30,* 473-495.

Cone, J. (1994). Appearing acts: Creating readers in a high school English class. *Harvard Educational Review, 64,* 450-473.

Constas, M. A. (1998). The changing nature of educational research and a critique of postmodernism. *Educational Researcher, 27*(2), 26-33.

Cooper, M., & Holzman, M. (1983). Talking about protocols. *College Composition and Communication, 34,* 284-293.

Cooper, M., & Holzman, M. (1985). Reply. *College Composition and Communication, 36,* 97-100.

Delpit, L. (1995). *Other people's children: Cultural conflict in the classroom.* New York: New Press.

Dewey, J. (1960). *How we think* (Rev. ed.). Lexington, MA: Heath. (Original work published 1933)

Dewey, J. (1962a). *A common faith.* New Haven: Yale UP. (Original work published 1934)

Dewey, J. (1962b). *Reconstruction in philosophy.* Boston: Beacon Press. (Original work published 1920)

Dewey, J. (1963). *Experience and education.* New York: Collier. (Original work published 1938)

Dewey, J. (1964). The relation of theory to practice in education. In R. Archimbault (Ed.), *John Dewey on education* (pp. 313-338). Chicago: U of Chicago P. (Original work published 1904)

Dewey, J. (1967). *Democracy and education.* New York: Free Press. (Original work published 1916)

Dewey, J. (1988). *The public and its problems.* Athens, OH: Swallow. (Original work published 1927)

Dewey, J. (1990). *The school and society;* and *The child and the curriculum.* Chicago: U of Chicago P. (Original work published 1902)

Durst, R. K., & Stanforth, S. C. (1996). "Everything's negotiable": Collaboration and conflict in composition research. In P. Mortensen & G. E. Kirsch (Eds.), *Ethics and representation in qualitative studies of literacy* (pp. 58-76). Urbana, IL: National Council of Teachers of English.

Dyson, A. H. (1984). Learning to write/learning to do school: Emergent writers' interpretations of school literacy tasks. *Research in the Teaching of English, 18,* 233-264.

Ede, L., & Lunsford, A. (1990). *Singular texts/plural authors.* Carbondale: Southern Illinois University Press.

Edelsky, C. (1994). Education for democracy. *Language Arts, 71,* 252-257.

Edelsky, C., & Boyd, C. (1993). Collaborative research: More questions than answers. In S. J. Hudelson & J. W. Lindfors (Eds.), *Delicate balances: Collaborative research in language education* (pp. 4-20). Urbana, IL: National Council of Teachers of English.

Eisner, E. W., & Peshkin, A. (1990). *Qualitative inquiry in education: The continuing debate.* New York: Teachers College Press.

Elbow, P. (1973). *Writing without teachers.* New York: Oxford UP.

Elbow, P. (1993). The uses of binary thinking. *Journal of Advanced Composition, 12,* 51-78.

Eldridge, M. (1998). *Transforming experience: John Dewey's cultural instrumentalism.* Nashville: Vanderbilt UP.

Elliott, J. (1991). *Action research for educational change.* Buckingham, UK: Open UP.

Emig, J. (1971). *The composing processes of twelfth graders.* Urbana, IL: National Council of Teachers of English.

Entes, J. (1994). The right to write a co-authored manuscript. In S. B. Reagan, T. Fox, & D. Bleich (Eds.), *Writing with: New directions in collaborative teaching, learning, and research* (pp. 47-60). Albany: State U of New York P.

Ericsson, K. A., & Simon, H. A. (1980). Verbal reports as data. *Psychological Review, 87,* 215-251.

Feiman-Nemser, S., & Melnick, S. (1992). Introducing teaching. In S. Feiman-Nemser & H. Featherstone (Eds.), *Exploring teaching: Reinventing an introductory course.* New York: Teachers College Press.

Feldman, A., & Atkin, J. M. (1995). Embedding action research in professional practice. In S. E. Noffke & R. B. Stevenson (Eds.), *Educational action research: Becoming practically critical* (pp. 127-137). New York: Teachers College Press.

Fishman, S. M. (1985). Writing-to-learn in philosophy. *Teaching Philosophy, 8,* 331-334.

Fishman, S. M. (1989). Writing and philosophy. *Teaching Philosophy, 12,* 361-374.

Fishman, S. M. (1993). Explicating our tacit tradition: John Dewey and composition studies. *College Composition and Communication, 44,* 315-330.

Fishman, S. M., & McCarthy, L. P. (1992). Is expressivism dead? Reconsidering its romantic roots and its relation to social constructionism. *College English, 54,* 647-661.

Fishman, S. M., & McCarthy, L. P. (1995). Community in the expressivist classroom: Juggling liberal and communitarian visions. *College English, 57,* 62-81.

Fishman, S. M., & McCarthy, L. P. (1996). Teaching for student change: A Deweyan alternative to radical pedagogy. *College Composition and Communication, 47,* 342-366.

Fishman, S. M., & McCarthy, L. P. (1998). *John Dewey and the challenge of classroom practice.* New York: Teachers College Press (co-published by the National Council of Teachers of English).

Fitts, K., & France, A. W. (Eds.). (1995). *Left margins: Cultural studies and composition pedagogy.* Albany: State U of New York P.

Flinders, M. (1997). *Just girls: Hidden literacies and life in junior high.* New York: Teachers College Press.

Flores, E., & Granger, S. (1995). The role of the collaborator in action research. In S. E. Noffke & R. B. Stevenson (Eds.), *Educational action research: Becoming practically critical* (pp. 165-179). New York: Teachers College Press.

Flower, L. S., & Hayes, J. R. (1985). Response to Marilyn Cooper and Michael Holzman. "Talking about protocols." *College Composition and Communication, 36,* 94-97.

Foucault, M. (1978). *Power/knowledge: Selected interviews and other writings, 1972-1977* (C. Gordon, Ed., & C. Gordon, L. Marshall, J. Mepham, & K. Soper, Trans.). New York: Pantheon Books.

France, A. W. (1993). Response. *College English, 55,* 549-550.

Freedman, A. (1993). Show and tell? The role of explicit teaching in the learning of new genres. *Research in the Teaching of English, 3,* 222-251.

Geertz, C. (1976). From the native's point of view: On the nature of anthropological understanding. In K. H. Basso and H. A. Selby (Eds.), *Meaning in anthropology* (pp. 221-237). Albuquerque: U of New Mexico P.

Geertz, C. (1983). The way we think now: Toward an ethnography of modern thought. In C. Geertz, *Local knowledge: Further essays in interpretive anthropology* (pp. 147-163). New York: Basic Books.

Geertz, C. (1988). *Works and lives: The anthropologist as author.* Stanford, CA: Stanford UP.

Glaser, B., & Strauss, A. (1967). *The discovery of grounded theory: Strategies for qualitative research.* New York: Aldine DeGruyter.

Goodman, K. S. (1996). Language development: Issues, insights, and implementation. In B. M. Power & R. S. Hubbard (Eds.), *Language development: A reader for teachers* (pp. 81-86). Englewood Cliffs, NJ: Prentice Hall. (Original work published 1989)

Goswami, D., & Stillman, P. R. (Eds.). (1987). *Reclaiming the classroom: Teacher research as an agency for change.* Portsmouth, NH: Boynton/Cook-Heinemann.

Graves, D. (1983). *Writing: Teachers and children at work.* Portsmouth, NH: Heinemann.

Guba, E. G. (1990). *The paradigm dialog.* Newbury Park, CA: Sage.

Hafernik, J. J., Messerschmitt, D. S., & Vandrick, S. (1997). Collaborative research: Why and how? *Educational Researcher, 26*(9), 31-35.

Hall, I., Campbell, C. H., & Miech, E. J. (1997). *Class acts: Teachers reflect on their own classroom practice.* Boston: Harvard Educational Review.

Harding, S. (1986). *The science question in feminism.* Ithaca, NY: Cornell University Press.

Harding, S. (1987). *Feminism and methodology: Social science issues.* Bloomington: Indiana UP.

Harris, J. (1989). The idea of community in the study of writing. *College Composition and Communication, 40,* 11-22.

Hayes, J. R., & Flower, L. S. (1983). Uncovering cognitive processes in writing: An introduction to protocol analysis. In P. Mosenthal, L. Tamor, & S. A. Walmsley (Eds.), *Research on writing: Principles and methods* (pp. 207-220). New York: Longman.

Headman, R. (1993). Parents and teachers as co-investigators. In M. Cochran-Smith & S. Lytle, *Inside/outside: Teacher research and knowledge* (pp. 220-230). New York: Teachers College Press.

Herder, J. G. (1966). *On the origin of language* (T. O. Churchill, Trans.). Chicago: U of Chicago P. (Original work published 1770)

Herrington, A. (1985). Writing in academic settings: A study of the contexts for writing in two college chemical engineering courses. *Research in the Teaching of English, 19*, 331-359.

Hesse, M. (1980). *Revolutions and reconstructions in the philosophy of science.* Bloomington: Indiana UP.

Hirtle, J. S. (1993). Connecting to the classics. In L. Patterson, C. M. Santa, K. G. Short, & K. Smith (Eds.), *Teachers are researchers: Reflection and action* (pp. 137-146). Newark, DE: International Reading Association.

Hofstadter, R. (1963). *Anti-intellectualism in American life.* New York: Knopf.

hooks, b. (1994). *Teaching to transgress: Education as the practice of freedom.* New York: Routledge.

Hopkins, D. (1985). *A teacher's guide to classroom research* (2nd ed.). Buckingham, UK: Open UP. (Originally published in 1985)

Hubbard, R. S., & Power, B. M. (1993). *The art of classroom inquiry: A handbook for teacher-researchers.* Portsmouth, NH: Heinemann.

Hursh, D. (1995). Developing discourses and structures to support action research for educational reform: Working both ends. In S. E. Noffke & R. B. Stevenson (Eds.), *Educational action research: Becoming practically critical* (pp. 141-153). New York: Teachers College Press.

Hymes, D. (1972). Introduction. In C. Cazden, V. P. John, & D. Hymes (Eds.), *Functions of language in the classroom* (pp. xi-lxii). New York: Teachers College Press.

Hymes, D. (1974). *Foundations in sociolinguistics: An ethnographic approach.* Philadelphia: U of Pennsylvania P.

Isakson, M. B., & Boody, R. M. (1993). Hard questions about teacher research. In L. Patterson, C. M. Santa, K. G. Short, & K. Smith (Eds.), *Teachers are researchers: Reflection and action* (26-34). Newark, DE: International Reading Association.

Jarratt, S. (1992). Feminism and composition: The case for conflict. In P. Harkin & J. Schilb (Eds.), *Contending with words: Composition in a postmodern era* (pp.105-125). New York: Modern Language Association.

Jordan, C., & Jacob, E. (1993). Ethnographic intervention: Applying anthropology to affect educational practice. In E. Jacob & C. Jordan (Eds.), *Minority education: Anthropological perspectives.* Norwood, NJ: Ablex.

Jumpp, D. (1996). Extending the literate community: Literacy over a life span. In H. Banford, M. Berkman, C. Chin, C. Cziko, B. Fecho, D. Jumpp, C. Miller, & M. Resnick et al. (Eds.), *Cityscapes: Eight views from the urban classroom.* Berkeley: National Writing Project.

Keller, E. F. (1982). Feminism and science. *Signs: Journal of Women in Culture and Society, 7*, 589-602.

Keller, E. F. (1985). *Reflections on gender and science.* New Haven: Yale UP.

Kerrigan, W. J. (1974). *Writing to the point: Six basic steps.* New York: Harcourt Brace Jovanovich.

Kinchloe, J. (1993). *Toward a critical politics of teacher thinking: Mapping the postmodern.* London: Bergin and Garvey.

Kuhn, T. S. (1962). *The structure of scientific revolutions.* Chicago: U of Chicago P.

Larsen, L. A. (1998). Home reading journals: Building bridges through literature. *Teacher Research: The Journal of Classroom Inquiry, 5,* 68-91.

Lather, P. (1991). *Getting smart: Feminist research and pedagogy with/in the postmodern.* New York: Routledge.

Lensmire, T. J. (1994). *When children write: Critical re-visions of the writing workshop.* New York: Teachers College Press.

Lincoln, Y. (1990). The making of a constructivist: A remembrance of transformations past. In E. G. Guba (Ed.), *The paradigm dialog* (pp. 67-87). Newbury Park, CA: Sage.

Lincoln, Y. S., & Guba, E. G. (1985). *Naturalistic inquiry.* Beverly Hills, CA: Sage.

Lu, M.-Z., & Horner, B. The problematic of experience: Redefining critical work in ethnography and pedagogy. *College English, 60,* 257-277.

Lyotard, J. F. (1992). *Postmodernism explained.* Minneapolis: U of Minnesota P.

Lytle, S. (1997). On *reading* teacher research. *Focus on Basics, 1,* 19-22.

Lytle, S., & Fecho, R. (1992). Meeting strangers in familiar places: Teacher collaboration by cross-visitation. In N. A. Branscombe, D. Goswami, & J. Schwartz (Eds.), *Students teaching, teachers learning* (pp. 296-317). Portsmouth, NH: Boynton/Cook Heinemann. (Orignial work published 1991)

MacIntyre, A. (1981). *After virtue: A study in moral theory.* Notre Dame, IN: U of Notre Dame P.

Mascia-Lees, F. E., Sharpe, P., & Cohen, C. B. (1989). The postmodernist turn in anthropology: Cautions from a feminist perspective. *Signs: Journal of Women in Culture and Society, 15,* 7-33.

Maxwell, J. A., & Lincoln, Y. S. (1990). Methodology and epistemology: A dialogue. *Harvard Educational Review, 60,* 497-512.

McCarthy, L. P. (1985). A stranger in strange lands: A college student writing across the curriculum. *Dissertation Abstracts International, 46-05A,* p. 1217. (University Microfilms No. AAG85-15414)

McCarthy, L. P. (1987). A stranger in strange lands: A college student writing across the curriculum. *Research in the Teaching of English, 21,* 233-265.

McCarthy, L. P., & Braffman, E. J. (1985). Creating Victorian Philadelphia: Children reading and writing the world. *Curriculum Inquiry, 15,* 121-151.

McCarthy, L. P., & Fishman, S. M. (1991). Boundary conversations: Conflicting ways of knowing in philosophy and interdisciplinary research. *Research in the Teaching of English, 25,* 419-468.

McCarthy, L. P., & Fishman, S. M. (1996). A text for many voices: Representing diversity in reports of naturalistic research. In P. Mortensen & G. E. Kirsch (Eds.), *Ethics and representation in qualitative studies of literacy* (pp. 155-176). Urbana, IL: National Council of Teachers of English.

McCarthy, L. P., & Walvoord, B. E. (1988). Models for collaborative research in writing across the curriculum. In S. McLeod (Ed.), *Strengthening programs for writing across the curriculum* (pp. 77-89). San Francisco: Jossey-Bass.

Miles, M. B., & Huberman, A. M. (1984). *Qualitative data analysis.* Beverly Hills, CA: Sage.

Mill, J. S. (1947). *On liberty*. Arlington Heights, IL: Harlan Davidson. (Original work published 1859)

Miller, S. (1994). New discourse city: An alternative model for collaboration. In S. B. Reagan, T. Fox, & D. Bleich (Eds.), *Writing with: New directions in collaborative teaching, learning, and research* (283-300). Albany: State U of New York P.

Mohr, M. M., & MacLean, M. S. (1999). *Teacher-researchers at work*. Berkeley, CA: National Writing Project.

Murray, D. M. (1968). *A writer teaches writing: A practical method of teaching composition*. Boston: Houghton Mifflin.

Myers, G. (1985). The social construction of two biologists' proposals. *Written Communication, 2,* 219-245.

Nelson, J. (1995). Reading classrooms as text: Exploring student writers' interpretive practices. *College Composition and Communication, 46,* 411-429.

Newkirk, T. (1996). Seduction and betrayal in qualitative research. In P. Mortensen & G. E. Kirsch (Eds.), *Ethics and representation in qualitative studies of literacy* (pp. 3-16). Urbana, IL: National Council of Teachers of English.

Newman, J. M. (1990). *Finding our own way: Teachers exploring their assumptions*. Portsmouth, NH: Heinemann.

Newman, J. M. (1998). *Tensions of teaching: Beyond tips to critical reflection*. New York: Teachers College Press.

Noffke, S. (1997). Professional, personal, and political dimensions of action research. In M. Apple (Ed.), *Review of research in education* (Vol. 22, pp. 301-343). Washington, DC: American Educational Research Association.

Noffke, S. E., & Stevenson, R. B. (Eds.). (1995). *Educational action research: Becoming practically critical*. New York: Teachers College Press.

Odell, L. (1987). Planning classroom research. In D. Goswami & P. R. Stillman (Eds.), *Reclaiming the classroom: Teacher research as an agency for change* (pp. 128-160). Portsmouth, NH: Boynton/Cook-Heinemann.

Orner, M., Miller, J. L., & Ellsworth, E. (1996). Excessive moments and educational discourses that try to contain them. *Educational Theory, 14,* 71-91.

Paley, V. G. (1995). *Kwanzaa and me: A teacher's story*. Cambridge: Harvard UP.

Patterson, L., Santa, C. M., Short, K. G., & Smith, K. (Eds.). (1993). *Teachers are researchers: Reflection and action*. Newark, DE: International Reading Association.

Patterson, L., & Shannon, P. (1993). Reflection, inquiry, action. In L. Patterson, C. M. Santa, K. G. Short, & K. Smith (Eds.), *Teachers are researchers: Reflection and action* (pp. 7-11). Newark, DE: International Reading Association.

Phillips, D. C. (1992). Subjectivity and objectivity: An objective inquiry. In E. E. Eisner & A. Peshkin (Eds.), *Qualitative inquiry in education: The continuing debate* (pp. 19-37). New York: Teachers College Press.

Phillips, D. L. (1993). *Looking backward: A critical appraisal of communitarian thought*. Princeton: Princeton UP.

Pradl, G. (1992). Response. In N. A. Branscombe, D. Goswami, & J. Schwartz (Eds.), *Students teaching, teachers learning* (pp. 318- 321). Portsmouth, NH: Boynton/Cook Heinemann.

Pratt, M. L. (1987). Linguistic utopias. In N. Fabb, D. Attridge, A. Durant, & C. McCabe (Eds.), *The linguistics of writing: Arguments between language and literature* (pp. 48-66). Manchester, UK: Manchester UP.

Pratt, M. L. (1991). Arts of the contact zone. *Profession 91* (pp. 33-40). New York: Modern Language Association.

Ray, R. (1993). *The practice of theory: Teacher research in composition.* Urbana, IL: National Council of Teachers of English.

Reagan, S. B., Fox, T., & Bleich, D. (Eds.). (1994). *Writing with: New directions in collaborative teaching, learning, and research.* Albany: State U of New York P.

Rilke, R. M. (1962). *Letters to a young poet.* New York: Norton. (Original letter written in 1903)

Roen, D. H., & Mittan, R. K. (1992). Collaborative scholarship in composition: Some issues. In G. Kirsch & P. Sullivan (Eds.), *Methods and methodology in composition research* (pp. 287-313). Carbondale: Southern Illinois UP.

Roman, L. G., & Apple, M. W. (1990). Is naturalism a move away from positivism? Materialist and feminist approaches to subjectivity in ethnographic research. In E. W. Eisner & A. Peshkin (Eds.), *Qualitative inquiry in education: The continuing debate.* New York: Teachers College Press.

Rosenblum, N. L. (1987). *Another liberalism: Romanticism and the reconstruction of liberal thought.* Cambridge: Harvard UP.

Rubin, D. L., & Piche, G. L. (1979). Development in syntactic and strategic aspects of audience adaptation skills in written persuasive communication. *Research in the Teaching of English, 13,* 293-316.

Schon, D. A. (1983). *The reflective practitioner: How professionals think in action.* San Francisco: Jossey-Bass.

Schulz, R. (1997). *Interpreting teacher practice: Two continuing stories.* New York: Teachers College Press.

Schuyler, P., & Sitterley, D. (1995). Preservice teacher supervision and reflective practice. In S. E. Noffke & R. B. Stevenson (Eds.), *Educational action research: Becoming practically critical* (pp. 53-59). New York: Teachers College Press.

Shannon, P. (1993). Introduction. In L. Patterson, C. M. Santa, K. G. Short, & K. Smith (Eds.), *Teachers are researchers: Reflection and action* (1-3). Newark, DE: International Reading Association.

Shockley, B., Michalove, B., & Allen, J. (1995). *Engaging families: Connecting home and school literacy communities.* Portsmouth, NH: Heinemann.

Shor, I. (1992). *Empowering education: Critical teaching for social change.* Chicago: U of Chicago P.

Shor, I. (1996). *When students have power: Negotiating authority in a critical pedagogy.* Chicago: U of Chicago P.

Short, K. G., Schroeder, J., Laird, J., Kauffman, G., Ferguson, M. J., & Crawford, K. M. (1996). *Learning together through inquiry: From Columbus to integrated curriculum.* York, ME: Stenhouse.

Smith, J. K. (1997). The stories educational researchers tell about themselves. *Educational Researcher, 26* (5), 4-11.

Stenhouse, L. (1975). *An introduction to curriculum research and development.* London: Heinemann.

Stenhouse, L. (1985a). Action research and the teachers' responsibility for the educational process. In J. Ruddock & D. Hopkins (Eds.), *Research as a basis for teaching: Readings from the work of Lawrence Stenhouse* (pp. 56-59). Portsmouth, NH: Heinemann. (Original seminars occurred 1981)

Stenhouse, L. (1985b). The case-study tradition and how case studies apply to practice. In J. Ruddock & D. Hopkins (Eds.), *Research as a basis for teaching: Readings from the work of Lawrence Stenhouse* (pp. 52-55). Portsmouth, NH: Heinemann. (Original paper presented 1982)

Stenhouse, L. (1985c). Curriculum research, artistry and teaching. In J. Rudduck & D. Hopkins (Eds.), *Research as a basis for teaching: Readings from the work of Lawrence Stenhouse* (pp. 102-111). Portsmouth, NH: Heinemann. (Original paper presented 1980).

Stenhouse, L. (1985d). How research can contribute to the improvement of teaching. In J. Rudduck & D. Hopkins (Eds.), *Research as a basis for teaching: Readings from the work of Lawrence Stenhouse* (pp. 49-51). Portsmouth, NH: Heinemann. (Original work published 1979)

Stenhouse, L. (1985e). The illuminative research tradition. In J. Rudduck & D. Hopkins (Eds.), *Research as a basis for teaching: Readings from the work of Lawrence Stenhouse* (pp. 31-32). Portsmouth, NH: Heinemann. (Original work published 1979)

Stenhouse, L. (1985f). The psycho-statistical paradigm and its limitations 2. In J. Rudduck & D. Hopkins (Eds.), *Research as a basis for teaching: Readings from the work of Lawrence Stenhouse* (pp. 25-30). Portsmouth, NH: Heinemann. (Original mimeo 1978)

Stenhouse, L. (1985g). Research as a basis for teaching. In J. Rudduck & D. Hopkins (Eds.), *Research as a basis for teaching: Readings from the work of Lawrence Stenhouse* (pp. 113-128). Portsmouth, NH: Heinemann. (Orignal paper presented 1979)

Stenhouse, L. (1985h). What counts as research. In J. Rudduck & D. Hopkins (Eds.), *Research as a basis for teaching: Readings from the work of Lawrence Stenhouse* (pp. 8-19). Portsmouth, NH: Heinemann. (Original work published 1981)

Stevenson, R. B., Noffke, S. E., Flores, E., & Granger, S. (1995). Teaching action research: A case study. In S. E. Noffke & R. B. Stevenson (Eds.), *Educational action research: Becoming practically critical* (pp. 60-73). New York: Teachers College Press.

Sullivan, P. (1994). Revising the myth of the independent scholar. In S. B. Reagan, T. Fox, and D. Bleich (Eds.), *Writing with: New directions in collaborative teaching, learning, and research* (pp. 11-30).

Swarts, H., Flower, L. S., & Hayes, J. R. (1984). Designing protocol studies of the writing process: An introduction. In R. Beach & L. S. Bridwell (Eds.), *New directions in composition research* (pp. 53-71). New York: Guilford Press.

Taylor, H. (1970). Enfranchisement of women. In A. S. Rossi (Ed.), *Essays on sexual equality* (pp. 93-121). Chicago: U of Chicago P. (Original work published 1851)

Tonnies, F. (1993). *Community and society* (C. P. Loomis, Trans.). New Brunswick, NJ: Transaction. (Original work published 1887)

Thompson, A., & Gitlin, A. (1995). Creating spaces for reconstructing knowledge in feminist pedagogy. *Educational Theory, 45,* 125-150.

Trimbur, J. (1989). Consensus and difference in collaborative learning. *College English, 51,* 602-616.

Trimmer, J. F. (Ed.). (1997). *Narration as knowledge: Tales of the teaching life.* Portsmouth, NH: Heinemann.

Ulichny, P., & Schoener, W. (1996). Teacher-researcher collaboration from two perspectives. *Harvard Educational Review, 66,* 496-524.

Van Maanen, J. (1988). *Tales from the field: On writing ethnography.* Chicago: U of Chicago P.

Wagner, J. (1997). The unavoidable intervention of educational research: A framework for reconsidering researcher-practitioner cooperation. *Educational Researcher, 26* (7), 13-23.

Walvoord, B. E. (1996). The future of writing across the curriculum. *College English, 58,* 58-79.

Walvoord, B. E., Hunt, L. L., Dowling, H. F., & McMahon, J. D. (1997). *In the long run: A study of faculty in three writing-across-the-curriculum programs.* Urbana, IL: National Council of Teachers of English.

Walvoord, B. E., & McCarthy, L. P. (1990). *Thinking and writing in college: A naturalistic study of students in four disciplines.* Urbana, IL: National Council of Teachers of English.

Wasser, J. D., & Bresler, L. (1996). Working in the interpretive zone: Conceptualizing collaboration in qualitative research teams. *Educational Researcher, 25* (5), 5-15.

Wilhelm, J. (1997). *You gotta be the book: Teaching engaged and reflective reading with adolescents.* New York: Teachers College Press.

Yancey, K., & Spooner, M. (1998). A single good mind: Collaboration, cooperation, and the writing self. *College Composition and Communication, 49,* 45-62.

Young, I. M. (1986). The ideal of community and the politics of difference. *Social Theory and Practice, 12,* 1-26.

Zeichner, K. M., & Gore, J. M. (1995). Using action research as a vehicle for student teacher reflection: A social reconstructionist approach. In S. E. Noffke & R. B. Stevenson (Eds.), *Educational action research: Becoming practically critical* (pp. 13-30). New York: Teachers College Press.

INDEX

ABOUT THE AUTHORS

STEPHEN M. FISHMAN teaches philosophy at the University of North Carolina Charlotte. Since attending his first Writing Across the Curriculum workshop in 1983, he has been studying student writing and learning in his classes. He is an alumnus of Camp Rising Sun, Rhinebeck, New York, an international scholarship camp founded in 1930 to promote world peace.

LUCILLE MCCARTHY teaches composition and literature at the University of Maryland Baltimore County. She is the co-author of *Thinking and Writing in College* with Barbara Walvoord (1990) and *The Psychiatry of Handicapped Children and Adolescents* with Joan Gerring (1988).

Together, Fishman and McCarthy have conducted a number of classroom studies. These have appeared in various journals, including *College English, Research in the Teaching of English,* and *College Composition and Communication*. In addition, they have co-authored a book, *John Dewey and the Challenge of Classroom Practice* (1998).